You've Got It
Made

Also by Diane Phillips

Happy Holidays from the Diva of Do-Ahead

Perfect Party Food

The Perfect Basket

The Ultimate Rotisserie Cookbook

The Soup Mix Gourmet

Pot Pies

It's a Wrap!

The Perfect Mix

Deliciously Easy Meals to
Make Now and Bake Later

You've Got It
Made

Diane Phillips

The Harvard Common Press
Boston, Massachusetts

The Harvard Common Press
535 Albany Street
Boston, Massachusetts 02118
www.harvardcommonpress.com

Printed in the United States of America

Printed on acid-free paper

Library of Congress Cataloging-in-Publication Data
Phillips, Diane.
You've got it made : deliciously easy meals to make now and bake later / Diane Phillips.
p. cm.
Includes index.
ISBN: 978-1-55832-350-6 (hardcover : alk. paper)
ISBN: 978-1-55832-351-3 (pbk. : alk. paper)
1. Cookery. 2. Entertaining. 3. Make-ahead cookery. I. Title.
TX714.P477 2008
641.5—dc22
2007025798

Special bulk-order discounts are available on this and other Harvard Common Press books.
Companies and organizations may purchase books for premiums or resale, or may arrange a
custom edition, by contacting the Marketing Director at the address above.

Book design by Ralph Fowler / rlf design
Cover photographs by Joyce Oudkerk Pool
Food styling by Dan Becker
Prop styling by Tabletop Props

2 4 6 8 10 9 7 5 3 1

To the gang at Great News!, my home on the range:

Ron, Devora, Allison, Sara, Aissa, Yvonne, Dionne, Tiffany, Sherri, Erika,

Kim, Nicole, Amanda, Deb, Pat, David, and the other staff members and

volunteers who make my time in their San Diego kitchen way too much fun—

thanks for making the Diva feel at home.

Acknowledgments

While writing this book many people added salt and spice to all that I did, and I would be remiss if I didn't thank them.

To my family members, who are extraordinary cheerleaders: Dr. Chuck, who survives weeks without a home-cooked meal even when I'm not on the road teaching but continues to exude good humor and encouragement—thanks, honey, I couldn't do this without you.

Daughter Carrie, her boyfriend, Eric, and our son, Ryan, all make me feel supported, loved, and special every day. Thanks, kids, I think it's time to eat!

My agent, Susan Ginsburg at Writers House, happens to be a remarkable woman, an incredibly savvy agent, and a treasured friend. I've enjoyed so much about our relationship but most of all the sharing of our lives—thanks for that, Susan. Her patient assistant, Emily Saladino, answers frantic e-mails and calls with grace and style; I'm grateful to have her there.

My buddy Lora Brody has been a mentor and role model to me since I met her, and she has generously led the way for me, with encouragement and laughter. We also share a passion for all things Red Sox!

Testing recipes for me in Carlisle, Pennsylvania, while juggling a full-time job and culinary school has been Robin Cox, an emerging star on the culinary horizon—you go, girl!

My work has been enriched by the relationships I've developed over the years, and I want to thank Lisa Callaghan and Patricia Claugh at All-Clad for their support, as well as Roy Johnson, the gang at Homewood Suites, Marissa Loper, and Spellbinders, who made my stays in Memphis so much fun.

I'd like to thank Sandra Maas and the crew at *Inside San Diego* on KUSI-TV for inviting me in and allowing me to have a great time. And I wouldn't be writing cookbooks without the support of cooking schools and students across the country and in France. Thanks and a toast to the staffs at Viking Culinary Arts Centers, Publix Supermarkets, Ramekins, Draeger's, Sur La Table, A Southern Season, Kitchen-Art, CooksWares, Great News!, The Kitchen Shoppe, and La Combe en Périgord.

Thanks to the dedicated and hardworking staff at The Harvard Common Press: publisher Bruce Shaw, executive editor Valerie Cimino, managing editor Jane Dornbusch and the production crew, publicist Howard Stelzer, the sales department (especially Betsy Young and Megan Weireter), and all the staff who have helped to make this book a reality. Thank you to my friend Ralph Fowler, of rlf design, for the terrific interior design, and to Andrea Chesman for her concise copyediting and great questions that kept the manuscript on target.

Lastly, thank you to you, dear reader, for taking the time to read and make use of this book. I hope you'll enjoy many nights of simple, do-ahead dinners in the years ahead with these easy and delicious ideas. Let me know how you do by visiting my Web site: www.dianephillips.com. Now, let's dig in!

Contents

Introduction

When someone mentions home cooking, you might remember a particularly great casserole that your mother made or an especially comforting plate of macaroni and cheese and wish that you could put that kind of meal on the table for your family. Baked comfort foods not only tantalize us with their aromas, they also satisfy us with their flavor. The aroma of a delicious baked chicken-and-rice casserole bubbling in a creamy sauce with a cheesy, crunchy topping makes the stress of the day go away, and everything becomes right with the world.

But time and its demands always seem to get in the way, don't they? The question "What's for dinner?" can send shivers up your spine. Too tired, stressed, and out of breath to think about food, you wait until you get home to realize that there isn't anything even remotely resembling dinner to be had in the fridge or freezer.

Well, the days of home-cooked meals don't have to be over for any of us; comfort foods can be on your table whenever you like, with just a little bit of planning ahead. That's where I come in. My tried and tested make-it-now, bake-it-later strategy will help you to become the Diva of Do-Ahead in *your* family.

Do-Ahead
Strategies

With a few simple steps and ingredients, and a little planning ahead, dinner can be waiting in your fridge or freezer most nights of the week. Defrosting in the microwave, or defrosting overnight in the refrigerator, then warming up in the oven is all that is needed to get you on your way to a hot, delicious, and simple home-cooked meal.

Getting Ahead of the Game

Teaching across the country as I do, I find that most home cooks are unsure of what will freeze well, how long different foods will keep in the freezer, and how long certain items will keep in the refrigerator. This makes storing your food seem complicated, but it doesn't have to be. My make-it-now, bake-it-later strategy works for many different types of meals. I think we all picture casseroles off the bat, but meats can be browned and additional ingredients added, and then the entire dish can be refrigerated or frozen. When the dish is baked, the meat can braise for a long period of time, developing rich flavor. Add fresh vegetables and you have a perfect, comforting dinner for your family or friends.

Planning is key here, and you will need to spend a few minutes, or maybe even an hour or two in some cases, planning how your meals will come together. Sauces, pastas, rice, and vegetables can be made ahead and refrigerated or frozen, and other components can be waiting to be added to the dish when you are ready. Then refrigerate or freeze them and *you've got it made* with terrific meals featuring terrific flavors any night of the week. The added benefit of the make-it-now, bake-it-later strategy is that you can usually freeze several meals at once with a few make-ahead sauces and different meat, chicken, or seafood combinations. Many people who work during the week take part of their Sundays to plan out their weeknight meals; with this strategy, you can even plan more than a week's worth of menus at once and have them ready to go in a relatively short period of time.

Make-It-Now Ingredients

Let's look first at your pantry and see if you have it stocked. I realize that you may have limited storage space, so pick the items you know that you will use and then add others as you begin to broaden your cooking repertoire.

Parmesan Cheese vs. Parmigiano-Reggiano Cheese

Parmigiano-Reggiano is a sublime cheese; some even call it the "undisputed King of cheeses." It comes from the Parma region of Italy. Only Parmesan cheese produced in the Parma region under the strictest guidelines can be labeled with the Parmigiano-Reggiano seal. (As an example of making the most of what you have, once the curds are separated from the whey and formed into wheels, the whey is fed to the pigs that eventually become prosciutto di Parma.) When I specify Parmigiano-Reggiano cheese in a recipe, I do so because I think the flavor of the finished dish will benefit from the finer and more expensive cheese. Domestic and imported Parmesans are different from Parmigiano-Reggiano since they are not produced under the same guidelines in the same region in Italy. That being said, there are many nice Parmesan cheeses on the market (no, the stuff in the green can is not one of them). When I specify Parmesan rather than Parmigiano-Reggiano, it is because the dish has so many other flavors that the finer cheese might get lost and using Parmesan is just fine for that dish.

Dry Pantry

Baking soda

Baking powder

Unbleached all-purpose flour
(I like King Arthur)

Cornmeal

Old-fashioned rolled oats

Panko crumbs

Bread crumbs

Tortillas:
flour and corn

Cornstarch

Cocoa powder:
Dutch-processed and regular

Chocolate chips
(your choice of flavors)

Sugar:
granulated sugar, light and dark
brown sugar, confectioners'
sugar, and raw sugar

Peanut butter

Jams

Honey

Rice:
white, wild, and Arborio

Pasta:
various shapes of dried
pasta, including no-bake
lasagna noodles

Tabasco or your favorite
hot sauce

Sun-dried tomatoes
packed in oil

Olive oil:
pure and extra-virgin

Vegetable oil:
canola or a blend of
vegetable oils

Nonstick cooking spray
(I like Baker's Joy for baked
goods; any of the others are fine
for casseroles)

Vegetable shortening
(Crisco is the Big Daddy
of them all)

Vinegar:
rice, white wine, red wine,
balsamic

Worcestershire sauce

Dry vermouth
(can be used in place of white
wine in any recipe and keeps
indefinitely in a cool, dry place)

Soy sauce

Tomato paste in a tube
(once opened, store in the
refrigerator)

Anchovy paste in a tube
(once opened, store in the
refrigerator)

Canned tuna packed in oil

Canned chopped clams

Canned tomatoes:
diced, whole plum,
ground peeled

Canned beans:
small white, kidney, garbanzo,
red kidney, refried, plain baked

Broth:
chicken, beef, seafood, vegetable

Artichoke hearts

Garlic (fresh)

Sweet onions:
    Spend the extra money on
    sweet onions, such as Vidalia,
    Texas Sweets or Texas 10-15s,
    Walla Walla, or Maui. These
    onions contain at least 6
    percent sugar and will add
    more personality and sweetness
    to your cooking.

Shallots

Potatoes:
    red, russet, Yukon gold, sweet

Dried spices

Refrigerator

Active dry yeast

Ketchup

Mustard:
    Dijon, yellow, whole-grain

Capers

Mayonnaise

Sour cream

Heavy cream

Unsalted butter

Cheeses:
    Blue, Boursin, Brie, sharp and
    mild cheddar, goat, Gruyère,
    Monterey Jack and pepper Jack,
    Jarlsberg, Munster, Parmigiano-
    Reggiano, Pecorino Romano,
    and aged provolone are among
    my favorites.

Why Unsalted Butter?

Years ago, chefs would only use unsalted butter because the salted butter had been preserved with the salt, thus it was often older than the unsalted butter. Nowadays, with refrigeration and shipping methods being what they are, both varieties are fresh, but with unsalted butter you can better control the amount of salt in a dish. Remember that a pound of butter contains 1 teaspoon of salt, so there is ¼ teaspoon of salt in each stick.

Remember to use a permanent marker to label packages with what they contain and a date (month and year they were frozen) before you put them in the freezer.

Chicken:
  breasts, thighs, wings

Turkey:
  boneless breasts, ground

Pork:
  tenderloins, lean chops, ground

Beef:
  steaks, pot roasts, ground

Frozen shrimp

Pasteurized lump crabmeat

Nuts:
  pecans, walnuts, almonds,
  pine nuts

Frozen vegetables:
  spinach, petite peas, corn

Phyllo dough

Puff pastry sheets

You've Got It Made Terms

Here's a quick primer on some of the language you will see throughout the recipes.

Bring to room temperature: Removing the casserole from the refrigerator and allowing the casserole to come to room temperature is essential for keeping your baking times accurate. If the casserole is placed in a preheated oven directly from the refrigerator, it will lower the temperature of your oven for one-quarter to one-half of the baking time, giving you uneven results and longer baking times. Please follow the directions in the individual recipes for bringing the dishes to room temperature before baking. If you forget (which I do frequently), adjust your cooking time by adding 15 to 20 minutes. Also, remember that the temperature of your kitchen will dictate how fast the dish will come to room temperature in the first place.

Preheat your oven: Preheating ovens is also very important, especially if you have a convection oven. When a convection oven is preheated (regardless of which setting you have chosen: convection bake, convection, bake, etc.), all the systems are working to preheat your oven, even the broiler, so don't put that casserole in until the oven is preheated, or else it will be browned, overcooked, and possibly burned. With older ovens, which may take longer to preheat, it's a good idea to have an oven thermometer to calibrate whether the oven is at the correct temperature.

Set in the center: If you are cooking something that contains a good deal of liquid, most of the time I will instruct you to bake until it is "set in the center;" this means that the liquid center is not sloshing around, and it should be firm. If you have tested it with a skewer, and a bit of liquid is still on the skewer, you will need to continue baking, checking at 5-minute intervals. (This result may be a factor of improper oven calibration; I highly recommend that you use an oven thermometer if you find that your baked goods are not done at the recommended times.)

Coat with nonstick cooking spray: I love the convenience of nonstick cooking sprays versus spreading butter or shortening in a baking dish. This is purely a matter of choice for me. If you choose to use butter, oil, or shortening, make sure the baking dish is thoroughly coated. If you use spray, spray it onto your pans over your open dishwasher; that way you won't get it onto your floor and end up dancing around in it!

Cover and store: Whatever you wish to use to cover your dishes when you refrigerate or freeze food is your choice (see Equipment, below). I love zipper-top plastic bags in all sizes for storage, because I know I can press out the air and guard against freezer burn; however, heavy-duty plastic freezer wrap and heavy-duty aluminum foil are also great for sealing your dishes. Keeping your food as airtight as possible is key to make-it-now, bake-it-later cooking.

Let it rest: Many times a dish will need to rest after cooking, so that the liquids in the dish can stabilize and, when you cut into the dish, the sauce doesn't run all over the place. This is particularly true with pasta and potato dishes. Meats and poultry often need to rest before they are cut, because the meats reabsorb the juices while resting. When you cut into them after a resting period, the juices from the meat won't run all over the cutting board; they will have stayed in the meat, making it succulent and delicious.

Equipment

My make-it-now, bake-it-later strategy doesn't require you to go out and buy a lot of new equipment for your kitchen, but there are some things that I think are essentials for this type of cooking. You probably already have many of them in your cupboards.

If you plan to prepare a lot of make-ahead dishes, it might be a good idea to look for sales on inexpensive glass or stoneware baking dishes in the sizes that you will use most often (9 x 13-inch or 9-inch square are two in particular, depending upon your family needs). That way, you won't have your very best oven-to-table

About Olive Oils

Olive oil is graded as extra-virgin, superfine, fine, and pure (or virgin), depending on its acidity. Extra-virgin olive oil has the least acidity and is used as a flavoring in dishes. Because it has a strong flavor, it can overpower other ingredients if you aren't careful. Use extra-virgin olive oil sparingly to add flavor to your dishes. When you want just a slight hint of olive oil, for sautéing or frying, use pure olive oil. Some reliable brands that are widely available are Filippo Berio, Bertolli, and Colavita.

ware in the freezer when you want to use it for something else. If you have a stack of baking vessels that you can freeze, and then transfer food into your "for company" dishes, all the better.

Oven-to-table bakeware: There are many different brands on the market, but by far the most reliable are those that can go from freezer to preheated oven. Make sure to ask the retailer if the type you are looking at is specifically made for that broad a use. Although baking frozen entrées isn't my first choice, because it takes a long time and some babying, knowing the dish will not shatter once it is exposed to heat in the oven is essential. I recommend the following sizes as essentials: 10-inch round, 9-inch square, 9 x 13-inch rectangular, and a 2-inch-deep pie plate. Later on, you can add other sizes if you feel you need them. When a recipe requires a 1-quart baking dish, you can use a 9-inch square, round, or oval baking dish.

Stainless steel sauté pans and skillets: Medium- and large-sized skillets and sauté pans are essential for caramelizing and browning ingredients that will go into your make-it-now, bake-it-later dishes. If you prefer nonstick cookware, make sure that the nonstick surface is anodized (like Scanpan brand) so that it will promote browning. Browning and caramelizing are important to the flavor of finished dishes. Many nonstick skillets and sauté pans won't brown meats or vegetables; rather, they will create steam, which will just add extra water, and not flavor, to your finished dish.

Dutch oven and stockpot: A 5- to 7-quart Dutch oven should take care of any recipes that are braised, and it is also great for soups and stews. A 5- to 7-quart stockpot will be necessary for cooking pasta and other grains, as well as sauces for lasagna and other pasta dishes.

Saucepans and sauciers: Saucepans are straight sided and come in sizes from 1 to 5 quarts. Saucepans are terrific for heating liquids and making sauces and small amounts of soup. Sauciers are rounded-bottom saucepans and my choice for making sauces and reducing liquids. Because the interior is rounded, a whisk can reach every part of the pan, leaving no lumpy bits of roux. Also, because the bottom is rounded, the surface area of the pan is wide and helps to reduce sauces rapidly.

Glass mixing bowls: Although this is a personal choice on my part, I love working with glass because I can see if everything is mixed together. When I use a ceramic or stainless steel bowl, some ingredients may still be unmixed on the bottom when I go to transfer the mixture to a pan.

Whisk: The huge balloon whisk at the gourmet shop may look like what you'd like, but a sauce whisk is the way to go for making creamy, lump-free sauces. The balloon whisk is for whipping cream and egg whites to high peaks. Sauce whisks have a narrow end, which will get into all parts of the saucepan or saucier when you are cooking roux. There are also flat whisks that work well for sauces.

Heatproof spatulas: Heat-tempered to 800+°F, these can go right into the dishwasher and don't absorb odors or stains.

Silicone baking liners: To help make cleanup a breeze and to have cookies literally slide off the sheets, these are a wonderful addition to your kitchen. Not only are there sheet pan–size liners, but they now come in round, square, and rectangular sizes to fit cake pans and casserole dishes. I recommend these for particularly sticky baked goods that might otherwise adhere to the pan. If you don't own these, parchment paper also works well.

Zipper-top plastic bags: Where would we be without these? I can store a 9-inch square or round pan in the 1-gallon size and a 9 x 13-inch casserole dish in a 2-gallon size bag. They are also helpful for storing leftovers and for refrigerating or freezing doughs for pies and other baked goods. I buy the freezer type for both refrigerating and freezing because they are thicker and stronger.

Heavy-duty plastic wrap: We all have our favorites when it comes to wrapping things airtight, and mine is Reynolds Heavy-Duty Plastic Wrap, because it doesn't seem to stick to itself when I cut it to seal a container. But there are lots of other brands on the market; just make sure to buy one that is labeled "heavy-duty." Glad makes a "press and seal" wrap that seals around the rim of awkwardly sized dishes and works well, too. I suggest this type of wrap for items that will be refrigerated or frozen for shorter periods of time.

Heavy-duty aluminum foil: If you aren't a fan of plastic wrap, heavy-duty aluminum foil (again, Reynolds is my favorite) works really well, but I find that if I want to protect foods from freezer burn, it's best to wrap them in foil, then seal them in a zipper-top plastic freezer bag. If I am freezing a dish that I plan to bake covered, I wrap it in foil rather than plastic wrap; that way I can use the same foil to cover it in the oven, too. Foil is also good for lining baking sheets.

Disposable aluminum baking pans: You can find these in your grocery store, and they come in handy for taking meals to a potluck or for when you are bringing a dish to someone's house and don't want to burden them with returning your dishes. They are expensive, though. And keep in mind that they don't conduct heat as well as porcelain, glass, or other heavy-duty bakeware. For those reasons, I don't recommend them for everyday make-it-now, bake-it-later use.

Storage and Kitchen Safety

According to the USDA, you can safely freeze almost any food, except canned foods or eggs in the shell. However, the USDA Web site also notes that "being able to freeze food and being pleased with the quality after defrosting are two different things." That's where I come in. When creating the recipes for this book, if I thought the quality of a dish after defrosting wasn't as good as before freezing (that is, if the integrity of the ingredients just wasn't the same), then I didn't recommend freezing those recipes. You will find this particularly in the seafood chapter. Raw meats, raw poultry, and the like will actually maintain their quality in the freezer longer than after they are cooked because there is moisture loss during cooking that adversely affects freezer shelf life.

Freezing Food

Any time you freeze a dish, make sure to squeeze all the air out of the container, whether it is a plastic bag or plastic freezer container. Air tends to react with the food and cause off odors, and it can also cause freezer burn, which affects flavor. Vacuum packing is the best way to freeze food, but vacuum-pack food-saver devices are expensive, and if you have space considerations, you are better off to invest in heavy-duty zipper-top plastic freezer bags in various sizes. Make sure that the container you are using is not too big for the food, so that the chance of any trapped air is minimal.

Keep your freezer at 0°F for optimal freezing. If you aren't sure if your freezer is at that temperature, buy a freezer thermometer to check, then adjust your freezer dial accordingly. As another way to check, ice cream should be frozen solid in a 0°F freezer, not soft or semisoft.

Most foods can be frozen. Some lose quality in the freezer, and I've pointed that out in each individual case throughout the book. But here are a few obvious items that don't freeze well: celery (high water content), salad greens (again, high water content), cooked and raw garlic (it loses its potency), hard-boiled eggs in the shell (don't ask), and salad dressing (it separates and turns gummy). Some items, like mayonnaise and sour cream, are not recommended for freezing, but if they are a component of a larger dish, say a dip or spread, it's perfectly fine to freeze that dish.

Defrosting Food

There are three safe ways to defrost foods:

1. Usually I recommend defrosting in the refrigerator, where small items will defrost much more quickly than, say, a roast or whole turkey. About 24 hours is normal defrosting time for average items, such as casseroles. Larger items, such as turkeys and roasts, will require 24 hours for every 5 pounds of weight. When defrosting food in the refrigerator, you also have the luxury of being able to store the thawed dish for a day or so before cooking it.

2. Enclose the dish to be defrosted in a *leakproof* plastic bag and submerge it in cold water, changing the water every 30 minutes. After thawing, cook the item immediately.

3. The microwave provides a great, safe way to thaw food, and the newer models can sense when the item is defrosted when you enter the weight of the frozen food into the touchpad. I use the microwave to defrost some foods, but for large items, such as a turkey or roast, I usually try to allow time to defrost in the refrigerator.

Once food is defrosted in the refrigerator, it is perfectly safe to refreeze it. There may be a bit of a loss of quality, however, since some moisture will be lost when defrosting the second time. If you have cooked the dish, and you then have leftovers from the previously frozen casserole dish, these leftovers can be refrozen without a problem.

The following chart gives you estimates for safe freezing and refrigerating of different types of foods. Some recommendations may be shorter than the USDA's guidelines, because I felt that the integrity of the flavor was compromised with the longer storage times allowed by the USDA. All the recipes in this book provide recommended storage times, but you will find this chart invaluable when you are preparing your own make-it-now, bake-it-later masterpieces.

Guidelines for Safe Food Storage

FREEZER

Fresh ground meats	3 to 4 months
Fresh lamb, beef, pork, veal	6 to 8 months
Bacon and sausage	1 to 2 months
Ham	1 to 2 months
Cooked meats	2 to 3 months
Meat casseroles	2 to 3 months
Whole chicken or turkey	12 months
Poultry parts	8 months
Cooked poultry	4 months
Poultry casseroles	2 to 3 months
Seafood (steaks, fillets)	4 months
Shellfish	3 months
Soups, stews, braises	2 to 3 months
Breads	2 to 3 months
Bread and pasta casseroles	2 to 3 months
Egg casseroles	6 to 8 weeks
Cakes	6 weeks
Cookies	2 months
Puff pastry dough	6 months or until expiration date

REFRIGERATOR

Egg casseroles	4 days
Ham, fully cooked (whole)	7 days
Meat and poultry casseroles	4 days
Cooked meats	3 days
Soups and stews	3 days
Fresh fish and shellfish	1 to 2 days
Fresh meats and poultry	1 to 2 days

Baking Frozen Food

In most of the recipes in this book, I recommend transferring the dish from the freezer to the refrigerator the day before baking because I think that gives the best results. But there will doubtless be times when you will want (or, let's face it, need) to bake something straight from the freezer.

To bake a solidly frozen entrée, it will take you at least 1½ times as long as baking a defrosted entrée. Multiply the cooking time called for in the recipe by 1½. Bake the frozen entrée covered with aluminum foil for the first 45 minutes of that time, then remove the foil and bake uncovered for the remaining amount of time. (Make sure the casserole dish you are using can go directly from freezer to pre-heated oven.) This method is not foolproof because all food and all ovens are a bit different, but once you remove the foil and begin baking the food "naked," periodically check on it to make sure that it isn't browning too fast. If it is, turn the oven down 25°F, and re-cover the dish with the foil.

If you get to the point where the casserole is cooked through but not browned on the top, a run under the broiler, or a torching with your crème brûlée torch, will give you a nice browned top. Make sure to insert an instant-read thermometer into the center of the casserole; it should register 165°F. If the dish is looking "done" but has not reached that temperature, then cover with foil and bake until it gets there.

Get Cooking

By following these simple formulas for preparation, storage, and baking, and finding a little time to plan ahead, you can turn the drudgery of weekday, weekend, and even special-occasion cooking into a more satisfying experience. Have fun!

Appetizers
and Small Bites

Appetizers are the delectable small tidbits, dips, and nibbles that whet appetites before the main course, or they can be the basis for a cocktail or grazing party, where the entire evening's offerings are a series of small plates. However you choose to serve appetizers, they are handy to have ready and waiting in your refrigerator or freezer for unexpected company, or for quiet nights at home when you might feel like having a few small bites rather than a full-on evening meal. And, of course, all of these appetizers are terrific for munching on while watching sports on TV or for bringing to a tailgate picnic.

Appetizers and Small Bites

Caramelized Onion and Gruyère Dip

A LITTLE BIT OF CARAMELIZED ONION makes most every savory dish taste better, and this warm dip served in a bread bowl is addictive with chips or veggies. My favorite way to eat this is to dip in with baguette slices. This tastes a bit like French onion soup, which is high on my delight list!

SERVES 6 TO 8

1 round loaf sourdough or sturdy French bread

2 tablespoons unsalted butter

1 tablespoon olive oil

2 medium-size sweet onions, such as Vidalias, coarsely chopped

1 teaspoon salt

1 teaspoon sugar

1 teaspoon dried thyme

One 8-ounce package cream cheese, softened

½ cup mayonnaise

2 cups shredded Gruyère or imported Swiss cheese

Make It Now

1. Slice the top off the loaf of bread and remove the insides with your hands or a sharp paring knife, leaving about a ¾-inch thickness of the inside shell. Reserve the inside of the bread for bread crumbs and set aside the shell.

2. Melt the butter with the oil in a medium-size skillet over medium heat. Add the onions, stirring to coat with the butter mixture. Sauté for about 3 minutes, until the onions begin to soften. Sprinkle with the salt, sugar, and thyme, and sauté for another 10 minutes, until the onions begin to turn golden, being careful that they don't burn. Transfer the contents of the skillet to a mixing bowl and allow to cool.

3. In the bowl of an electric mixer, beat the cream cheese and mayonnaise together until smooth, beginning at slow speed and increasing to medium. Fold in the onions and Gruyère cheese, and stir until blended. Spoon into the bread shell (if you decide not to use a bread shell, a 1-quart casserole dish will work just fine). Cover and refrigerate for up to 3 days or freeze for up to 2 months.

Bake It Later

1. Defrost the dip overnight in the refrigerator, if necessary.

2. Preheat the oven to 350°F. Bring the dip to room temperature for 20 minutes.

3. Bake for 20 minutes, until bubbling. Serve immediately.

Chile con Queso Dip

LITERALLY "CHILES WITH CHEESE," this spicy dip is a terrific starter for any party, but especially for a fiesta! I like to serve it with tortilla chips, but you can serve it with sturdy vegetable dippers (such as jicama and celery), hearty bread cubes, or even shrimp on skewers. SERVES 6 TO 8

2 tablespoons unsalted butter

1 clove garlic, minced

1/2 cup finely chopped sweet onion, such as Vidalia

2 tablespoons finely chopped jalapeño chile

1/2 teaspoon ground cumin

1/2 chipotle chile in adobo sauce, finely chopped, with 1/4 teaspoon sauce (see Diva Note)

1/2 cup finely chopped canned tomatoes, drained

1/4 cup milk

2 cups finely shredded Monterey Jack cheese

2 cups finely shredded mild cheddar cheese

Make It Now

1. Melt the butter in a medium-size saucepan over medium heat. Add the garlic, onion, jalapeño, cumin, and chipotle chile and adobo sauce and sauté for about 3 minutes, until the onion is softened. Add the tomatoes and cook for another 3 minutes, until any liquid from the tomatoes has evaporated.

2. Add the milk and remove the saucepan from the heat. Stir in the Monterey Jack and cheddar cheeses until melted and combined. Transfer the mixture to a 1-quart ovenproof casserole dish. Cover and refrigerate for up to 3 days or freeze for up to 1 month.

Bake It Later

1. Defrost the dip overnight in the refrigerator, if necessary.

2. Preheat the oven to 325°F. Bring the dip to room temperature for 30 minutes.

3. Bake for 20 to 30 minutes, until the dip is bubbling. Serve hot.

Queso Chile con Carne

Add ½ pound lean ground beef, crumbled Mexican chorizo, or spicy Italian sausage to the saucepan along with the onion. Sauté until the meat is cooked through, drain off the excess liquid from the pan, and proceed as directed.

Diva Note

Chipotle chiles in adobo sauce are smoked jalapeño chiles that are sold in cans or jars in the Latino section of your supermarket. An alternative is to sauté ½ teaspoon ground chipotle chile powder with the onion and jalapeños.

Cheddar Beer Dip with Smoked Sausage

THIS TANGY DIP, studded with nuggets of smoked sausage, is terrific served with chunks of bread, tortilla chips, pretzels, or sturdy crackers. The darker the beer you use, the stronger the flavor will be. You can serve it in a bread round (see Caramelized Onion and Gruyère Dip, page 15) or in an oven-proof baking dish. I don't recommend freezing this, as the amount of beer in the dip doesn't allow it to totally freeze, and it separates when reheated. SERVES 6 TO 8

2 tablespoons unsalted butter

½ cup finely chopped sweet onion, such as Vidalia

½ pound smoked sausage, cut into ½-inch pieces

2 tablespoons Dijon or whole-grain mustard

One 8-ounce package cream cheese

One 12-ounce bottle dark beer

4 cups shredded sharp white cheddar cheese

6 drops of Tabasco sauce

Make It Now

1. Coat the inside of a 1-quart baking dish with nonstick cooking spray.

2. Melt the butter in a medium-size saucepan over medium-high heat. Add the onion and sauté for 2 minutes, until the onion begins to soften. Add the sausage and cook until it is no longer pink in color and is cooked through, 8 to 10 minutes. Drain off any fat from the sausage.

3. Add the mustard, cream cheese, and beer, stirring until the cream cheese is melted. Remove from the heat and stir in the cheddar cheese, a handful at a time, until it is all incorporated. Add the Tabasco sauce, transfer to the baking dish, and let cool. Cover and refrigerate for up to 3 days.

Bake It Later

1. Preheat the oven to 350°F. Bring the dip to room temperature for about 30 minutes.

2. Bake the dip for 20 to 25 minutes, until bubbling. Serve warm.

VARIATION

Pacifico Chorizo Dip

Substitute Mexican chorizo for the smoked sausage; Pacifico, Dos Equis, or Corona beer for the dark beer; and pepper Jack cheese for the cheddar cheese.

Our Favorite Artichoke and Spinach Dip

THERE ARE LOTS OF VARIATIONS when it comes to artichoke dips, but this one is foolproof, and it has added color and flavor from spinach, too. Serve with tortilla chips, crackers, and baguette slices.

SERVES 6 TO 8

1 tablespoon unsalted butter

1 clove garlic, minced

One 10-ounce package fresh baby spinach, chopped

One 15.8-ounce can artichoke hearts, drained and coarsely chopped

1 cup mayonnaise

⅓ cup finely shredded Swiss cheese

⅔ cup freshly grated Parmesan cheese

Make It Now

1. Melt the butter in a medium-size skillet over medium-high heat. Add the garlic and sauté until softened, about 45 seconds. Add the spinach and sauté until there is no moisture in the bottom of the pan, about 4 minutes. Transfer the spinach mixture to a large bowl and allow to cool.

2. Stir in the artichoke hearts, mayonnaise, Swiss cheese, and Parmesan cheese, stirring to blend.

3. Transfer the mixture to a 1-quart baking dish. Cover and refrigerate for up to 2 days or freeze for up to 1 month.

Bake It Later

1. Defrost the dip in the refrigerator overnight, if necessary.

2. Preheat the oven to 350°F. Let the dip come to room temperature for about 30 minutes.

3. Bake the dip for 20 to 25 minutes, until the dip is bubbling and the cheese is beginning to turn golden brown. Serve hot or warm.

Smoked Salmon–Dill Puffs

FLECKED WITH NUGGETS of smoked salmon and fresh dill, these puffs are sure to disappear quickly. Whether you serve these with cocktails before dinner or as part of a brunch buffet, these pretty-in-pink puffs are a winner every time! SERVES 10 TO 12

3 ounces cream cheese, softened

½ cup sour cream

½ cup finely chopped or flaked smoked salmon

2 tablespoons chopped fresh dill

1 teaspoon finely grated lemon zest

1 sheet frozen puff pastry, defrosted

Make It Now

1. In a small bowl, stir together the cream cheese, sour cream, salmon, dill, and lemon zest until blended. At this point, you may cover and refrigerate for up to 3 days.

2. Coat the insides of standard-size muffin cups with non-stick cooking spray. On a lightly floured work surface, roll out the puff pastry into a 14-inch square and cut into 2-inch squares. Place a square of puff pastry into each cup and set aside.

3. Place about 1 tablespoon of the filling in the center of each puff pastry square. Bring up the opposite ends of the puff pastry to meet, and twist to seal the pastry. Cover with heavy-duty plastic wrap and refrigerate for up to 24 hours or freeze for up to 1 month. When the pastries are frozen solid, you can remove them from the muffin cups and store in zipper-top plastic bags, separated by waxed paper, parchment paper, or plastic wrap, so that they don't stick together.

1 large egg

2 tablespoons milk, cream, or water

Bake It Later

1. For refrigerated or defrosted pastries, preheat the oven to 400°F. For frozen pastries, preheat the oven to 375°F. If you are baking frozen pastries no longer in the muffin cups, arrange them on baking sheets lined with aluminum foil, parchment paper, or silicone liners.

2. In a small bowl, whisk together the egg and milk until blended. Brush the pastries with the egg wash. Bake refrigerated or defrosted pastries for 12 to 14 minutes, until golden brown. Bake frozen pastries for 19 to 21 minutes,

until golden brown. Remove to a cooling rack. Allow pastries in muffin cups to rest for about 2 minutes before trying to remove them from the pan. Serve warm or at room temperature.

Shrimp-Dill Puffs

Substitute ¼ pound cooked shrimp, finely chopped, for the salmon.

All Puffed Up

Puff pastry appetizers are simple to make and impressive to serve, and they can be ready and waiting in your freezer. Best of all, they can be baked frozen, directly from the freezer—what's not to love? Pepperidge Farm Puff Pastry sheets are the most widely available brand in the supermarket frozen-food section. Make sure to buy the sheets, because they also sell shells that you can fill, but the sheets roll out easily and you can get a large number of individual appetizers from one sheet. One sheet of puff pastry, rolled into a 14-inch square, will give you forty-nine 2-inch squares for small bites or about thirty pinwheel or palmier-type appetizers. If you make several different types and have them ready in the freezer, you can have an assortment of elegant appetizers any time you need them. I usually figure on three to four of these puff-pastry bites per person if it's the only thing served before dinner, and two to three per person if I am serving other appetizers.

Make sure that once the pastry is defrosted, you keep it chilled in the refrigerator if you don't plan to use it at once. If the pastry becomes warm, it will be hard to work with. Should this happen, just wrap it in plastic and stick it in the freezer for 10 minutes to firm it up.

The recipes on pages 20 to 24 can be baked and then frozen, if you wish. After baking and cooling as directed, freeze them in an airtight container for up to 1 month. Remove from the refrigerator 1 hour before baking, and bake in a 375°F oven for 5 minutes, until warmed through.

Baked Mushroom, Cheddar, and Bacon Puffs

ELEGANT AND DELICIOUS, these will become your favorite party appetizer. If you don't have enough muffin tins to make all the puffs at once, you can bake them in batches.

SERVES 10 TO 12

1 sheet frozen puff pastry, defrosted

2 tablespoons unsalted butter or olive oil

1/2 cup finely chopped sweet onion, such as Vidalia

3/4 pound white or cremini mushrooms, coarsely chopped

1 teaspoon salt

1/2 teaspoon freshly ground black pepper

1/2 cup mayonnaise

8 slices bacon, cooked crisp, drained, and crumbled

1 cup finely shredded sharp white cheddar cheese

Make It Now

1. Coat the insides of standard-size muffin cups with non-stick cooking spray. On a lightly floured work surface, roll out the puff pastry into a 14-inch square and cut into 2-inch squares. Place a square of puff pastry into each cup and set aside.

2. In a large skillet over medium heat, melt the butter. Add the onion and sauté for 2 to 3 minutes, until the onion is softened. Add the mushrooms and sauté until the mushrooms begin to color and the liquid in the pan has evaporated, 6 to 8 minutes. Mix in the salt and pepper and transfer to a bowl to cool.

3. When the mushroom mixture is cooled, stir in the mayonnaise, bacon, and cheese, and blend thoroughly.

4. Place about 1 tablespoon of the filling into the center of each puff pastry square. Bring up the opposite ends of the puff pastry to meet, and twist to seal the pastry. Cover with heavy-duty plastic wrap and refrigerate for up to 24 hours or freeze for up to 1 month. When the pastries are frozen solid, you can remove them from the muffin cups and store in zipper-top plastic bags, separated by waxed paper, parchment paper, or plastic wrap, so that they don't stick together.

1 large egg

2 tablespoons milk, cream, or water

1. For refrigerated or defrosted pastries, preheat the oven to 400°F. For frozen pastries, preheat the oven to 375°F. If you are baking frozen pastries no longer in the muffin cups, arrange them on baking sheets lined with aluminum foil, parchment paper, or silicone liners.

2. In a small bowl, whisk together the egg and milk until blended. Brush the pastries with the egg wash. Bake refrigerated or defrosted pastries for 12 to 14 minutes, until golden brown. Bake frozen pastries for 19 to 21 minutes, until golden brown. Remove to a cooling rack. Allow pastries in muffin cups to rest for about 2 minutes before trying to remove them from the pan. Serve warm or at room temperature.

Diva Note

I like the option of using muffin tins for this type of appetizer because the puffs will keep their shape, but if you don't have enough muffin tins, or don't want to bother, this alternative method works very well. Cut your puff pastry into squares as directed. Place the pastry squares on a cutting board, place the filling in the center of each square, then bring up the opposite corners and twist like a beggars' purse. Place these on cookie sheets and freeze. There's no need for muffin cups, and they can be baked on cookie sheets when you are ready. (Any of the puffs in this chapter can be done this way.)

Spinach and Feta Puffs

ALTHOUGH I LOVE TO EAT PHYLLO DOUGH APPETIZERS, they can be tedious to make with all the buttering and folding. This zesty filling does very well in puff pastry and takes half the time to wrap up. SERVES 10 TO 12

One 16-ounce package frozen chopped spinach, defrosted and squeezed dry

²/₃ cup mayonnaise

⅛ teaspoon freshly grated nutmeg

½ teaspoon garlic salt

1 cup crumbled feta cheese

1 sheet frozen puff pastry, defrosted

Make It Now

1. In a medium-size mixing bowl, combine the spinach, mayonnaise, nutmeg, garlic salt, and feta cheese until blended. At this point, you may cover and refrigerate for up to 3 days.

2. Coat the insides of standard-size muffin cups with non-stick cooking spray. On a lightly floured work surface, roll out the puff pastry into a 14-inch square and cut into 2-inch squares. Place a square of puff pastry into each cup and set aside.

3. Place about 1 tablespoon of the filling in the center of each puff pastry square. Bring up the opposite ends of the puff pastry to meet, and twist to seal the pastry. Cover with heavy-duty plastic wrap and refrigerate for up to 24 hours or freeze for up to 1 month. When the pastries are frozen solid, you can remove them from the muffin cups and store in zipper-top plastic bags, separated by waxed paper, parchment paper, or plastic wrap, so that they don't stick together.

1 large egg

2 tablespoons milk, cream, or water

Bake It Later

1. For refrigerated or defrosted pastries, preheat the oven to 400°F. For frozen pastries, preheat the oven to 375°F. If you are baking frozen pastries no longer in the muffin cups, arrange them on baking sheets lined with aluminum foil, parchment paper, or silicone liners.

2. In a small bowl, whisk together the egg and milk until blended. Brush the pastries with the egg wash. Bake refrigerated or defrosted pastries for 12 to 14 minutes, until golden brown. Bake frozen pastries for 19 to 21 minutes, until golden brown. Remove to a cooling rack. Allow pastries in muffin cups to rest for about 2 minutes before trying to remove them from the pan. Serve warm or at room temperature.

Pigs in a Blanket

ALTHOUGH THIS RECIPE is also in my book *Perfect Party Food* (The Harvard Common Press, 2005), these little sausages are such a great do-ahead item that I couldn't leave them out here. Plus, everyone loves them. I particularly like to roll the pastry in cheese to kick up the flavor, and adding different spices to the pastry also helps to make them special. SERVES 12 TO 14

2 cups finely shredded cheese, such as cheddar, Parmesan, pepper Jack, or Swiss

1 sheet frozen puff pastry, defrosted

¼ cup mustard (your favorite: sweet and hot, whole-grain, tarragon, Jack Daniels, Tabasco, honey mustard, champagne, or Creole)

One 1-pound package cocktail franks or mini smoked sausages

Make It Now

1. Line baking sheets with aluminum foil, parchment paper, or silicone liners.

2. Scatter the cheese on the work surface, as you would flour on a board, and roll out the puff pastry into a 14-inch square, turning several times to coat with the cheese. Brush the top of the pastry with the mustard and cut into 2-inch squares.

3. Place a frank across the center of each square of puff pastry and roll up the pastry to encase the frank; you should see the ends of the frank sticking out. Transfer to a prepared baking sheet. Repeat with the remaining franks and pastry, setting them 1 inch apart.

4. Cover with heavy-duty plastic wrap and refrigerate for up to 24 hours, or freeze on the baking sheet, transfer to zipper-top plastic bags, and freeze for up to 6 weeks.

Bake It Later

1. For refrigerated or defrosted pastries, preheat the oven to 400°F. For frozen pastries, preheat the oven to 375°F. If the pastries are not already on the prepared baking sheets, prepare the sheets by lining as above and place the pastries on them.

2. For refrigerated or defrosted pastries, bring them to room temperature and bake for 7 to 10 minutes, until the pastry is golden brown. For frozen pastries, bake for 13 to 16 minutes, until golden brown. Serve warm.

Baked Brie

THIS STAR APPETIZER will have guests oohing and ahhing, and it's so easy to make. The best part is that it can be frozen for up to 2 months. There are lots of choices for topping this showstopper, so you can tailor it to your particular menu and tastes. Serve with water crackers or baguette slices.

SERVES 12 TO 14

1 sheet frozen puff pastry, defrosted and kept chilled

One 10-inch wheel or two 4- to 6-inch wheels Brie cheese

1 1/2 cups Brandied Cranberries (page 28)

Make It Now

1. Sprinkle flour over a large work surface. Roll out the dough so that it is about twice the size of your Brie. Remove the wrapping (but not the rind) from the Brie and lay it in the center of the pastry. (If you are using the smaller wheels of Brie, place them side by side.) Cover the top of the Brie with the cranberries.

2. Taking hold of two opposing corners of the pastry, bring them to the middle of the Brie and twist into a knot. Repeat with the other two opposing corners to enclose the Brie in the pastry.

3. Transfer the pastry-wrapped Brie to an airtight container, and refrigerate for up to 2 days or freeze for up to 2 months.

Bake It Later

1. Defrost the Brie in the refrigerator overnight, if necessary.

2. Preheat the oven to 350°F. Place the Brie on a baking sheet, making sure to keep the pastry cold until you are ready to bake it.

3. Bake the Brie for 30 minutes, until the pastry is puffed and golden brown. Remove from the oven and allow to rest for at least 20 minutes. Using two large spatulas, transfer the Brie to a platter and serve.

Brandied Cranberries

One 10-ounce bag fresh or frozen cranberries

1 cup sugar

Grated zest of 1 orange

3 tablespoons freshly squeezed orange juice

2 tablespoons brandy or Grand Marnier

Combine all the ingredients in a medium-size saucepan, bring to a boil, and simmer for 20 minutes, until thickened. Remove from the heat and allow to cool.

VARIATIONS

Here are few simple toppings you can use in place of the Brandied Cranberries:

- Apricot or raspberry jam or orange marmalade

- Apple butter

- Sweet mango chutney

- Mild honey and finely chopped walnuts

- Sun-dried tomato, basil, or cilantro pesto

- Black olive tapenade

Prosciutto Palmiers

PALMIERS ARE TRADITIONALLY SERVED as caramelized sugar cookies (and are often known as elephant ears), but these are impressive savory appetizers to serve and are quick and easy to make. Just roll out the pastry, top with your favorite flavors (see variations on page 30), roll, and freeze. When you are ready to serve, remove the roll from the freezer, cut, and bake—nothing could be simpler or more elegant. If you like, roll the palmier log in finely chopped pecans or walnuts before cutting and baking for nutty cheesy palmiers. SERVES 10 TO 12 (2 PER PERSON)

½ cup freshly grated Parmesan cheese

1 sheet frozen puff pastry, defrosted

6 very thin slices prosciutto (a little less than ¼ pound)

Make It Now

1. Sprinkle half of the cheese over your work surface. Lay the puff pastry on top of the cheese and sprinkle the top with the remaining cheese. Roll the puff pastry into a 16 x 12-inch rectangle.

2. Lay the strips of prosciutto over the puff pastry. Starting from one long end and working toward the center, roll up the pastry until you reach the center. Roll the other long end toward the center, until the two rolls meet.

3. Wrap the palmier roll in heavy-duty plastic wrap and refrigerate for up to 2 days or freeze for up to 2 months.

Bake It Later

1. Preheat the oven to 400°F. Line 2 to 3 baking sheets with aluminum foil, parchment paper, or silicone liners.

2. Cut the roll into ½-inch slices and lay them on the prepared baking sheets about 1 inch apart.

3. For refrigerated or defrosted pastries, bake for 10 to 12 minutes, until puffed and golden brown. For frozen pastries, bake for 15 to 17 minutes, until puffed and golden brown. Serve warm or at room temperature.

Roll out the puff pastry on a flour-dusted work surface and omit the cheese. Fill with one of the following combinations in place of the prosciutto:

- ¼ cup basil pesto, sun-dried tomato pesto, or cilantro pesto blended with one 3-ounce package cream cheese, softened.

- ¼ cup olive tapenade blended with 3 ounces crumbled goat cheese or one 3-ounce package cream cheese, softened.

- ¼ cup Roquefort cheese blended with one 3-ounce package cream cheese, softened, and 1 tablespoon dry sherry.

- ¼ cup finely chopped sun-dried tomatoes blended with ¼ cup mascarpone cheese. (Roll out the dough on a work surface dusted with Parmesan cheese instead of flour for extra flavor.)

- One 3-ounce package cream cheese, softened, combined with ⅓ cup finely chopped black olives and ¼ cup finely chopped canned green chiles. (Roll out the dough on a work surface sprinkled with finely shredded mild cheddar cheese instead of the flour for extra flavor.)

Artichoke Nibblers

THESE LITTLE MINI-MUFFINS can be addictive, with their garlicky, creamy cheese flavor combined with nuggets of artichoke. One small bite equals lots of flavor. They can be tucked away in the freezer until you need a dynamite starter for dinner, or they can be served alongside grilled entrées.

SERVES 6

½ cup (1 stick) unsalted butter

4 cloves garlic, minced

4 cups fresh bread crumbs or finely torn bread from the inside of a loaf of sturdy white bread

One 6-ounce jar marinated artichoke hearts, drained and chopped

1 cup sour cream

1 cup freshly grated Parmesan cheese (see Diva Note)

Grated zest of 1 lemon

½ teaspoon freshly ground black pepper

Make It Now

1. Coat the insides of 24 mini-muffin cups with nonstick cooking spray.

2. Melt the butter in a large skillet over medium to medium-high heat. Add the garlic and sauté for about 2 minutes, until the garlic is fragrant, being careful not to let it brown.

3. Remove the pan from the heat and add the bread crumbs, tossing to coat. Transfer the bread to a large mixing bowl. Stir in the artichokes, sour cream, Parmesan, lemon zest, and pepper.

4. Using a small scoop, scoop the mixture into the prepared muffin cups so that each cup is three-quarters full. Cover with heavy-duty plastic wrap and refrigerate for up to 2 days or freeze for up to 1 month.

Diva Note

Parmesan cheese makes these appetizers into a sublime nibble, but if you choose to substitute more expensive Parmigiano-Reggiano, the difference is quite noticeable and for the better. Parmigiano-Reggiano has a subtle nutty flavor that will blend into the pastry and give you a deliciously extravagant appetizer. Either one will give you a great result; the Parmigiano takes these to another level.

1. Defrost the artichoke nibblers in the refrigerator overnight, if necessary.

2. Preheat the oven to 400°F. Let the appetizers come to room temperature for about 20 minutes.

3. Bake for 12 to 15 minutes, until golden brown. Remove from the oven, allow to rest for 3 to 5 minutes, transfer to a platter, and serve warm or at room temperature.

VARIATION

No mini-muffin tins? Never fear, you can spread the mixture in an 8-inch square baking dish coated with nonstick cooking spray. Bake for 15 to 17 minutes, until golden brown. Allow to rest for 5 minutes, then cut into squares and serve.

Jalapeño Pepper Poppers

THESE DELICIOUS LITTLE MUFFINLIKE APPETIZERS are studded with chiles, cheese, corn, and peppers. The batter keeps in the fridge for 3 days and can be frozen in muffin tins, and then defrosted and baked. They are the perfect snack for a Super Bowl party, or as a fun appetizer for a fajita party.

SERVES 8 TO 10

½ cup (1 stick) unsalted butter

½ cup finely chopped sweet onion, such as Vidalia

¼ cup finely chopped red bell pepper

¼ cup finely chopped jalapeño chile

1 cup corn kernels, fresh or defrosted frozen

One 8.5-ounce box Jiffy cornbread mix

½ cup milk

⅔ cup sour cream

½ cup mayonnaise

6 dashes of hot sauce of your choice

⅔ cup shredded mild cheddar cheese

⅓ cup shredded pepper Jack cheese

Make It Now

1. Coat the insides of 24 mini-muffin cups with nonstick cooking spray.

2. Melt the butter in a large skillet over medium heat. Transfer half to a large mixing bowl to cool. Add the onion, bell pepper, jalapeño, and corn to the skillet and sauté until the onion and pepper are softened, 3 to 4 minutes. Transfer the mixture to the mixing bowl and allow to cool.

3. Add the cornbread mix, milk, sour cream, mayonnaise, hot sauce, cheddar cheese, and pepper Jack cheese to the mixing bowl. Stir until blended. Using a small scoop, fill the muffin cups three-quarters full with the cornbread mixture. Cover and refrigerate for up to 3 days or freeze for up to 6 weeks.

Diva Note

Any leftover baked muffins can be refrozen in airtight containers for up to 1 month. Defrost and warm them, loosely tented with aluminum foil, in a 350°F oven for about 10 minutes.

1. Defrost the muffin batter in the refrigerator overnight, if necessary.

2. Preheat the oven to 375°F. Allow the batter to come to room temperature for about 20 minutes.

3. Bake for 20 to 30 minutes, until a toothpick inserted into the center of a muffin comes out with just a few crumbs adhering to it. Allow the muffins to cool in the tins for 5 minutes, then remove and serve warm.

VARIATION

Add 1 cup lump crabmeat or finely chopped cooked shrimp or chorizo to the batter.

Bacon-Wrapped Figs Stuffed with Blue Cheese

ONE OF MY MOST-REQUESTED RECIPES for grazing parties is bacon-wrapped dates with Parmesan, which has led me to try new variations on the theme. These crispy, sweet figs filled with piquant blue cheese are fast becoming my personal favorite! SERVES 8

8 strips bacon

16 dried figs

$\frac{1}{3}$ to $\frac{1}{2}$ cup crumbled blue cheese, such as Danish, Maytag, or Gorgonzola

Make It Now

1. Preheat the oven to 400°F. Line a baking sheet with aluminum foil or a silicone baking liner.

2. Lay the bacon on the baking sheet and bake for 5 to 7 minutes, until the bacon has rendered some fat but is still pliable. Drain on paper towels. Cut each strip of bacon in half and lay it on a cutting board. Slit the figs lengthwise, making a small pocket. Push about 1 teaspoon of the crumbled cheese into the pocket and close the slit.

3. Place the fig on the bacon and roll the bacon around the fig, securing with a toothpick. Repeat with the remaining bacon, figs, and cheese.

4. Transfer the figs to a 9 x 13-inch baking dish, placing them about $\frac{1}{2}$ inch apart. Cover, and refrigerate for up to 3 days or freeze for up to 1 month.

Bake It Later

1. Defrost the figs in the refrigerator overnight, if necessary.

2. Preheat the oven to 400°F. Let the figs come to room temperature for about 20 minutes.

3. Bake for 10 minutes, or until the bacon is crisp. Remove from the baking dish and serve hot or warm.

VARIATION

Try the figs stuffed with nuggets of sharp white cheddar or Parmigiano-Reggiano cheese.

Crab Melts

TUNA MELTS, CRAB MELTS, and even chicken melts are a great make-it-now, bake-it-later snack or light dinner entrée. To serve as an appetizer, cut the muffins into quarters and serve as finger food; otherwise serve two English muffin halves per person for an entrée.

SERVES 16 AS AN APPETIZER OR 8 AS A MAIN COURSE

One 3-ounce package cream cheese, softened

½ cup mayonnaise

2 teaspoons freshly squeezed lemon juice

1 teaspoon prepared horseradish

1 teaspoon Worcestershire sauce

½ cup finely chopped celery

3 green onions (white and tender green parts), finely chopped

1 cup finely shredded sharp cheddar cheese

1 pound lump crabmeat, picked over for cartilage and shells

8 English muffins, split in half

Make It Now

1. In a medium-size mixing bowl, mix together the cream cheese, mayonnaise, lemon juice, horseradish, and Worcestershire sauce until smooth. Stir in the celery, green onions, and cheese. Fold in the crab, being careful not to break up the lumps too much.

2. Spread the mixture on the split English muffins, lay the muffins on a baking sheet, cover with heavy-duty plastic wrap, and refrigerate for up to 3 days, or freeze for up to 1 month.

Bake It Later

1. Defrost the muffins in the refrigerator overnight, if necessary.

2. Preheat the oven to 400°F. Let the muffins come to room temperature for about 20 minutes.

3. Bake the melts for 15 to 20 minutes, until the tops are golden brown and bubbling. Serve immediately.

VARIATIONS

Substitute one of the following for the crabmeat:

- Two 8-ounce cans albacore tuna packed in vegetable oil, drained and flaked

- 2 cups finely diced or shredded cooked chicken

- 1 pound finely chopped cooked shrimp

Warm Seafood Spread

THIS SPREAD IS FILLED WITH LUMP CRABMEAT and clams and tastes sublime on crackers, baguette slices, or cucumber rounds. The spread keeps in the refrigerator for a few days, and you can freeze it for about 1 month. Freezing and baking this in a hollowed loaf of bread instead of the casserole dish is a nice way to present it, with no serving dish to clean up! SERVES 6 TO 8

One 8-ounce package cream cheese, softened

½ cup mayonnaise

2 green onions (white and tender green parts), chopped

1 tablespoon finely chopped fresh flat-leaf parsley

1 teaspoon prepared horseradish

1 teaspoon Worcestershire sauce

2 teaspoons dry white wine or dry vermouth

⅓ pound lump crabmeat, picked over for cartilage and shells

One 6-ounce can minced clams, drained

½ cup sliced almonds

Make It Now

1. In a medium-size bowl, beat together the cream cheese and mayonnaise. Add the green onions, parsley, horseradish, Worcestershire sauce, and wine, beating until the mixture is combined. Gradually fold in the crab and clams, stirring gently so as not to break up the lumps of crab.

2. Transfer the mixture to a 1-quart baking dish and sprinkle with the almonds. Cover and refrigerate for up to 3 days or freeze for up to 1 month.

Bake It Later

1. Defrost the casserole in the refrigerator overnight, if necessary.

2. Preheat the oven to 350°F. Let the casserole come to room temperature for about 20 minutes.

3. Bake for 20 to 25 minutes, until the spread is bubbling and the almonds are golden brown. Serve warm.

Bacon-Wrapped Shrimp with Many Basting Sauces

WE ALL KNOW THAT EVERYTHING TASTES BETTER WITH BACON, and shrimp are no exception! With the eight different basting-sauce options, you can give this classic finger food a unique personality. Partially cooking the bacon before wrapping the shrimp ensures that you won't overcook the shrimp, and they won't be swimming in grease. You can use this same bacon technique to wrap whole water chestnuts, scallops, and button mushrooms. SERVES 6 TO 8

12 strips bacon

1/2 cup basting sauce of your choice (recipes follow)

24 large or jumbo raw shrimp, peeled, deveined, and tail section left on if possible

Make It Now

1. Preheat the oven to 400°F. Line a baking sheet with aluminum foil or a silicone baking liner.

2. Lay the bacon on the baking sheet and bake for 5 to 7 minutes, until the bacon has rendered some fat but is still pliable. Drain on paper towels. Cut each strip in half.

3. Brush each strip of bacon with a thin layer of the basting sauce, place 1 shrimp on each piece of bacon, and wrap the bacon around the shrimp, securing with a 6-inch skewer.

4. Place in a 9 x 13-inch baking dish, cover, and refrigerate for up to 2 days, or freeze on cookie sheets until frozen, then transfer to zipper-top plastic bags and freeze for up to 2 weeks.

Bake It Later

1. Defrost the shrimp in the refrigerator overnight, if necessary.

2. Preheat the oven to 400°F.

3. Arrange the skewered shrimp on a rack on a rimmed baking sheet. Bake for 5 to 7 minutes, until the shrimp are pink, turning once to evenly brown the bacon. Serve immediately.

Plum-Chipotle Sauce

MAKES ABOUT ½ CUP

½ cup Asian plum sauce

1 teaspoon freshly squeezed lemon juice

½ teaspoon ground chipotle chile powder

Blend together the plum sauce, lemon juice, and chipotle chile powder. Store in the refrigerator for up to 2 weeks.

Maple-Dijon Sauce

MAKES ABOUT ½ CUP

⅓ cup Dijon mustard

3 tablespoons pure maple syrup

Blend together the mustard and maple syrup. Store in the refrigerator for up to 2 weeks.

Pesto Sauce

MAKES ABOUT ½ CUP

⅓ cup prepared pesto (sun-dried tomato, basil, or cilantro)

3 tablespoons mayonnaise

Blend together the pesto and mayonnaise. Store in the refrigerator for up to 5 days.

Sesame-Hoisin-Chili Sauce

MAKES ABOUT ½ CUP

½ cup hoisin sauce

1 teaspoon Asian chili garlic sauce

1 teaspoon toasted sesame oil

Blend together the hoisin sauce, chili garlic sauce, and sesame oil. Store in the refrigerator for up to 1 week.

Wasabi Sauce

MAKES ABOUT ½ CUP

½ cup mayonnaise

2 teaspoons wasabi powder

Blend together the mayonnaise and wasabi. Store in the refrigerator for up to 5 days. (The flavor will get hotter the longer it is stored.)

Mock Barbecue Sauce

MAKES ABOUT ½ CUP

⅓ cup ketchup

2 tablespoons light brown sugar

1 tablespoon Worcestershire sauce

6 dashes of hot sauce of your choice

Blend together the ketchup, brown sugar, Worcestershire sauce, and hot sauce. Store in the refrigerator for up to 1 week.

Bloody Mary Sauce

MAKES ABOUT ⅓ CUP

⅓ cup Bloody Mary mix or spicy tomato juice

2 teaspoons ketchup

1 teaspoon Worcestershire sauce

1 teaspoon celery salt

Blend together the Bloody Mary mix, ketchup, Worcestershire sauce, and celery salt. Store in the refrigerator for up to 1 week.

Apricot-Dijon Sauce

MAKES ABOUT ½ CUP

⅓ cup apricot preserves

2 tablespoons Dijon mustard

1 teaspoon freshly squeezed lemon juice

Blend together the preserves, mustard, and lemon juice. Store in the refrigerator for up to 1 week.

Honey-Teriyaki Chicken Wings

CHICKEN WINGS ARE SO VERSATILE, it's hard to put them in a category. Great starters for a casual party, served as part of the menu while watching sports on television, or offered as part of a buffet dinner, they are a terrific make-it-now, bake-it-later dish. I prefer the little drumettes, which look like tiny drumsticks, but you can also buy whole wings and split them at the joints. SERVES 8 TO 10

2 tablespoons vegetable oil

½ cup honey

1 cup soy sauce

¼ cup ketchup

1 tablespoon cornstarch

Juice from one 15.4-ounce can pineapple chunks

2½ to 3 pounds chicken wings (drumettes or whole wings split at the joints)

Make It Now

1. In a small saucepan, stir together the oil, honey, soy sauce, ketchup, cornstarch, and pineapple juice. (Reserve and refrigerate pineapple chunks.) Bring marinade to a boil, then remove from the heat and let cool to room temperature.

2. Place the chicken wings in a large zipper-top plastic bag and pour the sauce over the chicken. Seal the bag and turn the chicken in the bag to coat it. Refrigerate the chicken to marinate for at least 4 hours, or up to 2 days.

¼ to ⅓ cup sesame seeds

Reserved pineapple chunks

Bake It Later

1. Preheat the oven to 350°F. Line a baking sheet with aluminum foil or a silicone baking liner.

2. Pour the sauce and chicken onto the baking sheet, mix in the pineapple chunks, and sprinkle with the sesame seeds.

3. Bake the wings for 45 minutes, turning once, until the chicken is cooked through and the sesame seeds are golden brown. Remove from the oven and transfer to a serving platter. Serve warm, at room temperature, or cold.

Buffalo Baked Chicken Wings

THESE CLASSIC CHICKEN WINGS are baked rather than fried, but they don't lose a bit of flavor for it. Serve with the traditional accompaniments: chunky blue cheese dressing (recipe follows) and celery and carrot sticks. SERVES 8 TO 10

1 cup (2 sticks) unsalted butter

1 cup Frank's RedHot Sauce
(see Diva Note)

2½ to 3 pounds chicken wings
(drumettes or whole wings split at
the joints)

Make It Now

1. Melt the butter with the hot sauce in a medium-size saucepan over medium-low heat. Remove from the heat and let cool to room temperature.

2. Place the wings in a large baking dish and pour 1 cup of the buttery hot sauce over the wings, turning them in the dish to coat them with the sauce. Cover the dish and refrigerate, along with the remaining 1 cup of buttery hot sauce in a separate container, for up to 2 days.

Diva Note

The Anchor Bar in Buffalo, New York, originated the "Buffalo Wing" craze. Their recipe uses Frank's RedHot Original Cayenne Pepper Sauce, which is what I like to use. There are lots of other hot sauces on the market, but Frank's has a more balanced pepper flavor, while Tabasco and some others have a more pronounced vinegar flavor. If you can't find Frank's, try Crystal or your favorite brand of hot sauce.

1. Preheat the oven to 350°F.

2. Reheat the remaining buttery hot sauce in a saucepan over low heat.

3. Bake the wings for 45 minutes, turning once halfway through the baking time and basting with the remaining buttery hot sauce. Transfer to a serving platter and serve warm.

Buffalo Wing Blue Cheese Dressing

MAKES ABOUT 3 1/2 CUPS

1 1/2 cups mayonnaise

1/2 cup sour cream

1 tablespoon red wine vinegar

1 tablespoon freshly squeezed lemon juice

2 teaspoons Worcestershire sauce

1 teaspoon freshly ground black pepper

1 1/2 cups crumbled blue cheese

Combine all of the ingredients in a small bowl and stir to blend. Refrigerate for at least 2 hours, or for up to 4 days.

Maple-Chipotle Chicken Wings

SWEET, SMOKY, AND A BIT SPICY, these wings are perfect to nibble on as an appetizer, or you can serve them as part of a larger grazing menu with other south-of-the-border bites. SERVES 8 TO 10

2 tablespoons canola oil

½ cup finely chopped red onion

2 chipotle chiles in adobo sauce, drained and finely chopped

¼ cup pure maple syrup

½ cup ketchup

⅓ cup chicken broth

2½ to 3 pounds chicken wings (drumettes or whole wings split at the joints)

4 green onions (white and tender green parts), finely chopped, for garnish

¼ cup finely chopped fresh cilantro, for garnish

Make It Now

1. Heat the oil in a 2-quart saucepan over medium heat. Add the onion and chipotles and sauté for about 2 minutes, until the onion is fragrant and begins to soften.

2. Add the maple syrup, ketchup, and chicken broth and bring to a boil. Stir the mixture over medium-high heat until it begins to thicken, about 5 minutes. Remove from the heat and allow to cool.

3. Pour the sauce into a 2-gallon zipper-top plastic bag and add the wings. Seal the bag and refrigerate for at least 3 hours, or up to 24 hours.

Bake It Later

1. Preheat the oven to 350°F.

2. Transfer the wings and sauce to a 9 x 13-inch baking dish and bake for 35 to 45 minutes, turning the wings once and basting with the sauce, until the wings are glazed and cooked through. Sprinkle the green onions and cilantro over the wings before serving hot, cold, or at room temperature.

Macadamia-Crusted Chicken Tenders with Maui Sunset Sauce

A CRUNCHY COATING of finely chopped macadamia nuts and crispy panko crumbs gives these chicken tenders a lot of personality when served with the scarlet sweet-and-pungent sauce. Serve these as part of a grazing menu or as a starter before the main event. They can also be served warm over a green salad. SERVES 6

2 cups buttermilk

1 ½ pounds chicken breast tenders

1 teaspoon poultry seasoning

1 teaspoon freshly ground black pepper

½ cup (1 stick) unsalted butter, melted and cooled

1 ½ cups finely chopped salted or unsalted macadamia nuts

1 cup panko crumbs

1 teaspoon sweet paprika

2 cups Maui Sunset Sauce (page 46)

Make It Now

1. Combine the buttermilk, chicken tenders, poultry seasoning, and pepper in a large zipper-top plastic bag. Seal the bag and turn the chicken in the mixture to blend and coat. Refrigerate for at least 4 hours.

2. Line a baking sheet with aluminum foil, parchment paper, or a silicone baking liner.

3. Drain the chicken in a colander. Pour the butter into a shallow dish. In another shallow dish, combine the nuts, panko crumbs, and paprika. Dip the tenders into the butter, then into the nut mixture, pressing the nuts into the chicken to make them adhere. Lay the chicken strips onto the prepared baking sheet, continuing until all the chicken is breaded. Pour any remaining butter over the top of the tenders.

4. Cover with heavy-duty plastic wrap and refrigerate for up to 24 hours, or freeze for up to 6 weeks.

Bake It Later

1. Defrost the chicken in the refrigerator overnight, if necessary.

2. Preheat the oven to 400°F. Let the tenders come to room temperature for about 30 minutes.

3. Bake for 10 to 12 minutes, until the nuts are golden brown and the chicken is cooked through. Serve warm, at room temperature, or cold, with the Maui Sunset Sauce.

VARIATION

Turn this into a main dish by substituting 6 boneless, skinless chicken breasts halves for the chicken tenders. Bake at 400°F for 25 to 30 minutes.

Maui Sunset Sauce

A SWEET AND SPICY SAUCE, this not only pairs well with the crusted chicken tenders, but also with shrimp or pork on skewers. MAKES ABOUT 2 CUPS

½ cup dried apricots, finely chopped

¾ cup water

⅓ cup firmly packed brown sugar

½ cup rice vinegar

½ cup ketchup

1 clove garlic, minced

½ teaspoon finely minced fresh ginger

¼ teaspoon chili oil

1. Combine all of the ingredients in a 2-quart saucepan and bring to a boil. Reduce the heat to low, cover the pan, and simmer the sauce for 30 minutes, stirring, until thickened.

2. Let the sauce cool to room temperature and serve. It will keep in an airtight container in the refrigerator for up to 2 weeks.

Pasta and
Grain Bakes

Pasta and grains, such as grits, rice, and wild rice, lend themselves well to the make-it-now and bake-it-later strategy. You can have comforting main dishes and side dishes, from old-fashioned macaroni and cheese to elegant salmon and dill lasagna, in your fridge or freezer whenever you need them. Cooked pasta freezes well, and cooked rice (both white and wild) freezes beautifully.

When putting together a make-ahead pasta or rice dish, you need a bit more sauce than you might think. Since pasta and rice absorb liquid like sponges, it is necessary to thin the sauces a bit so that the starch can absorb them, which will thicken the sauce as it bakes in the oven. Most of the recipes here have a lot of sauce, but don't let that scare you, because the pasta, rice, or grain will absorb the sauce while the dish is baking. Any additional sauce that you may have left over can always be frozen; just remember to label it, otherwise you'll have little packages of no-name freezer-surprise sauces!

Pasta and Grain Bakes

Lasagne di Gubbio

THIS LASAGNA IS PATTERNED AFTER one that I had at Taverna del Lupo (Tavern of the Wolf), located in my grandmother's hometown of Gubbio, Italy. The original dish featured shaved black truffles over the top of each portion, which you can certainly include, but the dish itself is absolutely divine with its creamy cheese sauce and mushroom and ham filling. Think about buying a small bottle of black truffle oil and drizzling a bit over each portion before serving. The dish is terrific as an entrée or as a side dish to roasted beef or poultry. SERVES 10

FILLING

1/4 cup (1/2 stick) unsalted butter

1 pound white or cremini mushrooms (see Diva Note), stems removed and sliced 1/4 inch thick

ROMANO CREAM SAUCE

1/2 cup (1 stick) unsalted butter

1/2 cup unbleached all-purpose flour

3 cups chicken broth

2 1/2 cups whole milk

1 1/2 teaspoons salt, plus more as needed

1 teaspoon freshly ground black or white pepper, plus more as needed

1/2 teaspoon freshly grated nutmeg

1 1/2 cups freshly grated Pecorino Romano cheese

ASSEMBLY

One 9-ounce package no-cook lasagna noodles

1/4 pound boiled imported ham, diced

1 pound fresh mozzarella cheese, sliced 1/2 inch thick

1 cup freshly grated Pecorino Romano cheese

Make It Now

1. To make the filling, melt the butter in a large sauté pan over medium heat. Add the mushrooms and sauté until the liquid begins to evaporate and the mushrooms begin to color. Remove the mushrooms from the pan and set aside to cool. (You may cover and refrigerate the mushrooms for up to 2 days. Drain off any liquid that accumulates in the storage container before proceeding.)

2. To make the cream sauce, melt the butter in a medium-size saucepan over medium heat. Whisk in the flour and cook until white bubbles form on the surface. Cook the mixture for 2 to 3 minutes, until smooth and thick.

3. Gradually add the broth, whisking until blended. Add the milk, salt, pepper, and nutmeg. Increase the heat and bring the mixture to a boil, whisking constantly.

4. Remove the sauce from the stove and gradually stir in the cheese, until it melts. Add more salt and pepper, if desired.

5. To assemble the lasagna, coat the inside of a 9 x 13-inch baking dish with nonstick cooking spray.

6. Spread 1 cup of the cream sauce in the bottom of the pan, and top with a layer of lasagna noodles. Distribute some of the mushrooms and ham over the noodles. Top with a bit of the cream sauce, a few slices of fresh mozzarella, another layer of noodles, and another layer of

mushrooms and ham. Continue to layer, ending with a layer of noodles. You should have four layers. Top with the remaining cream sauce.

7. Sprinkle the casserole with the Romano cheese. Cover and refrigerate for up to 2 days or freeze for up to 1 month.

Bake It Later

1. Defrost the lasagna in the refrigerator overnight, if necessary.

2. Preheat the oven to 350°F. Allow the lasagna to come to room temperature for 30 minutes.

3. Bake, covered, for 30 minutes, then uncover and bake for an additional 10 to 15 minutes, until the sauce is bubbling and the cheese is golden brown on top. Allow the lasagna to rest for 5 to 10 minutes before cutting and serving.

Diva Note

White button or cremini mushrooms are my choice for this lasagna. They won't take over the flavor of the lasagna, just add to it. Don't try using dried mushrooms, because they will overpower the flavor of this dish, and portobello mushrooms may turn the lasagna an unattractive shade of UPS brown.

Salmon and Dill Lasagna

THIS LASAGNA IS A DELICIOUS ENTRÉE to serve for a special occasion or a dinner with friends. A splurge of your time and ingredients, it is filled with bright pink chunks of salmon and deep green dill. If you enjoy other seafood, substitute it for the salmon; firm white-fleshed fish, such as halibut, or shellfish, such as scallops, shrimp, and crab, all work well either by themselves or in combination with each other. SERVES 10 TO 12

FILLING

¼ cup (½ stick) unsalted butter

2 pounds salmon fillets

2 tablespoons dry white wine or dry vermouth

SEAFOOD CREAM SAUCE

½ cup (1 stick) unsalted butter

½ cup unbleached all-purpose flour

3 cups whole or 2 percent milk

⅔ cup reserved seafood cooking liquid or seafood stock (see Diva Note)

About ¾ cup heavy cream

Salt and white pepper to taste

Pinch of ground nutmeg

¼ cup chopped fresh dill, plus more for garnish

ASSEMBLY

One 9-ounce package no-cook lasagna noodles *or* three 12 x 8-inch sheets fresh pasta

1¼ cups freshly grated Parmigiano-Reggiano cheese

Make It Now

1. To prepare the filling, melt the butter over medium heat in a large skillet. Add the salmon and wine, cover, and poach for 10 minutes, or until the salmon is cooked through. It may still be a deep pink in the center, but will continue to cook as the lasagna is baked. Remove the salmon from the liquid, scrape off the skin, and break the salmon into chunks. Refrigerate until you are ready to assemble the lasagna. Drain the cooking liquid into a measuring cup and reserve. (At this point, you may refrigerate the salmon and cooking liquid for up to 24 hours.)

2. To make the seafood cream sauce, melt the butter in a 3-quart saucepan over medium heat. Whisk in the flour and cook until white bubbles form on the surface. Cook the mixture for 2 to 3 minutes, until smooth and thick. Gradually add the milk and reserved seafood cooking liquid, stirring constantly with a whisk, until the sauce comes to a boil. Add up to ¾ cup heavy cream and let simmer, stirring a few times, until the sauce coats the back of a spoon. Season with the salt, white pepper, nutmeg, and dill. (At this point, you may let cool, cover, and refrigerate for up to 3 days. Reheat to lukewarm so the sauce is easily spread before assembling the lasagna.)

3. To assemble the lasagna, coat the inside of a 9 x 13-inch baking dish with nonstick cooking spray. Spread a layer of the cream sauce over the bottom of the dish. Top with a layer of lasagna noodles, a thin layer of cream sauce, and half of the salmon. Cover with another layer of

lasagna noodles, cream sauce, and salmon. Top with a layer of lasagna noodles, the remaining cream sauce, and the grated cheese. Cover with aluminum foil and refrigerate for up to 24 hours.

Bake It Later

1. Preheat the oven to 350°F. Allow the lasagna to come to room temperature for 30 minutes.

2. Bake the lasagna, covered, for 1 hour, then uncover and bake another 10 to 15 minutes, until the sauce is bubbling and the cheese is golden brown on top. Allow the lasagna to rest for 10 to 15 minutes before serving.

Diva Note

Seafood stocks are now available in most grocery stores. My favorite is Superior Touch Better Than Bouillon brand lobster stock. If you can't find lobster stock, a mixture of equal parts chicken broth and clam juice will give you a seafood stock that isn't overpowering. Clam juice is sold in the canned clam section of the grocery store, where the tuna and other canned seafood are sold, or in the "gourmet" section.

Vegetarian Lasagna

THE THOUGHT OF TOFU IN LASAGNA would make my grandmother spin in her grave. So I thought, why not take her favorite vegetables, roast them, and then layer them between lasagna noodles, giving us an Old World dish with a New World flavor? I think she would approve, because these layers are stunning, with huge bold flavors. SERVES 10

1 large purple eggplant, ends trimmed and sliced into ½-inch rounds

3 medium-size zucchini, ends trimmed and sliced into ½-inch rounds

4 portobello mushrooms, stems and gills removed (see Diva Note)

1 large sweet onion, such as Vidalia, sliced into ½-inch rounds

1 cup olive oil

1 tablespoon salt

2 teaspoons freshly ground black pepper

1 teaspoon dried oregano

2 teaspoons dried basil

5 cups Quick Marinara Sauce (page 246)

One 9-ounce package no-cook lasagna noodles

½ cup finely chopped fresh flat-leaf parsley

2 cups finely shredded mozzarella cheese

1½ cups freshly grated Parmigiano-Reggiano cheese

Make It Now

1. Preheat the oven to 400°F. Line baking sheets with aluminum foil or silicone baking liners.

2. Arrange the eggplant, zucchini, mushrooms, and onion on the baking sheets, leaving space in between each piece. In a measuring cup, combine the olive oil, salt, pepper, oregano, and basil, stirring to blend. Liberally brush the vegetables with the mixture, and bake for 15 minutes, until the vegetables begin to color. Turn the vegetables and brush the other side with the oil. Roast for another 10 to 15 minutes, until the vegetables are cooked and beginning to turn golden. Remove to a cutting board and blot with paper towels to remove excess moisture. When cool enough to handle, cut the onion rings into quarters and slice the mushrooms ½ inch thick.

3. Coat the inside of a 9 x 13-inch baking dish with nonstick cooking spray. Spread a thin layer of marinara sauce over the bottom of the dish.

4. Lay some lasagna noodles over the sauce and top with the eggplant rounds. Sprinkle with some of the parsley and mozzarella cheese, and cover with another thin layer of sauce. Cover the sauce with another layer of noodles, all the zucchini, half the onion, more mozzarella

Diva Note

Portobello mushroom gills will turn your dishes black, so it's best to remove them before roasting. Use a teaspoon to scrape away the gills.

and parsley, and a thin layer of sauce. Cover the sauce with another layer of noodles, all the mushrooms, the remaining onion, some of the mozzarella and parsley, and a thin layer of sauce. End with a layer of noodles, the remaining sauce, parsley, and mozzarella, and the Parmigiano-Reggiano. Cover the casserole and refrigerate for up to 2 days or freeze for up to 1 month.

Bake It Later

1. Defrost the lasagna in the refrigerator overnight, if necessary.

2. Preheat the oven to 350°F. Allow the lasagna to come to room temperature for 30 minutes.

3. Bake, uncovered, for 40 to 50 minutes, until the sauce is bubbling and the cheese is golden brown on top. Allow to rest for 10 to 20 minutes before serving hot or at room temperature.

Lasagna

Lasagna is a show-stopping main course. There are several do-ahead options you may take advantage of while you are preparing lasagnas, and, in addition, the entire assembled lasagna can be refrigerated or frozen. Most lasagnas are baked in 9 x 13-inch baking dishes and will serve 10 to 12 people, but they can certainly be layered in smaller containers to serve 4 to 6. I like to use 8- or 9-inch square containers or loaf pans. All lasagnas freeze well, with the exception of the seafood lasagna, because the seafood's flavor and texture sometimes suffer in the freezing process. Since lasagna contains protein, vegetables, and starch, you need only serve a salad or vegetable on the side, and a light dessert; it really is the ultimate one-dish meal. That said, I sometimes will serve lasagna as a side dish as part of a large buffet. In that case, the traditional 9 x 13-inch baking dish will serve 16 to 20 people.

Barilla makes a thin lasagna noodle that needs no precooking or presoaking in water, and I recommend that you use those, as they are a real time and energy saver. If you use regular lasagna noodles, you may need a bit less sauce than what I've called for in these lasagna recipes.

Penne, Sausage, and Meatball Bake

THIS DELICIOUS CASSEROLE, with layers of spicy vodka cream sauce, penne, sausage nuggets, cut-up meatballs, and melted fresh mozzarella, is a terrific dish to serve for a winter company meal, or for a night when the gang is coming over to watch sports on TV. My friend and colleague Carol Blom-strom, the owner of Lotsa Pasta in San Diego, shared the recipe for this simple vodka cream sauce during a class she taught. It's a terrific, versatile sauce to use anytime. SERVES 10

MEATBALLS

1 slice crusty bread

2 tablespoons milk

½ cup finely chopped onion

1 clove garlic, minced

2 tablespoons finely chopped fresh flat-leaf parsley

1½ teaspoons salt

½ teaspoon freshly ground black pepper

¼ cup freshly grated Pecorino Romano cheese

1 large egg

½ pound lean ground pork

½ pound lean ground beef

½ cup olive oil

5 sweet Italian sausages

1 pound penne, cooked according to package directions

Carol's Spicy Vodka Cream Sauce (page 57)

8 ounces small fresh mozzarella balls, drained, *or* 1 large ball fresh mozzarella cut into small cubes

1 cup freshly grated Parmesan cheese

Make It Now

1. To make the meatballs, soak the bread and milk together in a large mixing bowl for 5 minutes. Add the onion, garlic, parsley, salt, pepper, Romano, and egg, and stir until blended.

2. Add the pork and beef and mix by hand until the meatball mixture is combined. Shape into balls 1 inch in diameter. (At this point, you may refrigerate for up to 2 days or freeze for up to 6 weeks.)

3. Preheat the oven to 350°F. Set a wire rack on a baking sheet. Heat the oil in a large skillet. Brown the meatballs on all sides, until they have formed a nice crust, about 10 minutes. Remove from the oil to the rack set on the baking sheet, and bake for 15 minutes, until the meatballs are cooked through. Remove from the oven and allow to cool. (At this point, you may refrigerate for up to 2 days or freeze for up to 1 month.) Cut the meatballs into quarters.

4. In a medium skillet over medium-high heat, brown the sausages on all sides. Prick the sausages with the sharp tip of a paring knife on all sides to allow some of the fat to drain off. Add ⅓ cup water to the pan, lower the heat, cover, and simmer until the sausages are cooked through and the water is absorbed. Cool the sausages and cut into ½-inch rounds.

5. To assemble the casserole, coat the inside of a 9 x 13-inch baking dish with nonstick cooking spray. Combine

the penne in a large bowl with 1½ cups of the vodka sauce, stirring until the penne is coated with the sauce.

6. Spread half the penne in the dish and top with the meatballs, sausage, and mozzarella cheese. Spread 1 cup of the vodka sauce over the mixture, then top with the remaining penne and vodka sauce and the Parmesan cheese. Cover and refrigerate for up to 3 days or freeze for up to 6 weeks.

Bake It Later

1. Defrost the casserole in the refrigerator overnight, if necessary.

2. Preheat the oven to 350°F. Allow the casserole to come to room temperature for about 30 minutes.

3. Bake, covered, for 30 minutes. Uncover and bake for another 20 minutes, until the sauce is bubbling and the cheese is golden brown on top. Allow to rest for 15 minutes before serving.

Carol's Spicy Vodka Cream Sauce

CAROL SERVES THIS as one of three sauces with her timpano, a many-layered baked pasta tower (see page 68).
The vodka sauce is simplicity itself, and her technique for
simmering the red pepper flakes in the vodka ensures
that the sauce has some nice heat, which is then tem-
pered by the addition of cream. MAKES 5 CUPS

1 cup vodka

2 teaspoons red pepper flakes

6 tablespoons unsalted butter

3½ cups whipping cream

One 32-ounce can crushed tomatoes (do not drain)

½ cup freshly grated Parmesan cheese

1. Pour the vodka into a small saucepan, stir in the red pepper flakes, and let sit for about 1 hour.

2. Bring the vodka to a boil and boil for about 4 minutes.
   Add the butter to the saucepan. When it has melted, stir
   in the cream and tomatoes and bring to a simmer. Simmer, uncovered, for 10 minutes. Remove from the heat
   and whisk in the Parmesan cheese. (At this point, you
   may cool the sauce and refrigerate for up to 3 days or
   freeze for up to 1 month.)

Chicken, Artichoke, and Penne Alfredo

THIS WARM AND INVITING CASSEROLE is a terrific dish to take to a potluck or to a friend who's feeling blue. Soothing and comforting, it's like grown-up mac and cheese, with lots of style. If you prefer a different pasta shape, fettuccine works well here, as does short rigatoni or shell-shaped pastas.

SERVES 10

½ cup (1 stick) unsalted butter

2 medium-size shallots, finely chopped

1 pound white mushrooms, sliced

One 16-ounce package frozen artichoke hearts, defrosted, *or* two 15.5-ounce cans artichoke hearts, drained and coarsely chopped

¼ cup unbleached all-purpose flour

2 cups chicken broth

1 cup heavy cream

3 tablespoons cream sherry

⅛ teaspoon ground nutmeg

Salt and freshly ground black pepper to taste

4 cups cooked chicken, cut into bite-size pieces

1 pound penne, cooked according to package directions

1 cup freshly grated Parmesan cheese

Make It Now

1. In a large skillet over medium heat, melt the butter. Add the shallots and sauté until the shallots are softened, about 3 minutes. Add the mushrooms and sauté for another 6 to 8 minutes, until the mushrooms have begun to color and their liquid has evaporated.

2. Add the artichoke hearts and stir to coat with the butter. Sprinkle the flour over the vegetables and cook for 2 to 3 minutes, stirring while they cook. Gradually add the broth, scraping up any bits stuck to the bottom of the pan. Bring the mixture to a boil. Add the heavy cream, sherry, and nutmeg. Season with salt and pepper.

3. Coat the inside of a 9 x 13-inch baking dish with nonstick cooking spray.

4. Transfer the sauce to a large mixing bowl and stir in the chicken and penne. Spread the mixture evenly into the baking dish and sprinkle the top with the Parmesan cheese. Cover and refrigerate for 2 days or freeze for up to 1 month.

Bake It Later

1. Defrost the casserole in the refrigerator overnight, if necessary.

2. Preheat the oven to 350°F. Allow the casserole to come to room temperature for about 30 minutes.

3. Bake the casserole for 30 to 40 minutes, until the sauce is bubbling and the cheese is golden brown on top. Allow to rest for 5 minutes before serving.

Spinach, Bacon, and Cheese Pasta Bake

THIS CREAMY, CHEESY CASSEROLE is flecked with bright green spinach and bathed in a robust cheese sauce flavored with bacon. A takeoff on pasta alla carbonara, it's a favorite at my house anytime we are craving a hearty, comforting casserole on the table. SERVES 10

½ cup (1 stick) unsalted butter

2 medium-size shallots, finely chopped

1 clove garlic, minced

Two 10-ounce bags fresh baby spinach

3 tablespoons unbleached all-purpose flour

½ cup chicken broth

1½ cups milk

4 dashes of Tabasco sauce

⅛ teaspoon ground nutmeg

1 cup freshly grated Parmesan cheese

½ cup freshly grated Pecorino Romano cheese

1 pound penne, cooked according to package directions

12 strips bacon, cooked crisp and crumbled

½ pound fresh mozzarella cheese, cut into ½-inch cubes

Make It Now

1. Melt the butter over medium heat in a large saucepan. Add the shallots and garlic and sauté until fragrant and softened, about 2 minutes. Add the spinach, toss to coat with the butter, and cook until it wilts, about 2 minutes.

2. Sprinkle the flour over the spinach and cook for about 3 minutes, stirring constantly. Gradually add the broth, milk, Tabasco sauce, and nutmeg, and stir until the mixture comes to a boil and thickens. Remove from the heat and stir in ½ cup of the Parmesan cheese and the Romano cheese, stirring until the cheeses have melted.

3. Coat the inside of a 9 x 13-inch baking dish with nonstick cooking spray. Sprinkle with 2 tablespoons of the remaining Parmesan cheese. Place the penne and sauce in a large bowl and stir to combine. Add the bacon and mozzarella cheese. Transfer to the prepared baking dish and sprinkle with the remaining Parmesan cheese. Cover and refrigerate for up to 2 days or freeze for up to 1 month.

Bake It Later

1. Defrost the casserole in the refrigerator overnight, if necessary.

2. Preheat the oven to 350°F. Allow the casserole to come to room temperature for about 30 minutes.

3. Bake for 30 minutes, until the sauce is bubbling and the cheese is golden brown on top. Allow to rest for 5 to 10 minutes before serving.

Pesto Ravioli Bake

SMALL AND SOPHISTICATED, these ravioli are delicious as a weeknight supper or as a side dish with grilled or roasted meats or seafood. Feel free to multiply this one for a large crowd, or try substituting tortellini for the ravioli. SERVES 4

¼ cup (½ stick) unsalted butter

1 clove garlic, minced

¼ cup unbleached all-purpose flour

2½ cups milk

4 dashes of Tabasco sauce

2 cups freshly grated Parmesan cheese

One 9-ounce package fresh cheese ravioli, cooked until a bit firmer than al dente and drained (see Diva Note)

½ cup basil pesto, store-bought or homemade

Diva Note

Because you are baking the ravioli, make sure you don't boil it for the full amount of time indicated on the package. It should be undercooked, or else it will fall apart when you try to serve the finished dish.

Make It Now

1. Melt the butter in a medium-size saucepan over medium heat. Add the garlic and sauté for 1 minute. Add the flour and whisk until white bubbles form on the surface. Continue to whisk for 2 minutes, then gradually add the milk and Tabasco sauce, whisking until the mixture comes to a boil and thickens. Remove from the heat and stir in 1 cup of the Parmesan cheese, stirring until the cheese melts. (At this point, you may cool the cheese sauce and refrigerate it for up to 3 days or freeze it for up to 1 month.)

2. Place the ravioli in a medium-size bowl and stir in 1 cup of the sauce, being careful not to break up the ravioli. Coat the inside of a 9-inch baking dish with nonstick cooking spray. Spread a thin layer of sauce over the bottom of the casserole dish and top with half the ravioli. Spread the pesto evenly over the ravioli, then top with the remaining ravioli and sauce. Sprinkle with the remaining 1 cup Parmesan cheese. Cover and refrigerate for 2 days or freeze for up to 1 month.

Bake It Later

1. Defrost the casserole in the refrigerator overnight, if necessary.

2. Preheat the oven to 350°F. Allow the casserole to come to room temperature for about 30 minutes.

3. Bake for 30 to 35 minutes, until the sauce is bubbling and the cheese is golden brown on top. Allow to rest for 5 to 10 minutes before serving.

Tuna Noodle Casserole

WHEN I WAS A CHILD, I would beg my mom to let me eat at my friends' homes on Friday nights, when their moms would serve tuna noodle casserole. My mother was appalled that I would want to eat something that was made with canned ingredients, but I have to admit, this '50s comfort food has a special place in my heart. When my husband (who grew up on casseroles) and I got married, I tried to make tuna noodle casserole with canned cream of mushroom soup, and it was a disaster! Since those early days, I've refined this dish using fresh ingredients to the point where you can call it gourmet comfort food. Feel free to use chicken or poached salmon in place of tuna. SERVES 6

6 tablespoons (¾ stick) unsalted butter

½ cup finely chopped onion

½ cup finely chopped celery

½ pound sliced white mushrooms

¼ cup unbleached all-purpose flour

1½ cups chicken broth

2 cups milk

4 dashes of Tabasco sauce

Salt to taste

1 pound medium-width egg noodles, cooked according to package directions

Two 6-ounce cans albacore tuna packed in olive oil, well drained and flaked into chunks

1 cup frozen petite peas, defrosted and drained

1 cup crushed potato chips

3 tablespoons freshly grated Parmesan cheese

Make It Now

1. Melt 4 tablespoons of the butter in a large skillet over medium heat. Add the onion and celery and sauté for about 3 minutes, until they begin to soften. Add the mushrooms and sauté until they begin to color and their liquid has evaporated.

2. Sprinkle the flour over the vegetables and stir until the flour disappears. Cook the vegetables for 2 minutes, and then gradually add the broth and milk, scraping up any bits that are stuck to the bottom of the pan. Add the Tabasco sauce and salt.

3. Coat the inside of a 9-inch baking dish with nonstick cooking spray. Spread a thin layer of the sauce over the bottom of the dish. Combine the noodles and 1½ cups of the sauce in a large bowl and stir until well mixed. Stir in the tuna and peas until they are evenly distributed.

4. Transfer the noodle mixture to the prepared pan, and cover with the remaining sauce. Melt the remaining butter, stir into the potato chips and Parmesan cheese in a small bowl, and sprinkle on top of the casserole. Cover and refrigerate for up 2 days or freeze for up to 1 month.

1. Defrost the casserole in the refrigerator overnight, if necessary.

2. Preheat the oven to 350°F. Allow the casserole to come to room temperature for about 30 minutes.

3. Bake the casserole for 30 minutes, until the sauce is bubbling and the top is golden brown. Serve hot.

Old-Fashioned Mac and Cheese with Variations

EVERYONE GREW UP ON A VERSION OF THIS COMFORT FOOD, whether it was the Day-Glo Kraft variety or a homemade creation; if you wanted to feel good, this was the dish to start you on your way. Many restaurants now feature their own versions of this childhood treat, and I'm pretty sure that they are pulling at our nostalgic memories when it's on the menu. I'm pretty fussy about my mac and cheese; I like it creamy, and I like the cheese to be sharp, cheddary, and full flavored. Getting what I want is sometimes not in the cards when I am eating out, but this version is by far my favorite, and I hope you'll enjoy it, too. Make sure to try all the variations. SERVES 6

½ cup (1 stick) unsalted butter

2 cloves garlic, minced

¼ cup unbleached all-purpose flour

2½ cups milk

1 teaspoon Dijon mustard

6 dashes of Tabasco sauce

2 cups finely shredded mild cheddar cheese

1½ cups finely shredded sharp cheddar cheese

1 pound elbow macaroni

1 cup fresh bread crumbs

2 tablespoons freshly grated Parmesan cheese

Make It Now

1. In a large saucepan over medium heat, melt 4 tablespoons of the butter. Add half of the minced garlic and sauté until fragrant and softened, 1 minute. Whisk in the flour and cook until white bubbles form on the surface. Cook the mixture for 2 to 3 minutes, until smooth and thick. Gradually add the milk, mustard, and Tabasco sauce, whisking until the mixture comes to a boil and thickens. Remove the pan from the heat, and add 1¾ cups of the mild cheddar cheese and 1 cup of the sharp cheddar cheese, stirring until the cheese is melted.

2. Coat the inside of a 9 x 13-inch casserole dish with non-stick cooking spray. Combine the macaroni and sauce in a large bowl and stir until well mixed. Transfer to the prepared dish.

3. Melt the remaining 4 tablespoons butter in a small sauté pan over medium heat. Add the remaining garlic and sauté for 1 to 2 minutes, until fragrant. Remove from the heat. Toss the garlic butter with the bread crumbs and Parmesan cheese. Stir in the remaining ¼ cup mild cheddar cheese and ½ cup sharp cheddar cheese. Sprinkle the mixture over the top of the mac and cheese. Cover and refrigerate for up to 2 days or freeze for up to 1 month.

1. Defrost the casserole in the refrigerator overnight, if necessary.

2. Preheat the oven to 375°F. Allow the casserole to come to room temperature for about 30 minutes.

3. Bake the mac and cheese for 30 to 40 minutes, until the sauce is bubbling and the topping is golden brown. Allow to rest for 5 to 10 minutes before serving.

VARIATIONS

Chipotle Mac and Cheese

Add 1 minced chipotle chile in adobo sauce to the garlic and butter in step 1, omit the Dijon mustard, and proceed as directed.

Blue Mac and Cheese

Omit the garlic in step 1, and add 1 tablespoon Worcestershire sauce to the sauce. Substitute 3 cups crumbled blue cheese for the mild and sharp cheddar cheeses. Top the casserole with ½ cup blue cheese mixed in with the garlic, Parmesan, and bread crumbs. Maytag is my favorite blue cheese, but others to try are Point Reyes, Gorgonzola (you may need a bit more), Stilton (you may need a bit less, so taste before adding the third cup), Saga blue, or Cambozola.

Garlic-Herb Mac and Cheese

Omit the mild and sharp cheddar cheeses, and add two 5.2-ounce packages Boursin garlic-herb cheese to the sauce.

Caramelized Onion Mac and Swiss Cheese

Substitute 3 cups finely shredded Gruyère cheese for the mild and sharp cheddar cheeses. Add caramelized onions (recipe follows) to the noodles and sauce in step 2.

Caramelized Onions

MAKES ABOUT 1 ½ CUPS

¼ cup (½ stick) unsalted butter

1 tablespoon olive oil

3 large sweet onions, such as Vidalias, thinly sliced

2 tablespoons sugar

2 teaspoons dried thyme

Melt the butter with the olive oil in a large skillet over medium heat. Add the onions and sauté until they soften. Add the sugar and thyme, and sauté until the onions begin to turn golden brown, 17 to 20 minutes. Drain off any excess oil. Caramelized onions will keep in the refrigerator for up to 3 days or in the freezer for up to 1 month.

Sausage-Stuffed Shells

SIMPLE TO PREPARE and have waiting in your freezer, stuffed shells are a terrific entrée or side dish to serve to your family and friends. This rich version is stuffed with sweet Italian sausage and then covered in both marinara sauce and cream sauce. SERVES 10 TO 12

One 12-ounce package large pasta shells

2 to 3 tablespoons pure olive oil

1 pound sweet Italian sausage, removed from its casings

3 tablespoons unsalted butter

3 tablespoons unbleached all-purpose flour

1½ cups beef broth

2 cups heavy cream

1 cup freshly grated Pecorino Romano cheese

1½ cups Quick Marinara Sauce (page 246)

Make It Now

1. Bring a large pot of water to a boil and cook the shells for 5 minutes. Drain and toss the hot shells with the olive oil to prevent sticking. Set aside.

2. Coat the bottom of a 9 x 13-inch baking dish with non-stick cooking spray.

3. In a large skillet over medium-high heat, cook the sausage meat, breaking it up into small pieces, until cooked through and no longer pink, 5 to 7 minutes. Drain on paper towels and set aside.

4. In a medium-size saucepan, melt the butter over medium heat. Whisk in the flour and cook until white bubbles form on the surface. Cook the mixture for 2 to 3 minutes, until smooth and thick. Gradually stir in the broth and bring to a boil. Stir in the cream and ½ cup of the cheese. Let cool, then spread 1 cup of the cream sauce over the bottom of the prepared dish.

5. Transfer 2 cups of the remaining cream sauce to a food processor or blender, add the sausage, and pulse until the sausage is finely ground. Stuff each of the shells with 2 to 3 tablespoons of the sausage mixture and set each shell, filling side up, in the prepared dish. Spread the marinara sauce over the shells. Use a small ladle to pour the remaining cream sauce over the marinara in a striped pattern. Sprinkle with the remaining ½ cup cheese. Let cool, then cover and refrigerate for up to 2 days or freeze for up to 2 months.

Bake It Later

1. Defrost the casserole in the refrigerator overnight, if necessary.

2. Preheat the oven to 350°F. Allow the casserole to come to room temperature for about 30 minutes.

3. Bake until the sauce is bubbling and the cheese is golden brown on top, 30 to 35 minutes. Serve hot.

Timpano

TIMPANO, A RECIPE YOU WON'T FIND IN MANY COOKBOOKS, was the centerpiece entrée featured in Stanley Tucci's classic movie, *Big Night*. Calabrian cooks make this decadently rich dish during Carnival time, to get rid of all the foods in the refrigerator that they can't eat during the Lenten season. Filled with layers of goodies, including pasta, sauce, hard-boiled eggs, meatballs, vegetables, and cheese, it is a masterpiece. Make sure to start the timpano a few days ahead of when you want to serve it; it's a production, but well worth it!

My friend Carol Blomstrom, who owns Lotsa Pasta restaurant in San Diego, teaches timpano classes to sold-out crowds. Her expertise in producing this marvelous creation is what inspired me to include it in this book. In many places the crust or casing for the timpano is pasta dough, but Carol feels that pizza dough will give you the best crust and will keep the filling from losing its shape. Her mantra during her class is "Keep it flat, keep it level, and keep it dry." That doesn't mean that your timpano will be dry, just that the more moisture you have in it, the less likely it is to hold its shape. You will need a large pan that has a 5- to 6-quart capacity and is at least 6 inches deep. I have a 5-quart Emile Henry flame-top casserole dish that works very well for this, and for a larger timpano, my 8-quart saucepan works terrifically. Make sure that whatever you use is oven-safe. SERVES 12

½ cup (1 stick) unsalted butter

1 pound cremini or white mushrooms, sliced

Salt and freshly ground black pepper to taste

2 cloves garlic, minced

Two 10-ounce bags fresh baby spinach, *or* one 16-ounce package frozen spinach, defrosted and squeezed dry

⅛ teaspoon ground nutmeg

¼ cup heavy cream

1 cup dried bread crumbs

2 pounds pizza dough, store-bought or homemade

1 pound penne, cooked according to package directions

1 cup Quick Marinara Sauce (page 246)

Make It Now

1. In a medium-size sauté pan over medium heat, melt 2 tablespoons of the butter. Add the mushrooms and sauté until the mushrooms begin to turn golden brown and their liquid has evaporated, 8 to 10 minutes. Season with salt and pepper, remove from the pan, and set aside. (At this point, you may refrigerate for up to 2 days.)

2. In a medium-size skillet over medium-high heat, melt another 2 tablespoons of the butter. Add the garlic and sauté for 1 minute. Add the spinach and sauté until wilted and the liquid in the pan has been absorbed, 5 to 7 minutes. Season with salt and pepper and add the nutmeg. Pour in the cream and simmer until the cream has almost evaporated. Remove the mixture from the pan and set aside. (At this point, you may refrigerate for up to 2 days or freeze for up to 1 month.)

1 cup freshly grated Parmesan cheese

3 cups Romano Cream Sauce (page 49)

8 meatballs (page 55), sliced

1 pound fresh mozzarella cheese, diced

4 hard-cooked eggs, sliced

1 pound sweet Italian sausage, sliced into ½-inch rounds

5 cups Carol's Spicy Vodka Cream Sauce (page 57)

1 cup basil pesto, store-bought or homemade

3. Coat the inside of a round 6-quart casserole dish with 5- to 6-inch sides with a generous coating of the remaining butter. Sprinkle the bread crumbs over the butter and tilt the pan to make sure that the pan is well coated with both butter and crumbs. Roll out 1 pound of the pizza dough until it is large enough to line the bottom and sides of the dish, with 1½ inches of overhang around the top. Fit the rolled-out dough into the dish.

4. Combine half of the penne with the marinara sauce in a small bowl and stir until well mixed. Spread it in the bottom of the dough-lined casserole dish. Sprinkle the penne with ½ cup of the Parmesan. Spread the spinach mixture over the penne in one layer. In another small bowl, combine the remaining penne with 1 cup of the Romano cream sauce. Stir until well mixed, and set aside.

5. Spread the sliced meatballs over the spinach layer in the dish and cover with about half of the mozzarella. Arrange the hard-cooked egg slices over the mozzarella, and cover with the sausage rounds. Arrange the remaining mozzarella over the sausage. Top with the sautéed mushrooms and finish with the penne in cream sauce. Sprinkle the penne with the remaining ½ cup Parmesan cheese.

6. Roll out the second piece of pizza dough and drape over the top of the timpano, bring up the flaps of the bottom piece, and roll the edges together toward the top. Cover the timpano and refrigerate for up to 3 days or freeze for up to 1 month.

1. Defrost the timpano in the refrigerator for 48 hours, if necessary.

2. Preheat the oven to 350°F. Allow the timpano to come to room temperature for 45 to 60 minutes.

3. Bake the timpano for 1½ hours, until golden brown on the top. If the dough seems to be browning too quickly, cover it with foil for the last 30 minutes of baking time. Remove to a wire rack and allow to rest for 30 minutes.

4. Warm the vodka sauce. Stir the pesto into the remaining 2 cups Romano cream sauce and keep warm.

5. The moment of truth: Make sure the sides of the timpano have pulled away from the sides of the baking dish. If they haven't, use a long offset spatula to gently loosen them. Invert the timpano onto a serving platter that is at least 2 inches larger than the dish. Cut a 3-inch circle in the center of the timpano (see Diva Note). Then, using a serrated knife, cut wedges from the center, like a pie. Garnish each piece with some of the vodka sauce and some of the pesto-cream sauce and serve. Leftover timpano wedges can be refrigerated and then reheated on individual plates in a 350°F oven for 15 minutes.

Diva Note

When cutting a wedding cake, caterers often cut a 3-inch circle in the center so they can cut wedges and the cake will not fall apart as they cut around the circle. This is also a good technique for timpano —if you try to cut wedges, it may in fact fall apart, because of the weight of each slice. If you cut a circle in the center, the rest of the timpano will hold up while you are slicing it.

Pasta Fagioli Casserole

PASTA FAGIOLI, or pasta with beans, is a dish traditionally made with leftovers by farmers from Southern Italy. Most of us have had some type of pasta fagioli soup, and this casserole is a twist on that. This recipe has beans, pasta, and vegetables mingling in a rosemary and red wine tomato sauce, with a crispy top. The addition of the rind from the Parmigiano-Reggiano gives this dish an extra boost of flavor. For a simple dinner, serve with focaccia and a green salad. SERVES 4 TO 6

2 tablespoons extra-virgin olive oil

½ pound sweet Italian sausage, removed from its casings

1 cup coarsely chopped sweet onion, such as Vidalia

1 clove garlic, minced

4 ribs celery, coarsely chopped

3 medium-size carrots, coarsely chopped

1 tablespoon chopped fresh rosemary

¼ cup red wine

1½ teaspoons salt

1 teaspoon freshly ground black pepper

One 14.5-ounce can diced tomatoes (do not drain)

Two 14.5-ounce cans beef or chicken broth

1-inch square rind of Parmigiano-Reggiano cheese, cut into small pieces

One 15.5-ounce can garbanzo beans, rinsed and drained

One 15.5-ounce can small white beans, rinsed and drained

One 15.5-ounce can red kidney beans, rinsed and drained

½ pound elbow macaroni, cooked according to package directions

Make It Now

1. Heat the oil in a Dutch oven over medium heat. Add the sausage and cook, breaking it apart and browning it, until it loses all of its pink color, 10 to 12 minutes. Remove all but 2 tablespoons of fat from the pan. Add the onion, garlic, celery, carrots, and rosemary and sauté for 4 to 5 minutes, until the vegetables begin to soften.

2. Add the wine, salt, and pepper, and boil until the wine is reduced to about 2 tablespoons (this shouldn't take long). Add the tomatoes, and bring the mixture to a boil, stirring well.

3. Pour in the broth and add the cheese rind and beans. Simmer the mixture, uncovered, for 25 minutes, until it thickens a bit. Add the pasta and simmer for another 10 minutes, until the liquid has thickened. Let cool, then cover and refrigerate for up to 2 days or freeze for up to 2 months.

½ cup freshly grated Parmigiano-
Reggiano cheese

1. Defrost the casserole in the refrigerator overnight, if necessary.

2. Preheat the oven to 350°F. Allow the casserole to come to room temperature for 30 to 40 minutes.

3. Sprinkle the cheese evenly over the top of the casserole. Bake for 20 to 25 minutes, until the sauce is bubbling and the cheese is golden brown on top. Serve hot in soup bowls.

VARIATIONS

- Substitute hot Italian sausage, turkey sausage, or apple-chicken sausage for the sweet Italian sausage.

- For a very good vegetarian dish, omit the sausage and use vegetable broth instead of the chicken or beef broth.

Noodle Kugel

KUGEL IS TRADITIONALLY SERVED during Jewish holidays, and it is up to the cook to decide whether the flavor will be sweet or savory. I prefer the sweet versions, balanced against the strong flavors of a main course, such as brisket or roasted poultry. Additions of fruits and spices also make kugels a nice change of pace from other starchy side dishes. SERVES 6

1 cup sour cream

8 ounces cream cheese, softened

1 cup sugar

1 teaspoon ground cinnamon

1 teaspoon pure vanilla extract

3 large eggs

1 pound thin egg noodles, cooked according to package directions

1 cup golden raisins

1 cup chopped dried apples

⅛ teaspoon ground nutmeg

¼ cup (½ stick) unsalted butter, melted

Make It Now

1. In a food processor or the bowl of an electric mixer, combine the sour cream, cream cheese, ¾ cup of the sugar, ½ teaspoon of the cinnamon, the vanilla, and the eggs until smooth.

2. Combine the noodles in a large bowl with the sour cream mixture and stir to mix well. Add the raisins, apples, and nutmeg and stir again.

3. Coat the inside of a 9 x 13-inch baking dish with nonstick cooking spray. Transfer the noodle mixture to the prepared dish. Combine the remaining ¼ cup sugar and ½ teaspoon cinnamon in a small bowl and sprinkle over the top of the casserole. Drizzle with the melted butter. Cover and refrigerate for up to 3 days, or freeze for up to 1 month.

Bake It Later

1. Defrost the casserole in the refrigerator overnight, if necessary.

2. Preheat the oven to 350°F. Allow the casserole to come to room temperature for about 30 minutes.

3. Bake the kugel for 40 to 45 minutes, until bubbling and golden brown. Let rest for 10 minutes before serving.

Arroz con Pollo Casserole

FLAVORS FROM SOUTH OF THE BORDER combine to give you a delicious one-dish meal, combining meat, vegetables, and rice in a flavorful chile-spiked sauce. The casserole freezes well and you can certainly vary the protein, using shredded beef or pork instead of the chicken. You can also serve it as a side dish on a buffet table. SERVES 10

1/2 cup (1 stick) unsalted butter

1 cup finely chopped sweet onion, such as Vidalia

1/2 teaspoon chipotle chile powder

3 tablespoons unbleached all-purpose flour

2 cups chicken broth

2 cups milk

1 teaspoon salt

1/4 cup chopped fresh cilantro

1 teaspoon ground cumin

1 red bell pepper, finely diced

2 cups frozen corn, defrosted and thoroughly drained

1 cup tomato puree

2 tablespoons tequila (optional)

2 tablespoons freshly squeezed lime juice

2 whole cooked chicken breasts, skin and bones removed and meat shredded

5 cups cooked white rice

2 cups sour cream, plus more for garnish

2 cups finely shredded Monterey Jack cheese

1 cup finely shredded mild cheddar cheese

1 Hass avocado, sliced into wedges, for garnish

Make It Now

1. Melt 1/4 cup of the butter in a medium-size saucepan over medium heat. Add 1/2 cup of the onion and the chipotle chile powder and sauté for 3 minutes, until the onion is softened. Sprinkle the flour on top of the onion, and whisk until white bubbles form on the surface. Cook for another 2 minutes, whisking constantly. Add the broth, milk, and salt, stirring until the mixture comes to a boil. Remove from the heat, stir in 2 tablespoons of the cilantro, and set aside.

2. Melt the remaining 1/4 cup butter in a large sauté pan over medium-high heat. Add the remaining 1/2 cup onion, the cumin, and the bell pepper and sauté for about 4 minutes, until the vegetables are softened. Stir in the corn, tomato puree, tequila (if using), lime juice, and chicken. Simmer for 15 minutes, until the mixture thickens. Remove from the heat and stir in the remaining 2 tablespoons cilantro.

3. Combine the rice in a large bowl with 1 cup of the chipotle-onion sauce and the sour cream. Mix well.

4. Coat the inside of a 9 x 13-inch casserole dish with non-stick cooking spray. Spread 1 cup of the chipotle-onion sauce on the bottom of the baking dish. Spread half of the rice mixture over the sauce. Cover with the chicken mixture, 1 cup of the Monterey Jack cheese, and the remaining rice mixture. Pour the remaining sauce over the rice, and top with the remaining 1 cup Monterey Jack cheese and the cheddar cheese. Cover the casserole and refrigerate for 3 days or freeze for up to 6 weeks.

Make-Ahead Rice Dishes

Rice can be tricky for make-ahead dishes, because when raw rice is added to liquid it tends to swell, and then will not cook correctly later on. To solve this problem, you will need to separate the flavorings from the rice until you are ready to bake. Some of the bases for rice can be made ahead and frozen in zipper-top plastic bags, then zapped in the microwave for you to use almost immediately. Others will need to be brought to a simmer on the stovetop, and then you are ready to bake. The easiest do-ahead rice casseroles are those that are made using already cooked rice, so if you are serving plain rice with a meal, be sure to make extra. Then you can freeze it and later you can make one of the delicious rice casseroles that I've designed for you.

Bake It Later

1. Defrost the casserole in the refrigerator overnight, if necessary.

2. Preheat the oven to 350°F. Allow the casserole to come to room temperature for about 30 minutes.

3. Bake the casserole, covered, for 30 minutes. Uncover and bake for an additional 20 to 25 minutes, until the sauce is bubbling and the cheese is golden brown on top. Allow the casserole to rest for 10 minutes, then top with additional sour cream and the avocado wedges and serve warm.

Red Beans and Rice

TRADITIONALLY SERVED ON MONDAYS in New Orleans, the day when the wash was done, the red beans could cook low and slow without any attention from the cook. This hearty dish, thick with beans, sausage, and vegetables in a spicy sauce, can soothe the heart and cure the blues.

SERVES 6 TO 8

1½ pounds andouille or other smoked sausage, cut into ½-inch rounds

1 cup chopped sweet onion, such as Vidalia

1 cup chopped celery

2 cloves garlic, minced

1 cup chopped green bell pepper

1 teaspoon dried thyme

½ teaspoon cayenne pepper

½ teaspoon salt

2 cups chicken broth

Two 15.5-ounce cans red beans, rinsed and drained

1 bay leaf

4 cups cooked white or brown rice

Make It Now

1. In a Dutch oven over medium heat, sauté the sausage until it renders some of its fat, 4 to 6 minutes. Add the onion, celery, garlic, bell pepper, thyme, and cayenne and sauté until the vegetables are softened, 6 to 8 minutes.

2. Add the salt, chicken broth, beans, and bay leaf and simmer for 45 minutes, until the mixture slightly thickens.

3. Coat the bottom of a large casserole dish or 9 x 13-inch baking dish with nonstick cooking spray. Line the bottom of the dish with the rice, and top with the red bean mixture. Cool, cover, and refrigerate for up to 3 days.

Bake It Later

1. Preheat the oven to 350°F. Allow the casserole to come to room temperature for about 30 minutes.

2. Bake, covered, for 30 minutes, until heated through and bubbling. Remove from the oven and serve immediately.

VARIATION

For an easy vegetarian version of this dish, omit the sausage and sauté the vegetables in 2 tablespoons olive oil. Substitute vegetable broth for the chicken broth.

Jambalaya Acadiana

WHEN THESE CREOLE COMFORT-FOOD AROMAS waft through your house, you can expect a crowd to gather around the oven. This simple dish, bursting with spicy sausage, shrimp, and rice, is the perfect one-dish meal. You can make the spicy base ahead of time and then refrigerate or freeze it. When you're ready to eat, just add the rice and broth and pop the whole shebang into the oven for 25 minutes; you end up with a terrific family-style meal for any day of the week. Making this in a Dutch oven allows you to take the dish from stovetop to freezer to stovetop to oven with ease. Consider adding your own favorite meats to this dish, and kick up the heat meter as you like with additional cayenne or your favorite Creole seasoning. I usually serve this with an assortment of hot sauces, which helps to get everyone talking about who has the highest heat tolerance! SERVES 6

1 tablespoon vegetable oil

3/4 to 1 pound andouille sausage or Polish kielbasa, cut into 1/2-inch pieces

1/2 cup chopped yellow onion

1/2 cup chopped celery

1/2 cup chopped green bell pepper

1 clove garlic, minced

1/2 teaspoon dried thyme

1 bay leaf

1/4 teaspoon dried oregano

Pinch of cayenne pepper

1/4 teaspoon dried basil

1/4 teaspoon freshly ground black pepper

One 14.5-ounce can diced tomatoes, drained

Make It Now

1. Heat the oil in a Dutch oven over medium heat. Add the sausage and sauté until browned, 8 to 10 minutes. If there is a lot of rendered fat, remove all but 2 tablespoons. Add the onion, celery, bell pepper, garlic, thyme, bay leaf, oregano, cayenne, basil, and black pepper and sauté for about 8 minutes, until the vegetables are soft and the onion is translucent.

2. Stir in the tomatoes and cook for about 5 minutes, or until most of the liquid has evaporated.

3. Cool, cover, and refrigerate for up to 3 days or freeze for up to 1 month.

1 cup converted white rice

2½ cups chicken broth

¾ pound medium-size shrimp, peeled, deveined, and tails removed

1. Preheat the oven to 350°F.

2. Bring the contents of the Dutch oven to a boil on the stovetop. Add the rice, and stir to coat the rice with the tomato mixture. Add the broth, scraping up any bits stuck to the bottom of the pan. Cover the pot and bake for 15 minutes.

3. Uncover the pot, stir the rice, and add the shrimp, pushing them under the rice. Bake for an additional 5 to 7 minutes. Allow to rest for 5 minutes before serving (this will allow the rice to continue to absorb the liquid in the pan).

Cranberry-Apple Wild Rice

WILD RICE IS ACTUALLY AN AQUATIC GRAIN that is grown in the northern areas of the United States and Canada. Although it is more expensive than regular rice, it is delicious in a casserole. It adapts well to many flavors, and, in particular, it's delicious with fruit. If you are in the mood to experiment, try substituting chopped dried apricots for the apples in this recipe. This is a fabulous side dish with simple roasted meats, poultry, and seafood. If you cook wild rice and have some left over, it freezes well for about 6 months. SERVES 6

¼ cup (½ stick) unsalted butter

¼ cup finely chopped yellow onion

½ teaspoon dried thyme

1 teaspoon salt

½ teaspoon freshly ground black pepper

½ cup dried cranberries

½ cup finely chopped dried apple

½ cup chicken broth

½ cup heavy cream

1 cup wild rice, cooked according to package directions

Make It Now

1. Melt the butter in a medium-size saucepan over medium heat. Add the onion and thyme and sauté until the onion softens, about 3 minutes.

2. Add the salt, pepper, cranberries, apple, broth, and cream. Simmer for about 3 minutes, until the apple begins to plump up. Stir in the wild rice.

3. Coat the inside of a 9 x 13-inch baking dish with nonstick cooking spray and transfer the rice mixture to the pan. Cool, cover, and refrigerate for up to 2 days or freeze for up to 1 month.

Bake It Later

1. Defrost the casserole in the refrigerator overnight, if necessary.

2. Preheat the oven to 350°F. Allow the casserole to come to room temperature for about 30 minutes.

3. Bake the casserole, covered, for 20 minutes, or until heated through. Serve hot.

Artichoke-Parmesan Rice

COMFORTING AND FULL OF FLAVOR, this casserole, bursting with artichoke hearts, ricotta, and rice, has an infusion of flavor from good-quality Italian cheese. Feel free to use other leftover cooked vegetables instead of, or in addition to, the artichokes; the flavors are particularly delicious with **asparagus, broccoli, cremini mushrooms, and spinach**. This is beautiful with simple roasted chicken or grilled steak. SERVES 6

2 tablespoons unsalted butter

1 clove garlic, minced

One 16-ounce package frozen artichoke hearts, defrosted and drained

Salt and freshly ground black pepper to taste

1 cup ricotta cheese

2 large eggs

1/8 teaspoon ground nutmeg

1/2 cup milk

1 1/2 cups freshly grated Parmigiano-Reggiano cheese

3 cups cooked white rice

Make It Now

1. Melt the butter in a medium-size sauté pan over medium heat. Add the garlic and sauté for 1 minute. Add the artichoke hearts, sprinkle with salt and pepper, and toss to combine. Remove from the heat and set aside to cool.

2. In a large mixing bowl, stir together the ricotta, eggs, nutmeg, milk, 1 cup of the Parmigiano-Reggiano, and the rice. Add the contents of the sauté pan and blend.

3. Coat the inside of a 2-quart casserole dish with nonstick cooking spray. Transfer the rice mixture to the baking dish and sprinkle with the remaining 1/2 cup Parmigiano-Reggiano.

4. Cool, cover, and refrigerate for up to 3 days or freeze for up to 1 month.

Bake It Later

1. Defrost the casserole in the refrigerator overnight, if necessary.

2. Preheat the oven to 350°F. Allow the casserole to come to room temperature for about 30 minutes.

3. Bake for 30 minutes, or until the casserole is bubbling and the cheese is golden brown on top. Allow to rest for 5 to 10 minutes before serving hot.

Baked Rice Pilaf

THIS IS A MASTER RECIPE to help you on your way to a great simple side dish. The base for this rice pilaf can be made ahead, then the rice added and baked when you are ready. The base for the pilaf can be refrigerated or frozen, and you should feel free to add your own special touches to it: try butter and Parmesan cheese to finish a chicken broth–based pilaf, dried porcini or sautéed white mushrooms to finish a beef broth–based pilaf, or curry and finely chopped mango chutney to finish a vegetable broth–based pilaf. SERVES 6

2 tablespoons unsalted butter

1/2 cup chopped sweet onion, such as Vidalia

1 teaspoon dried herbs (thyme, tarragon, sage, oregano, marjoram, or a combination)

2 1/2 cups chicken, beef, or vegetable broth

Make It Now

1. Melt the butter in a medium-size saucepan over medium heat. Add the onion and herbs and sauté for about 3 minutes, until the onion softens. Add the broth and bring to a boil. Simmer for about 3 minutes to infuse the flavor of the herbs into the broth.

2. Remove from the heat, cool, transfer the herb broth to a zipper-top plastic bag, and refrigerate for up to 3 days or freeze for up to 3 months.

1 cup converted white or brown rice

Bake It Later

1. Preheat the oven to 350°F. Defrost the broth and bring it to a boil in the microwave or on the stovetop.

2. Pour the broth into a 2-quart casserole dish and stir in the rice. Cover with aluminum foil and bake for 30 minutes, or until the liquid is absorbed. Allow to rest for 5 to 10 minutes before serving hot. You can freeze any leftover pilaf for up to 2 months.

Bacon and White Cheddar Grits Casserole

GRITS WERE NOT A STAPLE in my childhood household north of the Mason-Dixon Line, but when I tasted a side dish of bacon and white cheddar cheese grits at a small tavern, I decided that they were worthy of the make-it-now, bake-it-later strategy. Serve this with roasted meats, pork chops, or ham, or underneath barbecued shrimp. In the South, many cooks will flavor their grits only with salt and pepper, or if they do add cheese, it's a roll of garlic-flavored processed cheese. Trust me, you won't go back to plain grits once you taste these! SERVES 6

2 cups milk

2 cups chicken broth

1 teaspoon salt

½ teaspoon Tabasco or other hot sauce

½ teaspoon garlic powder

1 cup quick-cooking grits

3 tablespoons unsalted butter

4 large eggs, beaten

2 teaspoons Worcestershire sauce

5 strips bacon, cooked crisp and crumbled

2 cups finely shredded sharp white cheddar cheese

Make It Now

1. Coat the inside of a 9 x 13-inch baking dish with nonstick cooking spray.

2. Combine the milk, broth, salt, Tabasco sauce, and garlic powder in a large saucepan and bring to a boil. Stir in the grits and cook over low heat, stirring occasionally, for about 6 minutes. Remove from the heat, stir in the butter, and allow the mixture to cool for 5 minutes.

3. Gradually add the eggs and Worcestershire sauce to the slightly cooled grits, stirring to combine thoroughly. Add most of the bacon (reserving a bit to garnish the top) and 1½ cups of the cheese, stirring until most of the cheese is melted.

4. Transfer the grits to the prepared baking dish and sprinkle with the remaining bacon and cheese. Cover and refrigerate for up to 2 days or freeze for up to 1 month.

Bake It Later

1. Defrost the casserole in the refrigerator overnight, if necessary.

2. Preheat the oven to 350°F. Allow the casserole to come to room temperature for about 30 minutes.

3. Bake for 1 hour, or until the grits are puffed and the top is golden. Serve hot.

Hot
Dish

Casseroles, or "hot dishes," as they are called in the heartland, are combinations of protein, starch, and sometimes vegetables in a sauce, which are baked in the oven for a comforting and delicious meal. The casseroles in this chapter do not fall into the traditional categories, such as pasta-based dishes, or side dishes, or beef dishes; they are really equal parts of ingredients layered or mixed together to become a delicious and hearty main dish, such as oven-baked French toast for breakfast or brunch or hearty enchiladas for dinner. The beauty of a casserole is that the ingredients and their amounts don't have to be too precise, so you can usually mix and match ingredients if there is something that doesn't appeal to you in the recipe. The other bonus with a casserole is that you can revamp leftovers to make an entirely different meal later in the week, or you can freeze the casserole and have it next month!

Growing up in an Italian household, my mother never made tuna noodle casserole the way my friends' moms did, and I felt somewhat deprived. As I grew older, I realized that casseroles were part of our life, too, but they just were made very differently, like the pasta frittata that my mother would make with leftovers and serve for breakfast. The casseroles I present here are all true Diva-licious creations, with fresh ingredients and bold flavors to satisfy everyone in your home. These casseroles are terrific for weeknight family meals, but they certainly can be dressed up for entertaining, too.

Hot Dish

Cheese Enchiladas with Red Chile Sauce

I CALL THESE ENCHILADAS SPICY COMFORT FOOD: a slightly spicy red sauce covers tortillas oozing with two kinds of cheese, giving you a great dish for brunch, lunch, or dinner. If you like more heat, use pepper Jack cheese in the enchiladas and increase the amount of chili powder in the sauce. To dress up this main dish, serve your favorite Southwestern condiments on the side, such as guacamole, sour cream, salsa, and pickled jalapeños. SERVES 6

2½ cups Red Chile Sauce (page 86)

1½ cups finely shredded mild cheddar cheese

1 cup finely shredded Monterey Jack or pepper Jack cheese

½ cup sour cream

Twelve 6-inch corn tortillas

Make It Now

1. Coat the inside of a 9 x 13-inch baking dish with nonstick cooking spray. Spread about ¼ cup of the sauce over the bottom of the pan.

2. In a small bowl, combine 1 cup of the cheddar cheese, ½ cup of the Monterey Jack cheese, and the sour cream.

3. Dip a tortilla into the sauce to soften it. Place the softened tortilla on a flat surface and spread 2 to 3 tablespoons of the cheese filling down the center of the tortilla. Roll up the tortilla and place it seam side down in the baking dish. Repeat with the remaining tortillas. Spread the remaining sauce evenly over the tortillas in the pan, and sprinkle evenly with the remaining ½ cup cheddar and ½ cup Monterey Jack. Cover the casserole dish and refrigerate for 2 days or freeze for up to 1 month.

Bake It Later

1. Defrost the casserole in the refrigerator overnight, if necessary.

2. Preheat the oven to 350°F. Let the casserole come to room temperature for about 30 minutes.

3. Bake the enchiladas for 25 to 30 minutes, until the cheese is bubbling and beginning to turn golden brown. Serve hot.

Red Chile Sauce

MAKES ABOUT 2½ CUPS

2 tablespoons canola or vegetable oil

1 cup chopped onion

2 cloves garlic, minced

2 teaspoons chili powder

1 teaspoon ground cumin

Two 8-ounce cans tomato puree

1 teaspoon salt

¼ cup tequila

1. Heat the oil in a 2-quart saucepan over medium-high heat. Add the onion and sauté for 2 minutes, until it begins to soften slightly. Add the garlic, chili powder, and cumin, and cook, stirring, for about 1 minute, until the spices are fragrant, being careful not to burn the spices.

2. Lower the heat to medium and add the tomato puree, salt, and tequila, stirring to incorporate. Simmer for 20 minutes.

3. Taste for seasoning and adjust if desired. Let cool. At this point, you may transfer the sauce to an airtight container and refrigerate for up to 2 days or freeze for up to 1 month.

Chicken Enchiladas with Salsa Verde

THIS HEARTY AND COMFORTING ENTRÉE is filled with chicken and chiles and then covered with a tomatillo sauce. Since fresh tomatillos are not always available, I have jazzed up a store-bought tomatillo salsa (sometimes called salsa verde) with some fresh ingredients to give you a delicious and simple sauce to use on this and any number of Southwestern dishes. The sauce is awesome with nachos, too! If you decide that your family would prefer a red sauce for their chicken enchiladas, feel free to use Red Chile Sauce (opposite page) instead. SERVES 6

2½ cups Salsa Verde (page 88)

1 tablespoon vegetable or canola oil

½ cup finely chopped sweet onion, such as Vidalia

2 tablespoons diced canned green chiles, drained and rinsed

1 teaspoon ground cumin

2 cups shredded cooked chicken

1½ cups finely shredded Monterey Jack cheese

Twelve 6-inch corn tortillas (I like to use white corn tortillas)

1 cup finely shredded mild cheddar cheese

Make It Now

1. Coat the inside of a 9 x 13-inch baking dish with nonstick cooking spray and spread ⅓ cup of the salsa verde over the bottom of the pan.

2. Heat the oil in a small sauté pan over medium-high heat. Add the onion, chiles, and cumin and sauté until the onion begins to soften, about 2 minutes. Add the chicken and toss in the mixture to coat. Transfer the mixture to a bowl and allow to cool slightly. Stir in 1 cup of the Monterey Jack cheese.

3. Dip a tortilla into the salsa verde to soften it. Place the softened tortilla on a flat surface and spread about ¼ cup of the chicken filling in the center of the tortilla. Roll up the tortilla and place seam side down on top of the sauce in the prepared dish. Repeat with the remaining tortillas. Spread the remaining salsa verde over the enchiladas and cover with the remaining ½ cup Monterey Jack cheese and the cheddar cheese. Cover and refrigerate for up to 2 days or freeze for up to 1 month.

Bake It Later

1. Defrost the casserole in the refrigerator overnight, if necessary.

2. Preheat the oven to 350°F. Let the casserole come to room temperature for about 30 minutes.

3. Bake the casserole for 25 to 30 minutes, until the cheese is melted and turning golden brown. Serve hot.

VARIATION

Enchiladas Suiza

These are luxurious and quite different from traditional chicken enchiladas. Simply substitute finely shredded Gruyère or imported Swiss cheese for the Monterey Jack and cheddar.

Salsa Verde

MAKES ABOUT 2¼ CUPS

2 tablespoons vegetable oil

½ cup finely chopped sweet onion, such as Vidalia

1 clove garlic, minced

2 tablespoons diced canned green chiles, drained and rinsed

One 16-ounce jar tomatillo salsa

½ cup heavy cream

½ cup chopped fresh cilantro

Salt to taste

1. Heat the oil in a medium-size saucepan over medium-high heat. Add the onion, garlic, and chiles and sauté for 2 minutes, until the onion and garlic are fragrant and begin to soften.

2. Add the tomatillo salsa and simmer for 20 minutes, stirring occasionally, to blend the flavors. Remove from the heat and add the cream and cilantro. Taste for seasoning and add salt, if needed. Set aside to cool. Once cool, you can transfer the sauce to an airtight container and refrigerate for up to 2 days or freeze for up to 6 weeks.

Beef Enchiladas

THESE STICK-TO-YOUR-RIBS ENCHILADAS are a terrific weeknight dinner, and you can use any left-over roast beef or steak in the filling. If you are a heat lover, choose a spicier type of salsa to mix with the beef. Otherwise, these are about a 5 on a 10-point scale of hotness. SERVES 6

1 tablespoon vegetable oil

½ cup finely chopped sweet onion, such as Vidalia

2 cups shredded or julienned cooked roast beef or steak

½ cup medium-hot salsa, store-bought or homemade

Salt to taste

½ cup finely shredded cheddar cheese

2½ cups Red Chile Sauce (page 86)

Twelve 6-inch flour tortillas

1 cup finely shredded Monterey Jack cheese

Make It Now

1. Heat the oil in a small skillet over medium heat. Add the onion and sauté for about 2 minutes, until softened. Add the roast beef and stir to coat. Stir in the salsa and simmer for about 3 minutes, until thickened. Season with salt. Transfer to a bowl and let cool. When the mixture is cooled, stir in the cheddar cheese.

2. Coat the inside of a 9 x 13-inch baking dish with nonstick cooking spray and spread about ⅓ cup of the chile sauce in the bottom of the pan.

3. Dip a tortilla into the remaining sauce to soften. Place the softened tortilla on a flat surface and spread 3 to 4 table-spoons of the filling down the center of the tortilla. Roll it up and place the enchilada seam side down on top of the sauce in the prepared dish. Repeat with the remaining tortillas.

4. Spread the remaining chile sauce over the tortillas and cover with the Monterey Jack cheese. Cover the casserole and refrigerate for up to 2 days or freeze for up to 1 month.

Bake It Later

1. Defrost the casserole overnight in the refrigerator, if necessary.

2. Preheat the oven to 350°F. Let the casserole come to room temperature for about 30 minutes.

3. Bake for 25 to 30 minutes, until the cheese is melted and the casserole is bubbling. Serve hot.

Seafood Enchiladas

I'M NOT SURE THAT YOU WILL FIND THIS DISH SERVED IN MEXICO, but you certainly find it on up-scale American menus along the southwestern coast. These enchiladas are covered in a creamy cilantro-flecked sauce, and bursting with salmon, halibut, shrimp, crab, or lobster. Each seafood choice is terrific, so it's really up to you which type you choose. Although you can freeze these, I don't recommend it because so much seafood that you buy has been previously frozen. There is some loss in flavor and texture when refreezing, so my recommendation is to refrigerate the enchiladas, then bake them, but if your seafood has never been frozen, you can freeze them for about 2 weeks. SERVES 6

3 tablespoons unsalted butter

3 tablespoons unbleached all-purpose flour

1 cup seafood stock or bottled clam juice

2½ cups milk

½ cup finely chopped fresh cilantro

½ teaspoon freshly ground black pepper

Salt to taste

2 cups chopped cooked seafood (choose firm-fleshed fish, such as salmon, halibut, or sea bass, or shrimp, crab, or lobster)

2 cups finely shredded Monterey Jack cheese

Twelve 6-inch flour or white corn tortillas

1½ cups sour cream, for garnish

Chopped cilantro for garnish

Make It Now

1. Melt the butter in a medium-size saucepan over medium heat. Whisk in the flour and cook until white bubbles form on the surface. Continue to cook the mixture for 2 to 3 minutes, until smooth and thick. Gradually stir in the seafood stock and milk, whisking until blended. Bring the mixture to a boil, stirring constantly. Remove the sauce from the heat and add the cilantro and pepper. Add salt, and let cool.

2. Place the seafood in a large bowl and stir in ½ cup of the cooled sauce and ½ cup of the cheese.

3. Coat the inside of a 9 x 13-inch baking dish with nonstick cooking spray. Spread ¾ to 1 cup sauce in the bottom of the pan.

4. Place a tortilla on a flat surface, spread a thin layer of sauce on it, then arrange 3 to 4 tablespoons of filling down the center of the tortilla and roll up. Place the tortilla seam side down in the prepared dish. Repeat with the remaining tortillas.

5. Spread the remaining sauce over the tortillas and sprinkle with the remaining 1½ cups of cheese. Cover and refrigerate for up to 2 days or freeze (only fresh seafood) for up to 2 weeks.

Enchiladas

A casserole of enchiladas is a great main dish to have waiting in the freezer, and you can make several different flavors to keep on hand. Cheese enchiladas, corn tortillas stuffed with your favorite cheeses and topped with a red chile sauce, make a delicious dinner, served with a fruit or vegetable salad. Chicken enchiladas feature chicken, chiles, a bit of sautéed onion, and sour cream in corn tortillas and can be with covered with either a green tomatillo or a red chile sauce and a molten layer of melting cheese for a satisfying weeknight dinner, or they can be dressed up for a company dinner with a little guacamole, sour cream, and pico de gallo to serve on the side. Beef enchiladas are a great way to use leftover roast beef and are best served in flour tortillas with a red chile sauce (page 86) or ranchero sauce (page 110). For the seafood lovers in the crowd, seafood enchiladas make an elegant yet casual main course for family or friends. All of these enchilada recipes can be doubled or tripled easily for larger crowds.

Bake It Later

1. Defrost the casserole in the refrigerator overnight, if necessary.

2. Preheat the oven to 350°F. Let the casserole come to room temperature for about 30 minutes.

3. Bake for 20 to 25 minutes, until the sauce is bubbling and the cheese is beginning to turn golden brown. Serve hot, garnished with the sour cream and cilantro.

Moussaka

MOUSSAKA IS A PRODUCTION LIKE A LASAGNA, where the parts can be made a few days ahead of assembling the dish, and then the entire casserole can be refrigerated or frozen. Eggplant is layered with a meaty sauce, and then covered with a cheesy cream sauce to give you a spectacular dish to serve to guests. I have also made this with ground turkey in place of the beef and lamb, and it works very well. Although this recipe is made in a 9 x 13-inch casserole dish, if you would prefer to make it in two 9-inch square baking dishes, that will work, too. The baking time will be about 5 to 7 minutes shorter for the smaller casseroles. SERVES 8

BROILED EGGPLANT

Two large purple eggplants, cut into 1/2-inch-thick slices

3/4 cup olive oil

1 1/2 teaspoons salt

1/2 teaspoon freshly ground black pepper

BEEF AND LAMB FILLING

2 tablespoons olive oil

2 cloves garlic, minced

1 cup finely chopped sweet onion, such as Vidalia

1 pound lean ground beef

3/4 pound lean ground lamb

1/2 teaspoon ground cinnamon

1/3 cup red wine

Two 8-ounce cans tomato sauce

Salt and freshly ground black pepper to taste

1/2 cup chopped fresh flat-leaf parsley

Make It Now

1. To make the eggplant, preheat the broiler for 10 minutes. Line baking sheets with heavy-duty aluminum foil. Lay the eggplant slices on the baking sheets.

2. In a small bowl, combine the olive oil, salt, and pepper. Brush both sides of each slice of eggplant with some of the oil. Broil for about 7 minutes on each side, or until the slices begin to turn golden. Allow the eggplant to cool on the sheets. (At this point, you may refrigerate for up to 3 days or freeze for up to 1 month.)

3. To make the filling, heat the oil in a large skillet over medium heat. Add the garlic and onion and sauté for about 3 minutes, until the onion begins to soften. Add the beef, lamb, and cinnamon and sauté, breaking up the meat and cooking until the meat is no longer pink, 10 to 15 minutes. Drain off any excess liquid from the pan.

4. Add the wine to the pan and cook to deglaze, stirring to scrape up and mix in any cooked pieces of food. Allow some of the wine to evaporate, about 2 minutes. Add the tomato sauce and bring the mixture to a simmer. Simmer, uncovered, until the mixture is quite thick, about 30 minutes. Add salt and pepper and stir in the parsley. At this point, you may cool and refrigerate for up to 4 days or freeze for up to 6 weeks.

CREAM SAUCE

1/4 cup (1/2 stick) unsalted butter

1/4 cup unbleached all-purpose flour

3 cups milk

1 1/2 teaspoons salt

1/2 teaspoon freshly ground black pepper

1/8 teaspoon freshly ground nutmeg

1 cup freshly grated Pecorino Romano cheese or Kefalotiri cheese

4 large egg yolks

5. To make the cream sauce, melt the butter in a medium-size saucepan over medium heat. Whisk in the flour and cook until white bubbles form on the surface. Cook the mixture for 2 to 3 minutes, until smooth and thick.

6. Gradually whisk in the milk, and add the salt, pepper, and nutmeg. Whisk until the mixture comes to a boil. Remove the sauce from the heat and stir in 1/2 cup of the cheese. Cool the mixture slightly, then stir in the egg yolks. (At this point, you may refrigerate for up to 2 days.)

7. To assemble the moussaka, coat the inside of a 9 x 13-inch baking dish or two 9-inch square baking dishes with nonstick cooking spray. Lay about one-third of the eggplant slices in the dish, cutting them to fit snugly if necessary.

8. Spread half of the meat filling over the eggplant, and then top with another layer of eggplant. Top the eggplant with the remaining meat filling, and then with the remaining eggplant. Pour the cream sauce over the casserole and sprinkle with the remaining 1/2 cup cheese. Cover and refrigerate for up to 2 days or freeze for up to 6 weeks.

Bake It Later

1. Defrost the casserole in the refrigerator overnight, if necessary.

2. Preheat the oven to 350°F. Let the moussaka come to room temperature for 35 to 45 minutes.

3. Bake the casserole for 50 to 60 minutes, or until the casserole is bubbling and the cheese has turned golden brown. Allow to rest on a wire rack for 15 to 20 minutes, then serve hot.

Egg Stratas

A lot quicker than flipping endless omelets for breakfast, and way more fun, these tasty stratas are sandwiched with lots of fillings to give your breakfast or brunch style and flavor. Stratas, which are like savory versions of French toast, are also great paired with a salad. They are formulaic in nature, but once you have the basic concept you can take off on your own flights of culinary fantasy, using leftovers to prepare delightful creations that will have your family up early when they catch a whiff of the aromas coming from your oven. Stratas can be baked in large baking dishes, as they are here, or in ramekins or muffin pans (for 15 to 17 minutes), or in two 9-inch baking dishes (for 30 minutes). Here's a plain, basic recipe to get you started.

> 8 large eggs
> 2 cups milk
> 1 teaspoon salt
> 6 dashes of Tabasco sauce
> 8 cups torn bread, crusts removed (see Diva Note)
> $2\frac{1}{2}$ cups grated or shredded cheese of your choice
> 3 tablespoons unsalted butter, melted

Make It Now

1. Coat the inside of a 9 x 13-inch baking dish with nonstick cooking spray.
2. In a large bowl, whisk together the eggs, milk, salt, and Tabasco sauce. Add the bread and stir to coat all the bread. Transfer half of the mixture to the prepared dish, sprinkle with $1\frac{1}{4}$ cups of the cheese, top with the remaining bread mixture, and spread the remaining $1\frac{1}{4}$ cups cheese over the top. Drizzle with the melted butter.
3. Cover and refrigerate for up to 2 days, or freeze for up to 1 month.

Bake It Later

1. Defrost the casserole overnight in the refrigerator, if necessary.
2. Preheat the oven to 350°F. Let the casserole come to room temperature for about 30 minutes.
3. Bake the casserole for 40 to 45 minutes, until the top is puffed and golden brown. Let the casserole rest for about 5 minutes, then serve hot.

Diva Note

Use a nice bread with some structure, such as a country white. Avoid spongy sandwich bread.

Ham, Gruyère, and Spinach Strata

HAM AND CHEESE IS A CLASSIC COMBINATION when made into a sandwich; here I've turned it into a strata and added spinach for a little color and flavor. This can be a great way to use leftover ham and turn your table into a French bistro, all with a few do-ahead tips and a preheated oven. I like this best in a 9 x 13-inch casserole dish, but you can certainly prepare this in muffin tins or ramekins if you like. SERVES 8

8 large eggs

2 cups milk

1 tablespoon Dijon mustard

1 teaspoon salt

6 dashes of Tabasco sauce

8 cups torn soft French or Italian bread, crusts removed

2 tablespoons unsalted butter

2 shallots, finely chopped

1 pound smoked ham, excess fat removed and cut into ½-inch dice (about 1½ cups)

One 16-ounce package frozen chopped spinach, defrosted and squeezed dry

⅛ teaspoon freshly grated nutmeg

¼ teaspoon freshly ground black pepper

Salt to taste

2½ cups shredded Gruyère or imported Swiss cheese

3 tablespoons unsalted butter, melted

Make It Now

1. Coat the inside of a 9 x 13-inch baking dish with nonstick cooking spray.

2. In a large bowl, whisk together the eggs, milk, mustard, salt, and Tabasco sauce. Add the bread, and stir to coat all the bread. Set aside while you make the ham and spinach mixture.

3. Melt the butter in a medium-size sauté pan over medium-high heat. Add the shallots and sauté for about 3 minutes, until the shallots begin to soften. Add the ham and sauté for 3 minutes, until the ham begins to color and is coated with the butter and shallot. Add the spinach and sauté until there is no liquid left in the pan. Sprinkle with the nutmeg and pepper, stir, and season with salt. Transfer the mixture to a bowl and let cool.

4. Spread half of the bread mixture in the prepared pan. Spread the ham-spinach mixture over the bread mixture and sprinkle with 1¼ cups of the cheese.

5. Spread the rest of the bread mixture over the cheese and sprinkle with the remaining 1¼ cups cheese. Drizzle with the melted butter. Cover and refrigerate for up to 2 days or freeze for up to 1 month.

1. Defrost the casserole in the refrigerator overnight, if necessary.

2. Preheat the oven to 350°F. Let the casserole come to room temperature for 30 to 45 minutes.

3. Bake the casserole for 40 to 50 minutes, until puffed, golden, and set in the middle. Let rest for 5 minutes before serving hot.

Roasted Tomato and Mozzarella Strata

INTENSELY FLAVORED, ROSEMARY-SCENTED ROASTED TOMATOES are a beautiful addition to this dish, which is inviting, comforting, and a terrific breakfast, lunch, or brunch entrée. Try varying the cheese by using an herbed chèvre or Boursin in place of the mozzarella. SERVES 8

8 large eggs

2 cups milk

1 teaspoon salt

6 dashes of Tabasco sauce

8 cups torn soft Italian bread, crusts removed

3 cups Oven-Roasted Tomatoes (page 98)

Two 8-ounce balls fresh mozzarella cheese, cut into ½-inch pieces

½ cup freshly grated Parmesan cheese

3 tablespoons unsalted butter, melted

Make It Now

1. Coat the inside of a 9 x 13-inch baking dish with nonstick cooking spray.

2. In a large bowl, whisk together the eggs, milk, salt, and Tabasco sauce. Add the bread and stir to coat all the bread. Transfer half of the mixture to the prepared dish. Spread all of the tomatoes over the bread layer and top with all of the mozzarella. Cover with the remaining bread mixture, sprinkle with the Parmesan cheese, and drizzle with the melted butter. Cover and refrigerate for up to 2 days or freeze for up to 1 month.

Bake It Later

1. Defrost the casserole in the refrigerator overnight, if necessary.

2. Preheat the oven to 350°F. Let the casserole come to room temperature for about 30 minutes.

3. Bake the casserole for 40 to 50 minutes, until the strata is puffed, golden, and set in the center. Let rest for 10 to 15 minutes before serving hot.

Oven-Roasted Tomatoes

IN ITALY, when the tomatoes in the markets aren't quite up to par, cooks sometimes oven-roast them to give them a more intense flavor. These tomatoes are delicious served over pasta, used as a filling for a strata or lasagna, stirred into cooked rice, chopped for a bruschetta topping, or used in a sauce for grilled meats, poultry, or seafood. MAKES ABOUT 3 CUPS

Two 28-ounce cans peeled whole tomatoes, drained

1/2 cup extra-virgin olive oil

2 teaspoons dried basil

1 teaspoon finely chopped fresh rosemary leaves

1/2 cup chopped red onion

6 cloves garlic, coarsely chopped

1 1/2 teaspoons salt

1/2 teaspoon freshly ground black pepper

1. Cut the tomatoes in half and put them in a large nonreactive bowl. Stir in the olive oil, basil, rosemary, onion, garlic, salt, and pepper, being careful not to tear the tomatoes. Cover the tomatoes and refrigerate for up to 3 days.

2. Preheat the oven to 375°F. Line a baking sheet with a silicone baking liner or aluminum foil.

3. Pour the tomato mixture onto the prepared pan, spreading it out in a single layer. Bake until the tomato liquid is absorbed and the tomatoes have firmed up and turned a deep red color, 45 to 60 minutes.

4. Transfer the tomato mixture to a heatproof glass bowl and let it mellow at room temperature for about 6 hours. You may cover and refrigerate the tomatoes for up to 4 days or freeze for up to 3 months. Defrost in the refrigerator overnight and bring to room temperature before using.

Artichoke, Salmon, and Boursin Strata

STUNNING IN APPEARANCE AND AWESOME IN TASTE, this simple strata will have your family and friends talking about it long after it has been served and consumed. The color and taste combinations of bright pink poached salmon, light green artichoke hearts, and creamy herb-flecked Boursin make this a dish for celebrations! I don't recommend freezing this because it contains seafood, and the seafood may have been frozen previously, but it keeps well in the fridge for 2 days before baking. If the salmon hasn't been frozen, you can freeze this for up to 2 weeks. SERVES 8

8 large eggs

2 cups milk

1 teaspoon salt

6 dashes of Tabasco sauce

2 cups poached salmon (not canned), flaked

One 16-ounce package frozen artichoke hearts, defrosted and coarsely chopped, *or* two 14.5-ounce cans artichoke hearts, drained and coarsely chopped

8 cups torn white bread, crusts removed

Two 5.2-ounce packages garlic-herb Boursin cheese, chilled (see Diva Note)

3 tablespoons unsalted butter, melted

Make It Now

1. Coat the inside of a 9 x 13-inch baking dish with nonstick cooking spray.

2. In a large bowl, whisk together the eggs, milk, salt, Tabasco sauce, salmon, and artichoke hearts. Add the bread and stir to coat all the bread. Crumble the Boursin into the bowl, reserving about half of one of the packages.

3. Pour the bread mixture into the prepared baking dish. Crumble the remaining Boursin and sprinkle it over the top of the casserole. Drizzle the melted butter over the Boursin, then cover and refrigerate for up to 2 days.

Bake It Later

1. Preheat the oven to 350°F. Let the casserole come to room temperature for about 30 minutes.

2. Bake the casserole for 40 minutes, until puffed, golden, and set in the middle. Let rest for 5 to 10 minutes before serving hot.

Diva Note

It's easiest to crumble soft cheeses like Boursin and goat cheese when they are chilled; if they are at room temperature they won't crumble at all and will become a sticky mess.

Smoked Salmon–Sour Cream Crustless Quiche

LUXURIOUS SMOKED SALMON, enveloped in sour cream, chives, and dill, bakes with a surprising and delicious addition of hash-brown potatoes. The potatoes give the quiche body and structure so that there is no need for a bottom crust, and the quiche is delectable with the potatoes in the mix. Try making these in mini-muffin tins for elegant small-bite appetizers, too (bake them for only 10 minutes). Quiche is generally made in a straight-sided pan, and some pans have a removable bottom, which is great for seeing the entire pie in its glory, but for this crustless quiche, use a pie plate or a solid quiche pan that is at least 2 inches deep, and serve the quiche from the pan rather than trying to remove it first. I recommend freezing this quiche only after baking it. If you decide to do that, bake the quiche for 20 minutes, allow it to cool completely, then cover and freeze for up to 1 month. Reheat in a preheated 350°F oven, covered with aluminum foil, for 10 to 15 minutes. SERVES 6

4 large eggs

1/2 cup sour cream, plus more for garnish

1/2 cup heavy cream

2 tablespoons finely chopped fresh dill

2 tablespoons finely chopped fresh chives or green onions (white and tender green parts)

4 ounces smoked salmon, chopped or flaked (see Diva Note)

1 1/2 cups frozen hash-brown potatoes, defrosted and squeezed dry

Make It Now

1. Coat the inside of a 2-inch deep, 9-inch quiche or pie pan with nonstick cooking spray.

2. In a large bowl, whisk together the eggs, sour cream, heavy cream, dill, chives, and salmon until blended. Stir in the hash browns until blended. Transfer the mixture to the prepared pan, cover, and refrigerate for up to 2 days.

Diva Note

There are two types of smoked salmon on the market. One is cold-smoked at a low temperature and cured with salt, spices, and brine, giving you a salmon that has to be sliced and chopped before adding to the quiche. The other is hot-smoked at a higher temperature, resulting in a drier salmon that can be flaked. Either type is fine in this recipe; they each have a different texture but both give the quiche a lovely flavor.

Optional garnishes: sour cream, finely chopped fresh dill, finely chopped fresh chives

Bake It Later

1. Preheat the oven to 350°F. Let the quiche come to room temperature for 20 to 30 minutes.

2. Bake the quiche for 25 to 30 minutes, or until puffed, golden, and set in the center. Let cool for at least 10 minutes before cutting. Garnish with additional sour cream, dill, and chives, if desired. Serve warm, at room temperature, or cold.

Cremini and Caramelized Onion Quiche

EARTHY CREMINI MUSHROOMS, sweet caramelized onions, and Gruyère cheese make this quiche memorable. It's delicious served warm or at room temperature, and I've even eaten it cold for breakfast. This quiche and a green salad are my idea of the perfect informal lunch or light supper.

SERVES 6

½ cup (1 stick) unsalted butter

1 pound cremini mushrooms, trimmed and sliced

Salt and freshly ground black pepper to taste

1 tablespoon olive oil

3 large sweet onions, such as Vidalias, thinly sliced

2 teaspoons finely chopped fresh thyme

1 tablespoon sugar

4 large eggs

1 cup heavy cream

1 tablespoon Dijon mustard

Pastry for 9-inch pie (see Diva Note)

Make It Now

1. Melt 4 tablespoons of the butter in a large skillet over medium-high heat. Add the mushrooms and sauté until their liquid has evaporated and the mushrooms begin to color, about 10 minutes. Season the mushrooms with salt and pepper, transfer to a large bowl, and set aside.

2. In the same skillet, melt the remaining 4 tablespoons butter with the olive oil over medium-high heat. Add the onions and sauté until the onions begin to turn translucent, about 8 minutes. Add the thyme and sugar, and sauté until the onions begin to turn golden brown, about 10 minutes longer. Transfer the onions to the bowl with the mushrooms and stir to blend. Allow the vegetables to cool slightly.

3. In a medium-size mixing bowl, whisk together the eggs, cream, and mustard. Pour into the bowl with the vegetables. Cover and refrigerate for up to 3 days.

2 cups finely shredded
Gruyère cheese

Bake It Later

1. Preheat the oven to 375°F.

2. Coat the inside of a 2-inch-deep, 9-inch quiche or pie pan with nonstick cooking spray. Lay the pastry in the pan and trim the edges to fit the pan. Crimp or flute the edges of the pastry around the edge of the pan.

3. Pour the vegetable custard over the pastry and sprinkle the top with the cheese. Bake for 15 minutes, reduce the heat to 350°F, and bake for an additional 30 minutes, until the quiche is puffed, golden, and set in the center. Let rest for at least 10 minutes before cutting. Serve warm or at room temperature.

Diva Note

If you enjoy making your own pastry crust, then I recommend that you do it for this quiche, but if you don't enjoy making pastry, there are several brands of either fresh (in the refrigerated section of the grocery store) or frozen pie pastry that will work here. Follow the defrosting directions on the package for frozen pastry.

Baked Benedict Casserole

I LOVE EGGS BENEDICT, the classic dish with poached eggs perched atop Canadian bacon and English muffins, but I don't like the tedious last-minute preparation of the hollandaise sauce and poached eggs, so I came up with a casserole that has all the elements of eggs Benedict but without the hassles, and I guarantee that you will love it. This recipe is easily doubled, if you'd like to make it for a larger group. SERVES 8

3 tablespoons unsalted butter, softened

4 English muffins, split in half

8 slices Canadian bacon

6 large eggs

1 cup mayonnaise

2 tablespoons freshly squeezed lemon juice

1 teaspoon dry mustard

4 dashes of Tabasco sauce

Make It Now

1. Coat the inside of a 9 x 13-inch baking dish with nonstick cooking spray. Spread the butter over the cut sides of the English muffins, and arrange the muffins in the prepared pan. Cover each muffin half with a slice of Canadian bacon. Set aside.

2. In a large bowl, whisk together the eggs, mayonnaise, lemon juice, dry mustard, and Tabasco sauce. Pour the mixture over the muffins in the prepared pan, tilting to make sure that the liquid touches the bottom to soak into the muffins on both sides. Cover the pan, and refrigerate for up to 2 days or freeze for up to 1 month.

Bake It Later

1. Defrost the casserole in the refrigerator overnight, if necessary.

2. Preheat the oven to 350°F. Let the casserole come to room temperature for 30 minutes.

3. Bake the casserole for 45 minutes, until puffed, golden, and set in the center. Let rest for 10 minutes. Cut into 8 squares, using the muffins as your guide.

Midwest Breakfast Casserole

THROUGHOUT MUCH OF THE COUNTRY, you will find Cracker Barrel restaurants, where they serve a side dish called hash-brown casserole. I've taken that casserole and turned it into a delicious main dish with the addition of sausage and eggs. This can be made in individual 4-ounce ramekins instead of the 9-inch baking dish, but bake the ramekins for only 15 to 17 minutes, until set. SERVES 6

½ pound bulk pork sausage
(Jimmy Dean is my favorite brand)

½ cup chopped onion

3 tablespoons unbleached all-purpose flour

1½ cups milk

6 dashes of Tabasco sauce

2 cups finely shredded sharp cheddar cheese

1½ cups frozen shredded hash-brown potatoes, defrosted

3 green onions (white and tender green parts), thinly sliced

6 large eggs, beaten

Make It Now

1. Coat the inside of a 9-inch baking dish with nonstick cooking spray.

2. Cook the sausage in a large sauté pan over medium heat until it is no longer pink, breaking it up with a fork, 8 to 10 minutes. Drain off any excess liquid in the pan, add the onion, and sauté for another 2 to 3 minutes. Sprinkle in the flour, and stir until the flour is combined and coats the sausage and onion. Cook for about 2 minutes, stirring constantly.

3. Slowly pour in the milk and stir up the bits from the bottom of the skillet. Bring to a boil and add the Tabasco sauce.

4. Stir in 1 cup of the cheese and continue stirring until the cheese melts. Cool for 10 minutes. Add the hash browns, green onions, and eggs, stirring until the mixture is combined. Pour into the prepared baking dish and sprinkle with the remaining 1 cup cheese. Cover and refrigerate for up to 2 days or freeze for up to 1 month.

Bake It Later

1. Defrost the casserole in the refrigerator overnight, if necessary.

2. Preheat the oven to 350°F. Let the casserole come to room temperature for about 30 minutes.

3. Bake the casserole for 25 to 35 minutes, until puffed, golden, and set in the center. Let rest for 10 minutes before serving hot.

VARIATIONS

Eastern Ham Casserole

Substitute 2 cups finely diced smoked ham sautéed in 2 tablespoons unsalted butter for the sausage.

Southern Turkey Casserole

Substitute 2 cups finely diced smoked turkey sautéed in 2 tablespoons unsalted butter for the sausage.

Totally Veggie Western Casserole

Substitute 2 cups diced green, yellow, and red bell peppers sautéed in 2 tablespoons unsalted butter for the sausage.

Diva Note

Clarified butter is simply butter without the milk solids and whey (a watery liquid), which are removed after the butter is melted. It is important to use clarified butter in phyllo dough preparations because the water and milk solids will make the phyllo soggy rather than crispy when it bakes. Many markets now sell clarified butter (look for it where they sell regular butter or in the cheese section), but it's also quite easy to make yourself. To clarify butter, melt it in a small saucepan and skim all the foam off the top. Carefully pour off the clear butter, leaving any milk solids in the bottom of the pan. Refrigerate the butter until ready to use. One cup of butter will make ¾ cup of clarified butter.

Spinach, Gruyère, and Egg Strudels

WORKING WITH PHYLLO DOUGH CAN SEEM DAUNTING, but it's really quite simple to handle, and the results are worth the work. These strudels are an eye-appealing centerpiece for a brunch, with their creamy sauced eggs and bright green spinach encased in a crackly dough. The great thing about phyllo is that it freezes really well, so you can have these little packets ready in your freezer to serve at a moment's notice! SERVES 10 TO 12

5 tablespoons unsalted butter

3 tablespoons unbleached all-purpose flour

1½ cups whole or 2 percent milk

1 cup finely shredded Gruyère cheese

1½ teaspoons salt

Pinch of cayenne pepper

¼ teaspoon plus a pinch of ground nutmeg

Three 10-ounce packages fresh baby spinach, *or* two 16-ounce packages frozen chopped spinach, defrosted and squeezed dry

½ teaspoon freshly ground black pepper

8 large eggs, beaten

1 pound phyllo dough, defrosted

1 cup (2 sticks) unsalted butter, melted and clarified (see opposite page)

½ cup plain dried bread crumbs

Make It Now

1. Melt 3 tablespoons of the butter in a 2-quart saucepan over medium heat. Whisk in the flour and cook until white bubbles form on the surface. Cook the mixture for 2 to 3 minutes, until thick and smooth. Gradually add the milk, whisking until the sauce is smooth and begins to boil. Remove from the heat and stir in the cheese, ½ teaspoon of the salt, the cayenne pepper, and a pinch of nutmeg. Set aside in a large bowl to cool.

2. Melt 1 tablespoon of the remaining butter in a large skillet over medium heat. Add the spinach and sauté for 3 minutes, until the fresh spinach is wilted, or the frozen spinach is dry.

3. Sprinkle with the remaining 1 teaspoon salt, the black pepper, and the remaining ¼ teaspoon nutmeg. Remove from the skillet and add to the sauce in the bowl.

4. Wipe out the skillet and melt the remaining 1 tablespoon butter over medium-low heat. Add the eggs and scramble until just set, but still pretty wet. Remove from the heat and stir into the spinach mixture. Cool, cover, and chill in the refrigerator. (At this point, you may refrigerate for up to 3 days.)

5. Remove the phyllo from the package, unroll it, and place it on a clean kitchen towel. Cover with another kitchen towel to keep it from drying out. Line a baking sheet with aluminum foil, parchment paper, or a silicone baking liner.

6. Arrange a phyllo sheet on a work surface, keeping the others covered with the towel. Liberally brush the phyllo with clarified butter and sprinkle with about 1 teaspoon of the bread crumbs. Fold the sheet in half lengthwise. Brush the surface with more butter and sprinkle with another teaspoon of bread crumbs. Spoon ⅓ cup of the filling 1 inch in from the short end of the pastry sheet. Fold the edge of the pastry over the filling and brush with clarified butter. Fold the sides of the pastry in toward the middle, brush with clarified butter, and sprinkle with 1 teaspoon bread crumbs. Starting at the end with the filling, fold the dough over the filling, rolling it up to form a package. Brush the top and bottom with clarified butter and place on the prepared sheet, seam side down. Repeat to make 12 packages. Cover and refrigerate for up to 2 days or freeze for up to 6 weeks. (Once the packages are frozen, they can be transferred to zipper-top plastic bags or storage containers, with the layers separated by plastic wrap or waxed paper.)

Bake It Later

1. Defrost the strudels in the refrigerator overnight, if necessary. (Frozen phyllo packets can also go straight from the freezer into the oven, but will take a little longer to bake, 20 to 30 minutes.)

2. Preheat the oven to 375°F. Place the strudels on a baking sheet lined with aluminum foil, parchment paper, or a silicone baking liner. Let the packets come to room temperature for 15 minutes.

3. Bake the strudels until puffed and golden, about 15 minutes. Let cool for 5 minutes before serving.

Chile Relleno Soufflé

THIS IS A CLASSIC RECIPE WITH A NEW TWIST: a dynamite ranchero sauce that perks it up considerably! This favorite standby can be a lifesaver on a busy weeknight, or you can serve it on Sunday morning for breakfast or brunch in a pool of ranchero sauce. SERVES 6

Two 7-ounce cans whole green chiles, drained and rinsed

2 cups finely shredded Monterey Jack cheese

2 cups finely shredded mild cheddar cheese

4 large eggs

2 tablespoons unbleached all-purpose flour

1 teaspoon salt

6 dashes of Tabasco sauce

One 12-ounce can evaporated milk

2 cups Ranchero Sauce (page 110), at room temperature

Make It Now

1. Coat the inside of a 9 x 13-inch baking dish with nonstick cooking spray. Split the chiles down the center and rinse them, removing any seeds. In a medium-size bowl, combine the Monterey Jack and cheddar cheeses.

2. Lay out the chiles on a flat surface and fill each with about 2 tablespoons each of the Monterey Jack and cheddar cheeses. Roll up the chiles, and place them seam side down in the prepared baking dish.

3. In a large bowl, whisk together the eggs, flour, salt, Tabasco sauce, and evaporated milk until blended. Pour over the chiles in the prepared pan. Cover and refrigerate for up to 2 days.

Diva Note

This casserole freezes well after baking. Bake for 45 minutes, remove from the oven, let cool completely, cover, and freeze for up to 1 month. Defrost the casserole in the refrigerator overnight and bring to room temperature for about 30 minutes. Bake at 350°F, covered, for 10 minutes. Spread the ranchero sauce over the top, cover, and bake for an additional 5 to 7 minutes, until heated through.

1. Preheat the oven to 350°F. Let the casserole come to room temperature for 30 minutes.

2. Bake the casserole for 45 minutes, until puffed and golden. Remove from the oven and spread 1 cup of the ranchero sauce over the top of the soufflé. Bake for another 10 to 15 minutes, until the center is set. Let rest for 10 minutes before cutting. Pool a little ranchero sauce on each plate and serve a square of the soufflé in the center of the sauce, or serve the extra sauce warmed on the side.

Ranchero Sauce

MAKES ABOUT 4 CUPS

2 tablespoons vegetable oil

2 large onions, thinly sliced

2 cloves garlic, minced

1 medium-size green bell pepper, thinly sliced

1 medium-size red bell pepper, thinly sliced

1 teaspoon ground cumin

1 teaspoon salt

$\frac{1}{8}$ teaspoon chili powder

2 tablespoons tequila

4 cups tomato puree

1. Heat the oil in a large, deep skillet over medium-high heat. Add the onion and sauté until softened, about 3 minutes. Add the garlic, green and red bell peppers, cumin, salt, and chili powder and cook for 8 to 10 minutes, stirring to prevent the vegetables and spices from sticking or burning.

2. Add the tequila and allow it to reduce. Add the tomato puree and bring to a boil. Reduce the heat to low and simmer until the sauce is thickened, about 30 minutes. (At this point, you may let cool, cover, and refrigerate for up to 5 days or freeze for up to 2 months.) Serve warm or at room temperature.

Bananas Foster French Toast

A CLASSIC NEW ORLEANS DESSERT combo of caramelized bananas in brown sugar, rum, and butter, bananas Foster makes for great French toast, to give you a decadent and delicious morning wake-up call! I recommend making this in two 9-inch cake pans or pie plates, because you can turn them out onto platters for serving. Otherwise, a 9 x 13-inch dish is fine because, when your guests dig in, they will find the goodies on the bottom. SERVES 8

½ cup (1 stick) unsalted butter

⅔ cup firmly packed light brown sugar

½ cup dark rum

4 bananas, ripe but still firm, cut into ½-inch-thick slices

1 cup granulated sugar

8 large eggs

2 cups heavy cream

2 teaspoons ground cinnamon

One 1-pound loaf bread, tough crusts removed and torn into small pieces (about 8 cups)

Make It Now

1. Coat the inside of two 9-inch round cake pans or pie plates or one 9 x 13-inch baking dish with nonstick cooking spray.

2. Melt the butter in a medium-size sauté pan over medium-high heat. Add the brown sugar and stir until the sugar is melted. Add the rum, and stir until the mixture is combined.

3. Divide the brown sugar mixture between the two pans, or pour into the bottom of the 9 x 13-inch baking dish. Arrange the banana slices on top of the sugar mixture.

4. In a large bowl, whisk together the granulated sugar, eggs, heavy cream, and cinnamon. Add the bread and stir to blend. Spread the bread mixture over the bananas. Cover and refrigerate for up to 3 days or freeze for up to 1 month.

Bake It Later

1. Defrost the casseroles overnight in the refrigerator, if necessary.

2. Preheat the oven to 350°F. Let the casseroles come to room temperature for about 20 minutes.

3. Bake the French toast for 40 to 45 minutes, or until the bread is golden brown and the banana mixture is bubbling. Allow to rest on wire racks for 5 to 10 minutes before removing from the pans and serving hot.

Over-the-Top Chocolate French Toast
with Vanilla Custard Sauce

THIS FRENCH TOAST, oozing with three types of melted chocolate and rich French toast batter, is a winner for breakfast, and I know some people who like to serve it as a dessert. Either way, try your own favorite chocolate combinations in this deluxe combo. Serve this with the vanilla custard and freshly sliced strawberries or raspberries to send it even further over the top. SERVES 8

1 cup sugar

8 large eggs

2 cups heavy cream

1 tablespoon pure vanilla extract or vanilla bean paste (see Diva Note)

One 1-pound loaf egg bread, such as challah or brioche, *or* 1 pound leftover croissants, torn into small pieces

1/3 cup milk chocolate chips

2/3 cup semisweet chocolate chips

1/3 cup bittersweet chocolate chips

3 tablespoons unsalted butter, melted

Make It Now

1. Coat the inside of a 9 x 13-inch baking dish with nonstick cooking spray.

2. In a large bowl, whisk together the sugar, eggs, heavy cream, and vanilla. Add the bread, and stir to blend. Add three types of chocolate chips, and stir to blend.

3. Pour the mixture into the baking dish and drizzle with the butter. Cover and refrigerate for up to 2 days or freeze for up to 1 month.

Diva Note

Vanilla bean paste is awesome; it will give you a punch of vanilla flavor in cooked dishes. I use it for all cooked desserts, because it won't evaporate the way vanilla extract does. The paste is far superior to using vanilla beans, as well, because sometimes you'll get dried-out vanilla beans that aren't worth the money you paid for them. A small jar of paste will last for a year in your pantry, but it will be gone before that! You can find vanilla bean paste in gourmet food stores.

Vanilla Custard Sauce
(recipe follows), warmed

Bake It Later

1. Defrost the casserole overnight in the refrigerator, if necessary.

2. Preheat the oven to 350°F. Let the casserole come to room temperature for about 30 minutes.

3. Bake the casserole for 35 to 40 minutes, or until the top is golden brown and the chips are melted. Serve warm, passing the sauce on the side.

Vanilla Custard Sauce

THIS CUSTARD SAUCE is delicious not only with French toast, but also with fruit cobblers, crisps, and pies.

MAKES ABOUT 2½ CUPS

3 tablespoons sugar

2 tablespoons cornstarch

2 cups milk

3 large egg yolks

1 teaspoon vanilla bean paste (see Diva Note)

1. In a small saucepan, whisk together the sugar, cornstarch, milk, and egg yolks until smooth. Place over medium heat, and whisk until the mixture thickens slightly and comes to a boil.

2. Remove from the heat and transfer to a heatproof glass bowl. Press plastic wrap against the surface to prevent a skin from forming. Refrigerate the sauce for at least 4 hours, or up to 4 days, or freeze for up to 1 month. Defrost when ready to use. Serve warm, at room temperature, or cold.

French Toast

Whether you call it French toast, bread pudding, or *pain perdu* (literally "lost bread"), bread soaked in eggs has been around for a long time, but on these pages we'll take a formula and then add personality and flavors for panache. Since I'm a great believer in having one fabulous recipe and then adapting it with other flavors, I hope that these recipes will have you inventing your own special French toast. Vary the breads (don't forget those leftover croissants and doughnuts!) and the flavorings to come up with your own versions. These recipes are baked in a 9 x 13-inch baking dish, but they can also be baked for 20 minutes in 12 muffin cups or individual ramekins.

These are rich recipes. If someone you're serving has a diet that restricts fat, you can prepare the custard using egg substitute and evaporated skim milk in place of the eggs and cream, and omit the butter drizzle. But keep in mind that the lower-fat products are not as thick as real eggs and cream, so you will have to add about 1 cup more bread and cook the French toast about 10 minutes longer.

No-Fear Flipping

Sometimes turning a dish over onto a serving plate can fill you with fear and trepidation. To flip with confidence, make sure your serving dish is at least 2 to 3 inches larger than the baking dish. Place the serving dish on top of your baking dish, then grasp your serving dish and baking dish (use potholders here—I find the big mitts work best) and flip the dish over. You can practice by filling a baking dish with rolls, or some other food like fruit, and flipping until you feel confident doing it. Although I think the Bananas Foster French Toast (page 111) is spectacular when it's turned with its "beauty shot" side up, it's also perfectly fine to serve it without flipping.

Strawberry Mascarpone French Toast

THIS IS A RIFF ON A DISH that was published in my book *Perfect Party Food* (The Harvard Common Press, 2005). The recipe in that book called for sandwiches to be made with bread, mascarpone, and strawberries, then covered with custard and baked. This is similar, and just as delicious, but without the extra steps, and that's what I love! If you would like to use frozen strawberries, make sure to defrost and drain them well, as they tend to bleed when mixed with the bread and custard. This is also awesome made with blueberries, raspberries, blackberries, and/or peaches. SERVES 8

1¼ cups sugar

8 large eggs

2 cups heavy cream

2 teaspoons ground cinnamon

One 1-pound loaf bread, tough crusts removed and torn into small pieces (about 8 cups)

2 cups mascarpone cheese, softened

2 cups fresh or frozen sliced strawberries

3 tablespoons unsalted butter, melted

Make It Now

1. Coat the inside of a 9 x 13-inch baking dish with nonstick cooking spray. In a large bowl, whisk together 1 cup of the sugar, the eggs, heavy cream, and cinnamon. Add the bread and stir to blend.

2. Pour half of the bread mixture into the baking dish. In a small bowl, stir together the mascarpone, the remaining ¼ cup sugar, and the berries. Dot the top of the French toast with the cheese mixture, spreading it to the edges as best you can (dip an offset spatula into warm water to help spread). Top with the remaining bread mixture and drizzle with the melted butter. Cover and refrigerate for up to 2 days or freeze for up to 1 month.

Bake It Later

1. Defrost the casserole overnight in the refrigerator, if necessary.

2. Preheat the oven to 350°F. Let the casserole come to room temperature for about 30 minutes.

3. Bake the casserole for 35 to 40 minutes, or until the top is golden brown. Allow it to rest for 10 minutes, then serve warm.

PB&J French Toast

I KNOW, YOU'RE THINKING I've had too many egg-and-cream concoctions, and my brain has turned to French toast, but this classic combo is an all-time favorite. Your kids won't ever turn up their noses at breakfast again! And for those of you in living in Red Sox nation, make sure to try the "fluffernutter" variation. SERVES 8

½ cup peanut butter (reduced fat is okay)

1 cup sugar

6 large eggs

1¾ cups heavy cream

2 teaspoons vanilla bean paste (see Diva Note, page 112) or pure vanilla extract

8 cups torn bread cubes (egg bread, such as brioche or challah, or soft white bread with the crust on is fine)

1 cup good-quality strawberry jam or your favorite jam (see Diva Note)

3 tablespoons unsalted butter, melted

½ cup chopped roasted and salted peanuts

Make It Now

1. Coat the inside of a 9 x 13-inch baking dish with nonstick cooking spray.

2. In the bowl of an electric mixer, cream together the peanut butter and sugar at low speed. Add the eggs, one at a time, incorporating after each addition. Slowly pour in the cream, beating until the mixture is blended. It may appear curdled, but that is okay. Add the vanilla bean paste and mix to incorporate.

3. Place the bread cubes in a large bowl. Pour the peanut-butter mixture over the bread cubes and stir until all the cubes are coated.

4. Transfer half of the bread mixture to the prepared pan, dot the top with the strawberry jam, and then spread the jam with an offset spatula to within about ½ inch of the sides of the pan. Spread the remaining bread mixture over the jam, drizzle with the melted butter, and sprinkle with the peanuts. Cover the baking dish and refrigerate for up to 2 days or freeze for up to 1 month.

Diva Note

Although some people think that PB&J should consist only of grape jelly and peanut butter, jelly doesn't bake very well. But the strawberry jam is a great substitute. You may also use grape jam, if you prefer.

1. Defrost the casserole overnight in the refrigerator, if necessary.

2. Preheat the oven to 350°F. Let the casserole come to room temperature for about 30 minutes.

3. Bake the casserole for 35 to 40 minutes, or until the top is golden brown and the casserole is bubbling. Serve warm.

VARIATION

Fluffernutter French Toast

Marshmallow Fluff is a New England pantry staple, and it makes this French toast even dreamier. Substitute an equal amount of Marshmallow Fluff for the strawberry jam, and proceed as directed. When cut, the French toast oozes marshmallow heaven.

French Toast Cobblers

HERE IS ANOTHER VARIATION ON OVEN-MADE FRENCH TOAST, but in this dish the fruit is on the bottom, baking and bubbling, and the French toast is on the top, getting crispy and delicious. This is a great way to use up lots of fresh fruit in the summer or leftover breads. I have made this with left-over croissants, doughnuts, angel food cake, and challah, all with great success. Think of this recipe as a basic tried-and-true formula, and mix and match your fruits, nuts, and flavorings according to my suggestions (opposite page). I know that you'll find yourself serving this time and again, with your own favorite flavor combinations, to rave reviews! SERVES 8

6 large eggs

$2/3$ cup whole or 2 percent milk

1 tablespoon flavoring of your choice (such as amaretto, rum, Chambord, pure vanilla extract, or lemon extract)

2 tablespoons sugar

$1/8$ teaspoon ground cinnamon

One 8-ounce loaf good-quality white bread, crusts removed and torn into pieces

FRUIT

8 cups fresh fruit, peeled, cored or pitted, and coarsely chopped, *or* two 16-ounce bags frozen fruit, defrosted and well drained

$1/2$ cup sugar

1 teaspoon ground cinnamon

Pinch of freshly grated nutmeg

1 tablespoon cornstarch

TOPPING

1 cup sugar

2 teaspoons ground cinnamon

$1/2$ cup chopped or sliced nuts

3 tablespoons unsalted butter, melted

Make It Now

1. In a large bowl, whisk together the eggs, milk, flavoring, sugar, and cinnamon until blended. Add the bread and stir to coat. (At this point, you may cover and refrigerate for up to 2 days.)

2. To prepare the fruit, in another large bowl, combine the fruit, sugar, cinnamon, nutmeg, and cornstarch, stirring gently to combine. Pour into a 9 x 13-inch baking dish. (At this point, you may cover and refrigerate for up to 2 days.)

3. To make the topping, in a small bowl, combine the sugar, cinnamon, and nuts. Set aside.

4. Spread the bread mixture over the fruit in the baking dish. Sprinkle with the topping and drizzle with the melted butter. Cover and refrigerate for up to 2 days or freeze for up to 1 month.

Cobbler Combinations

FRUIT	FLAVORING	NUTS
Peaches	Amaretto	Sliced almonds
Blueberries	Lemon zest	Sliced almonds
Raspberries and peaches	Amaretto	Sliced almonds
Raspberries and blueberries	Chambord or brandy	Chopped pecans
Sweet cherries	Brandy or vanilla extract	Chopped pecans
Blueberries and peaches	Rum	Chopped hazelnuts
Pineapple or mango	Rum or coconut extract	Chopped macadamia nuts
Pears	Brandy	Chopped walnuts or pecans

Bake It Later

1. Defrost the casserole in the refrigerator overnight, if necessary.

2. Preheat the oven to 350°F. Allow the casserole to come to room temperature for about 30 minutes.

3. Bake for 45 to 50 minutes, until the toast is golden brown and the fruit is bubbling. Serve hot.

Diva Note

I love raspberries, but they can be expensive, and they tend to fall apart in this dish, so it's best to combine them with another fruit, giving you the flavor of raspberry, but the structure of the other fruit.

The Main Dish
Meat

With beef, pork, and lamb, the dinner choices are as varied as the meats, from old-fashioned beef stew covered with a Boursin cheese–mashed potato crust to a new version of osso buco using pork instead of veal, baked on a creamy bed of Parmesan polenta. For all the dishes in this chapter, I've chosen boneless cuts of meat that will cook quickly in their braising liquids; then they are either refrigerated or frozen, ready to be popped into the oven for a final cooking. Most stews and braises actually taste better after they have been refrigerated for a couple of days, allowing the flavors to deepen and develop. Using wine and acidic ingredients, such as balsamic vinegar and citrus, not only helps to perk up flavors but also aids in tenderizing the meat, ensuring melt-in-your-mouth goodness in every bite. Many of these recipes can be made in individual ovenproof crocks or served family style from your favorite casserole dish or Dutch oven. Ovenproof crocks are a great way to make individual portions to store in the freezer for smaller households. No matter how you serve these meals, make sure to accompany them with lots of crusty bread to soak up the scrumptious sauces.

The Main Dish: Meat

Asian Braised Short Ribs

MY FRIEND RICK RODGERS makes braised short ribs that are famous, the result of having been featured as the dish of the year by *Bon Appétit* magazine. His classic American version is warm and comforting, with the short ribs meltingly tender when braised. My version uses soy sauce, ginger, and garlic, giving this classic American fare an Asian twist. The ribs are perfect to serve with soba noodles or rice. SERVES 6

2 tablespoons olive oil

4 pounds boneless beef short ribs

3 cloves garlic, minced

2 teaspoons finely grated fresh ginger

1 cup finely chopped onion

½ cup soy sauce

¼ cup mirin (rice wine) or dry sherry

Two 14.5-ounce cans beef broth

Make It Now

1. Heat the oil in a 5- to 7-quart Dutch oven over medium heat. Brown the short ribs a few pieces at a time, removing the meat from the pan as it browns. Add the garlic, ginger, and onion to the pan and sauté until the onion begins to turn translucent, 5 to 7 minutes.

2. Return the ribs to the pan, and slowly add the soy sauce, rice wine, and broth. Simmer for 45 minutes, skimming off any foam that forms on the top of the broth.

3. Let cool, then transfer to a large zipper-top plastic freezer bag, and refrigerate for up to 3 days or freeze for up to 2 months.

2 tablespoons cornstarch mixed with 3 tablespoons water

2 teaspoons toasted sesame oil

4 green onions (white and tender green parts), chopped

Bake It Later

1. Defrost the short ribs in the refrigerator overnight, if necessary. Remove and discard any excess fat from the surface of the sauce.

2. Preheat the oven to 350°F. Transfer the ribs and sauce to a Dutch oven and allow them to come to room temperature for about 20 minutes.

3. Bake the short ribs, covered, for 1 hour. Stir in the cornstarch mixture and bake, covered, for another 10 minutes, until the sauce thickens.

4. Stir in the sesame oil and sprinkle the green onions over the top before serving.

Cornbread-Chili Bake

THIS EASY CASSEROLE IS A TERRIFIC WEEKNIGHT DINNER that you can pull from the freezer in the morning and serve piping hot that night. The cornbread covers the chili, so it will come out of the oven with its own crust! A fruit or vegetable salad can complete this simple do-ahead dinner.

SERVES 6

CHILI

2 tablespoons olive oil

1½ pounds lean ground beef (or substitute ground turkey)

1 teaspoon salt

½ teaspoon freshly ground black pepper

1 cup finely chopped sweet onion

2 cloves garlic, minced

2 tablespoons chili powder

1 teaspoon ground cumin

½ teaspoon dried oregano

2 tablespoons cornmeal or masa harina

Two 16-ounce cans tomato sauce

One 14.5-ounce can beef broth

One 15.5-ounce can red kidney beans, drained and rinsed

CORNBREAD

1½ cups yellow cornmeal

½ cup unbleached all-purpose flour

1 tablespoon sugar

1 tablespoon baking powder

1 teaspoon salt

2 large eggs

¾ cup milk

2 tablespoons unsalted butter, melted

6 dashes of Tabasco or other hot sauce

1 cup finely shredded mild cheddar cheese

Make It Now

1. Coat the inside of a 3-quart or 9 x 13-inch casserole dish with nonstick cooking spray.

2. To make the chili, heat the oil in a large stockpot over medium heat. Add the beef, sprinkle with the salt and pepper, and add the onion. Sauté until the meat has lost its pink color, 6 to 8 minutes. Drain off and discard any excess fat from the pan. Add the garlic, chili powder, cumin, and oregano, and sauté for another 2 minutes, being careful not to burn the spices. Add the cornmeal and stir until it clings to the meat and onions. Slowly add the tomato sauce and beef broth, scraping up any bits that cling to the bottom of the pot. Bring the sauce to a boil, stirring so that the chili doesn't stick to the pot. Reduce the heat, add the beans, and simmer for 20 minutes, stirring frequently. Let the chili cool slightly and transfer it to the prepared baking dish.

3. To make the cornbread, combine the cornmeal, flour, sugar, baking powder, and salt in a large bowl, stirring to aerate the ingredients. Add the eggs, milk, butter, and Tabasco, stirring until the ingredients are moistened. Stir in the cheese (the batter will be stiff).

4. Spread the batter over the cooled chili. Cover and refrigerate for up to 2 days or freeze for up to 1 month.

Bake It Later

1. Defrost the casserole in the refrigerator overnight, if necessary.

2. Preheat the oven to 375°F. Allow the casserole to come to room temperature for about 30 minutes.

3. Bake the casserole for 30 minutes, until the chili is bubbling, the cornbread is golden brown, and a toothpick inserted into the cornbread comes out clean. Serve immediately.

VARIATION

Since I designed this chili to serve a family, I've toned down the heat. If you would like a spicier chili, add more chili powder (make sure to sauté it first). You can also add 2 teaspoons minced jalapeños to the onion when sautéing.

Diva Notes

Make sure to sauté the spices with the meat and onion because the spices are meant to "bloom" in the fat, releasing their oils and becoming fragrant. If you just dump the spices into the chili, you will have a very different end result; the ingredients will take on an acrid taste and smell.

———

Another way to make this dish is in individual ovenproof soup bowls, using ½ to ¾ cup chili topped with about ½ cup of the cornbread batter, depending upon the size of your bowls. Bake for 15 to 18 minutes, until the cornbread is golden brown.

Beef Stroganoff Casserole

AS A CHILD I THOUGHT THIS DISH WAS VERY EXOTIC, with its creamy mushroom sauce. Nowadays people don't seem to make beef stroganoff, and it's a shame, because it's a terrific do-ahead entrée. I like to make it a one-dish meal by including noodles on the bottom. Although beef fillet is pricey, it cooks quickly and you don't need much to make this satisfying dinner. SERVES 6

NOODLES

1 pound medium-width egg noodles, cooked according to package directions

1 teaspoon salt

½ teaspoon freshly ground black pepper

2 tablespoons unsalted butter

BEEF AND VEGETABLES

1½ pounds beef fillet, cut into 1- x ½-inch strips

1 teaspoon salt, plus more as needed

¾ teaspoon freshly ground black pepper, plus more as needed

3 tablespoons unsalted butter

1 large onion, thinly sliced

1 teaspoon sugar

1 teaspoon fresh thyme leaves

1 pound white mushrooms, sliced

½ pound cremini mushrooms, sliced

1½ cups beef broth

⅔ cup heavy cream

Make It Now

1. Coat the inside of a 9 x 13-inch baking dish or 3-quart casserole dish with nonstick cooking spray. Toss the noodles with the salt, pepper, and butter. Spread the noodles evenly in the baking dish. (At this point, you may cover with plastic wrap and refrigerate for up to 2 days.)

2. Sprinkle the beef with the salt and pepper. Melt 1 tablespoon of the butter in a large skillet over medium heat. Add the meat, a few pieces at a time, browning the meat on all sides. Remove the meat from the pan as it is browned and set aside.

3. Melt the remaining 2 tablespoons butter in the pan and add the onion, sugar, and thyme, sautéing until the onion begins to turn golden, 8 to 10 minutes. Add the white and cremini mushrooms and sauté for another 5 minutes, until the liquid in the pan is just about evaporated. Stir in the beef broth and scrape up any bits that have stuck to the bottom of the pan. Return the meat to the pan and simmer gently for about 3 minutes. Add the cream, turn off the heat, and season with salt and pepper.

4. Pour the beef and sauce over the noodles in the pan and let cool. Cover and refrigerate for up to 2 days, or freeze for up to 6 weeks.

Bake It Later

1. Defrost the casserole in the refrigerator overnight, if necessary.

2. Preheat the oven to 350°F. Allow the casserole to come to room temperature for about 30 minutes.

3. Bake the casserole, covered, for 30 minutes. Uncover and bake for an additional 10 minutes, until the sauce is bubbling. Serve immediately.

Diva Note

Stroganoff recipes traditionally use sour cream instead of heavy cream. However, sour cream sometimes curdles with heat, and I find that heavy cream complements the meat and vegetables beautifully.

Italian-Style Pot Roast

A LEAN EYE OF THE ROUND ROAST MAKES A DELICIOUS POT ROAST to braise with vegetables and herbs in an aromatic sauce of wine and tomatoes. An eye of the round roast looks like a filet mignon in that it is a solid piece of virtually fat-free meat that slices into portions easily. That being said, it is expensive and not as tender as the filet, so it needs a long braise to become tender. Other, less expensive alternatives are a rump roast or sirloin tip roast. Neither of these will slice into the neat, uniform slices that the eye of the round does, but they will become tender and delicious when simmered in the sauce, which is delicious over pasta, potatoes, or rice. This dish can serve you well as a "go to" meal for company. SERVES 6 TO 8

2 cloves garlic, minced

2 teaspoons salt

1 teaspoon freshly ground black pepper

3 pounds eye of the round roast, tied

2 tablespoons olive oil

1 cup finely chopped onion

1 cup finely chopped celery

1 cup finely chopped carrot

1 tablespoon finely chopped fresh rosemary

1 cup red wine

One 32-ounce can crushed tomatoes

1 cup beef broth

Make It Now

1. Make a paste of the garlic, salt, and pepper and rub this all over the roast. Heat the oil in a 4- to 5-quart Dutch oven over medium heat. Brown the roast in the oil on all sides. Remove from the pan and set aside. Add the onion, celery, carrot, and rosemary and sauté until the vegetables are softened, about 5 minutes. Add the wine and allow the wine to boil for about 1 minute. Add the tomatoes and beef broth, stir to blend, then return the meat to the pan. Simmer the meat in the sauce for 45 minutes.

2. Remove from the heat and let the meat and sauce cool. Transfer to a large zipper-top plastic freezer bag and refrigerate for up to 3 days or freeze for up to 3 months.

Diva Note

A liquid is simmering when the bubbles that form in the liquid just gently break the surface. Cooking meat at a rolling boil will make it tough and stringy, so be patient and make sure that the sauce is simmering and the meat is not bouncing around in the sauce!

Bake It Later

1. Defrost the pot roast in the refrigerator overnight, if necessary.

2. Preheat the oven to 350°F. Place the roast and sauce in a baking dish and allow it to come to room temperature for about 30 minutes.

3. Bake, occasionally basting with the sauce, for 90 minutes or until the meat is tender and registers 170°F on an instant-read thermometer. Remove from the oven and allow the meat to rest for 20 minutes. While the meat is resting, remove excess fat from the sauce with a flat spoon, or by gently blotting the surface of the sauce with a paper towel. There is so little fat on this cut of meat that the paper towel trick works well. Boil the sauce down if it is thin. Remove the string from the meat, carve, and serve with the sauce drizzled over the top.

Oven-Barbecued Beef

BARBECUED BEEF SANDWICHES ARE A STAPLE IN MY HOUSE when folks are watching sports on TV. I love a beefy barbecue sauce, with a hint of sweetness from brown sugar and molasses and some zest from Tabasco sauce. This meal is a snap to put together, then it's baked until the meat is tender and falling apart. Serve this with soft potato rolls and cole slaw on the side. SERVES 6

2 tablespoons olive oil

Salt and freshly ground black pepper to taste

1 flat-cut 4- to 5-pound beef brisket

2 large onions, thinly sliced

6 cloves garlic, minced

1 cup ketchup

1 cup beef broth

One 16-ounce can tomato sauce

1/2 cup firmly packed light brown sugar

1/4 cup dark molasses

1/4 cup whole-grain mustard

1 tablespoon Tabasco sauce

Make It Now

1. Heat the oil over medium heat in a 5- to 7-quart Dutch oven. Sprinkle the salt and pepper over the beef and add to the Dutch oven. Brown the meat on each side, remove from the pan, and set aside. Add the onions and garlic to the pan and sauté until the onions are softened, 4 to 5 minutes. Stir in the ketchup, broth, tomato sauce, brown sugar, molasses, mustard, and Tabasco sauce, scraping up any browned bits from the bottom of the pan. Return the meat to the pan, cover, and simmer for 1 hour.

2. Remove the meat from the sauce and let both cool. Trim any fat from the meat and thinly slice the meat against the grain at a 30-degree angle. Lay the meat in a 3-quart casserole dish or a 9 x 13-inch baking dish. Spoon the sauce over the meat. Cover and refrigerate for up to 3 days or freeze for up to 2 months.

Bake It Later

1. Defrost the beef in the refrigerator overnight, if necessary. Remove any excess fat that may have congealed on the surface of the sauce.

2. Preheat the oven to 350°F. Allow the dish to come to room temperature for about 30 minutes.

3. Bake for 2 to 3 hours, until the meat is falling-apart tender and the sauce is thick.

4. Remove any accumulated fat from the sauce and serve warm.

Beef Pot Pie with Boursin–Mashed Potato Crust

THIS ABSURDLY DELICIOUS PIE is perfect for a special occasion. The creamy herbed Boursin gives the potatoes a bit of attitude, and the wine- and sage-flavored beef stew is the perfect complement. Feel free to serve this in either individual ovenproof soup bowls or in a large casserole dish. SERVES 6

BEEF STEW

1 teaspoon salt

½ teaspoon freshly ground black pepper

2 cloves garlic, crushed

2 tablespoons olive oil

2 pounds lean beef sirloin, cut into 1-inch pieces

1½ cups full-bodied red wine, such as Burgundy or Cabernet

2 cups beef broth

2 teaspoons dried sage

1 bay leaf

¼ cup warm water

3 tablespoons unbleached all-purpose flour

1 tablespoon unsalted butter

1 pound white mushrooms, cut in half

BOURSIN MASHED POTATOES

4 large baking potatoes, cut into 1-inch pieces (peeled or unpeeled)

One 5.2-ounce package Boursin cheese, softened

¼ cup sour cream

2 tablespoons unsalted butter

Salt and freshly ground black pepper to taste

Make It Now

1. To make the beef stew, mash together the salt, pepper, and garlic to form a paste, and rub it over the surface of the meat. Heat the oil in a 5- to 7-quart Dutch oven over medium heat. Add the meat, a few pieces at a time, and cook until browned, removing the meat as it is browned. When all of the meat is browned, return it to the pan and add the wine. Bring to a boil, then simmer the meat in the wine for 10 minutes to reduce the liquid and concentrate the flavor. Add the broth, sage, and bay leaf, and simmer the stew for 1½ hours, until the meat is tender.

2. Remove the meat from the sauce and bring the sauce to a boil. In a small bowl, stir the water and flour together until smooth. Whisk the mixture into the sauce and return the sauce to a boil. Return the meat to the sauce.

3. Melt the butter in a large skillet over medium heat and add the mushrooms. Sauté until the mushrooms are golden and their liquid has evaporated, 8 to 12 minutes. Add the mushrooms to the stew. Cool the stew, remove the bay leaf, cover, and refrigerate for up to 3 days or freeze for up to 3 months.

4. To make the mashed potatoes, place the potatoes in salted water to cover. Bring to a boil and boil the potatoes until tender, about 15 minutes. Drain thoroughly and return to the pan, shaking the potatoes over the heat briefly to dry them out.

5. Using an electric mixer at low speed, beat the Boursin, sour cream, and potatoes together, increasing the speed to medium until the potatoes are smooth. Stir in the butter and season with salt and pepper. Cover the potatoes and refrigerate for up to 2 days or freeze for up to 6 weeks.

2 tablespoons unsalted butter

Bake It Later

1. Defrost the beef stew and the mashed potatoes in the refrigerator overnight, if necessary. Remove any excess fat that may have accumulated on the top of the stew.

2. Preheat the oven to 350°F. Allow the stew and potatoes to come to room temperature for about 30 minutes.

3. Pour the stew into a 3-quart casserole dish or a 9 x 13-inch baking dish. Spread a 1-inch layer of the potatoes over the stew, covering it. Dot the potatoes with tiny slivers of the butter. Bake the stew for 45 to 50 minutes, until the potatoes are golden brown and the stew is bubbling. Allow the casserole to rest for about 10 minutes before serving.

RUSSET BAKING POTATOES make the fluffiest mashed potatoes, but I love to mash red potatoes and Yukon golds as well. They will give you a denser texture, but the Boursin and the other ingredients will help to make them light and airy, like a soufflé. If you like lumps or skin-on mashed potatoes, you can certainly prepare them that way, but if you plan to pipe the potatoes through a pastry bag, make sure to peel the potatoes.

Diva Note

If you want to tap your "inner Martha," pipe the potatoes over the casserole dish using a pastry bag with a large star tip.

Pepper Steak Casserole

THIS IS A GREAT ONE-DISH WONDER, with sautéed steak, peppers, and onions in a balsamic-flavored tomato sauce sitting atop a bed of rice. It's terrific as a weeknight dinner, but it also lends itself to being taken to a potluck or to a friend who's been under the weather. Any way you serve it, it's a delicious meal. SERVES 6

2 tablespoons olive oil

2 large onions, thinly sliced

2 cloves garlic

1 large green bell pepper, thinly sliced

1 large red bell pepper, thinly sliced

1 teaspoon dried basil

1 teaspoon salt, plus more to taste

1/2 teaspoon freshly ground black pepper, plus more to taste

1 pound beef sirloin, cut into 1/2-inch-thick strips

1/4 cup balsamic vinegar

1 beef bouillon cube

Two 15.5-ounce cans crushed tomatoes

4 cups cooked white rice

Make It Now

1. Heat the oil in a large skillet over medium heat. Add the onions and garlic and sauté for 1 minute, until the garlic is fragrant. Add the green and red bell peppers, basil, salt, and pepper, and sauté until the peppers begin to soften, 7 to 8 minutes. Remove the pepper mixture from the pan and set aside. Increase the heat to high, add the beef, and sauté until it loses its red color. Add the vinegar to the pan and bring it to a boil to reduce it. Add the bouillon cube, tomatoes, and reserved pepper mixture to the pan. Simmer for 10 minutes. Season with salt and pepper.

2. Coat the inside of a 9 x 13-inch casserole dish with non-stick cooking spray. Spread the rice in the pan, top with the beef and pepper mixture, and let cool. Cover and refrigerate for up to 2 days or freeze for up to 6 weeks.

Bake It Later

1. Defrost the casserole in the refrigerator overnight, if necessary.

2. Preheat the oven to 350°F. Allow the casserole to come to room temperature for about 30 minutes.

3. Bake the pepper steak, covered, for 30 minutes. Remove the cover and bake for an additional 20 minutes, until the sauce is bubbling. Serve immediately.

Braised Sirloin with Zinfandel and Cremini Mushroom Sauce

THIS DELICIOUS BRAISED SIRLOIN is just waiting for the chance to star at your next dinner party. The beef and vegetables are sautéed and then simmered in a wine and beef broth to give you an elegant dinner. SERVES 6

2 tablespoons olive oil

3 pounds beef sirloin, cut into 1-inch cubes

1½ teaspoons salt, plus more to taste

1 teaspoon freshly ground black pepper, plus more to taste

2 cloves garlic, minced

2 teaspoons dried thyme

1 pound cremini mushrooms, cut in half, tough stems removed if necessary

1½ cups Zinfandel

Two 14.5-ounce cans beef broth

Make It Now

1. Heat the oil in a 5- to 7-quart Dutch oven over medium heat. Sprinkle the meat with the salt and pepper, and add the meat in small batches, making sure not to crowd the pan. Cook until the meat is browned and remove from the pan as it is browned.

2. Add the garlic, thyme, and mushrooms to the pan and sauté until the mushroom liquid has evaporated. Return the meat to the pan, add the wine and broth, and bring to a simmer. Cover and simmer the meat for 20 minutes. Add more salt or pepper, if desired. Let cool, then transfer the mixture to a large zipper-top plastic freezer bag and refrigerate for up to 3 days or freeze for up to 2 months.

Diva Note

Many of my cooking students ask what to do if they want to omit the wine from recipes. There really is no substitute for wine in recipes, but if you must, you can substitute broth for the wine. Additional herbs will punch up the flavor as well.

1 cup pearl onions, peeled

2 cups baby carrots

12 small potatoes, such as fingerling, Yukon gold, red, or white new potatoes

¼ cup (½ stick) unsalted butter, softened (optional)

¼ cup unbleached all-purpose flour (optional)

Bake It Later

1. Defrost the meat in the refrigerator overnight, if necessary. Remove any fat that has formed on the surface of the sauce and let the meat come to room temperature for about 30 minutes.

2. Pour the beef and sauce into a 7-quart Dutch oven. Add the onions, carrots, and potatoes. Simmer for 1 hour, until the meat and potatoes are tender when pierced with the tip of a sharp knife. If you want a thicker sauce, mix together the butter and flour. Bring the stew to a boil and stir in bits of the butter mixture until the sauce is thickened to your taste. Serve immediately.

Filet Mignon Pizzaiola

SENSATIONAL TO SERVE FOR COMPANY with a side of pasta, these filet mignons are seared, covered with a delicious homemade cremini mushroom pizza sauce, sprinkled with a combination of cheeses, and baked to give you a great meal for a tiny bit of effort. SERVES 6

¼ cup olive oil

2 cloves garlic, crushed

2½ teaspoons salt

1 teaspoon freshly ground black pepper

Six 1-inch-thick filet mignon steaks, trimmed of fat

1 cup finely chopped red onion

1½ teaspoons dried oregano

½ teaspoon dried basil

1 pound cremini mushrooms, sliced

½ cup full-bodied red wine, such as Chianti, Burgundy, or Cabernet

One 32-ounce can crushed tomatoes

1 teaspoon sugar

1½ cups finely shredded Monterey Jack, mozzarella, or Munster cheese

½ cup freshly grated Parmesan cheese

Make It Now

1. Make a paste of the oil, garlic, 1 teaspoon of the salt, and ½ teaspoon of the pepper. Spread the paste over both sides of the meat, turning the meat to coat thoroughly.

2. Heat a dry skillet over high heat and sear the filets on one side for 3 minutes, until evenly browned but not cooked through. Sear the other side for 2 minutes, until browned. Remove the meat from the skillet, cool, cover, and refrigerate while making the sauce.

3. In the same pan, sauté the onion, oregano, and basil until the onion is softened but not browned. Add the mushrooms and cook until they begin to color. Add the wine and deglaze the pan, bringing the wine to a boil and scraping up any loose bits from the bottom of the pan. Add the tomatoes, the remaining 1½ teaspoons salt, the remaining ½ teaspoon pepper, and the sugar. Simmer the sauce for 45 minutes, stirring a few times to make sure that the sauce doesn't sick to the bottom of the pan. Remove from the heat and let cool.

4. Spread 1 cup of the sauce in a baking dish that will fit the filets comfortably, without crowding them. Set the filets on top of the sauce, and cover each filet with a few table-spoons of the remaining sauce. Combine the Monterey Jack and Parmesan cheeses in a bowl, and sprinkle them evenly over the sauce. Cover and refrigerate for up to 24 hours, or freeze for up to 1 month.

Bake It Later

1. Defrost the steaks in the refrigerator overnight, if necessary.

2. Preheat the oven to 400°F. Allow the steaks to come to room temperature for 20 minutes.

3. Bake for 10 to 15 minutes, until the filets are medium-rare (140°F on an instant-read thermometer) and the cheese is bubbling. Remove from the oven and allow to rest for 5 minutes before serving.

Pork Chop and Stuffing Bake

THIS DISH FROM THE HEARTLAND can be absolutely scrumptious or bland and tasteless. I'm hoping you'll try this version, because it's a delicious one-dish meal to serve to family and friends. The cornbread stuffing gets its punch from pork sausage and apples, and the thick-cut pork chops bake beneath an apple cider sauce to give you a dish fit for company or a special weeknight. SERVES 6 TO 8

4 cups crumbled cornbread
(see Diva Note)

³/₄ pound bulk pork sausage
(I like Jimmy Dean original or sage
flavor)

¹/₂ cup finely chopped onion

¹/₂ cup finely chopped celery

1 cup coarsely chopped apple
(Granny Smith or other tart
firm apple)

2 teaspoons dried thyme

1 teaspoon dried sage, crumbled

1 teaspoon salt, plus more to sprinkle
on the pork

¹/₂ teaspoon freshly ground black
pepper, plus more to sprinkle on
the pork

¹/₂ cup milk

1 cup chicken broth

1 large egg, beaten

3 tablespoons olive oil

8 thick-cut pork loin chops, about
³/₄ inch thick (¹/₃ pound each)

2 tablespoons unsalted butter

2 tablespoons all-purpose flour

1 cup apple cider

1 cup beef broth

1¹/₂ teaspoons chopped fresh thyme

¹/₂ cup heavy cream

Make It Now

1. Place the cornbread in a large mixing bowl. Coat the inside of a 9 x 13-inch baking dish with nonstick cooking spray.

2. Sauté the sausage in a large skillet over medium heat, breaking it up into small pieces, until it is no longer pink. Drain all but 1 tablespoon of fat from the pan. Add the onion, celery, apple, dried thyme, sage, salt, and pepper to the pan and sauté the vegetables, stirring frequently, until they are softened, 5 to 7 minutes. Stir in the milk and chicken broth, scraping up any bits from the bottom of the pan. Transfer the mixture to the bowl with the cornbread and stir to blend thoroughly. Add the egg and mix well. Spread the mixture in the prepared casserole dish.

3. Heat the oil in a large skillet over medium-high heat. Sprinkle the pork chops evenly with salt and pepper and sauté until golden brown on each side. Remove from the pan and place atop the stuffing in the baking dish. Cover and refrigerate while preparing the sauce.

4. In the same skillet, melt the butter over medium-high heat. Add the flour and whisk for 3 minutes. Slowly add the cider, beef broth, and fresh thyme and bring the mixture to a boil. Add the cream. Let cool, then pour over the pork chops in the prepared pan. Cover and refrigerate for up to 2 days or freeze for up to 1 month.

Bake It Later

1. Defrost the pork in the refrigerator overnight, if necessary.

2. Preheat the oven to 325°F. Allow the pork to come to room temperature for 20 minutes.

3. Bake the pork chops, covered, for 45 to 55 minutes, until the chops are cooked through and register 160°F on an instant-read thermometer. Serve hot.

Diva Note

To make the cornbread, use one 8.5-ounce box Jiffy cornbread. Bake according to the directions on the box, cool, and crumble. You should have 4 cups. You can also use your favorite cornbread recipe that fills a 9-inch square pan.

Stuffed Pork Tenderloin

PORK TENDERLOIN STUFFED WITH A BREAD STUFFING flavored with golden raisins, fennel, and thyme is a terrific company meal that can be ready and waiting anytime in the refrigerator or freezer.

SERVES 6

Two 1-pound pork tenderloins

2 teaspoons salt

½ teaspoon freshly ground black pepper

2 tablespoons unsalted butter

½ cup finely chopped onion

½ cup finely chopped celery

½ cup finely chopped fresh fennel

2 teaspoons finely chopped fresh thyme

½ cup finely chopped golden raisins

4 cups fresh bread crumbs

1 large egg

¼ cup olive oil

1 cup balsamic vinegar

2 tablespoons firmly packed light brown sugar

2 cups beef broth

Make It Now

1. Slit a pork tenderloin down the center lengthwise, leaving about ½ inch attached so you can open the tenderloin like a book. Place the pork on a long sheet of plastic wrap and cover with another sheet of plastic wrap. Pound the pork until it is uniform in thickness. Repeat with the other tenderloin. Sprinkle the pork with the salt and pepper.

2. Melt the butter in a medium-size sauté pan over medium heat. Add the onion, celery, fennel, and thyme and sauté until the vegetables become translucent, about 5 minutes. Add the raisins to the pan and toss to combine. Transfer the mixture to a large bowl and let cool. Add the bread crumbs to the bowl and toss to blend. Stir in the egg and mix to blend. Spread the filling on the pork tenderloins, leaving about ¾ inch on all sides without filling. Roll up each piece of pork from the long side and tie with kitchen twine or secure with toothpicks. Refrigerate for at least 1 hour before proceeding, to help the filling firm up.

3. Heat the oil in a large skillet over medium heat. Add the pork and brown on all sides. Remove the pork from the pan, pour in the vinegar, and scrape up any bits on the bottom of the pan. Add the brown sugar and bring to a boil. Stir in the broth and return the pork to the pan. Cover and simmer for 10 minutes. Remove from the heat and let cool. If desired, transfer to a 9 x 13-inch baking dish. Cover and refrigerate for up to 2 days or freeze for up to 6 weeks.

Bake It Later

1. Defrost the tenderloins in the refrigerator overnight, if necessary. Remove any excess fat that may have accumulated on the top of the sauce. Transfer to a 9 x 13-inch baking dish or Dutch oven, if necessary.

2. Preheat the oven to 350°F. Allow the tenderloins to come to room temperature for 20 minutes.

3. Bake the pork and sauce, covered, for 20 minutes. Uncover and bake for an additional 10 to 15 minutes, basting twice with the sauce. Allow the meat to rest for 10 minutes, then remove the string or toothpicks and slice the meat into 1-inch medallions. Pool some of the sauce on the plates, then arrange 2 or 3 medallions on the sauce. Drizzle with additional sauce, if desired.

Pork Osso Buco with Parmesan Polenta

THIS DELICIOUS STEW, based on the classic Milanese dish but made here with pork instead of veal, is a real crowd-pleaser. Instead of serving this with the traditional risotto, I pair it with a bed of Parmesan-flavored polenta that will bake along with the pork, absorbing the flavors of the sauce. SERVES 6

PARMESAN POLENTA

4 cups chicken broth

1 cup instant polenta

3 tablespoons unsalted butter, softened

½ cup freshly grated Parmesan cheese

PORK OSSO BUCO

1 tablespoon unsalted butter

1 tablespoon olive oil

2 pounds pork tenderloin, cut into 1-inch pieces

Salt and freshly ground black pepper to taste

½ cup finely chopped onion

½ cup finely chopped carrot

½ cup finely chopped celery

2 teaspoons dried sage

One 14.5-ounce can diced tomatoes, undrained

½ cup white wine

1 cup chicken broth

1 cup beef broth

2 tablespoons finely chopped fresh flat-leaf parsley

2 cloves garlic, minced

1 teaspoon freshly grated orange zest

1 teaspoon freshly grated lemon zest

Make It Now

1. To make the polenta, coat the inside of a 9 x 13-inch baking dish with nonstick cooking spray. Bring the broth to a boil in a large saucepan. Add the polenta, whisking until smooth. Cook the polenta, stirring, until it thickens, 10 to 12 minutes. Remove from the heat and stir in the butter and cheese.

2. Allow the polenta to cool slightly, then transfer it to the prepared baking dish. (At this point, you may cover and refrigerate for up to 2 days or freeze for up to 6 weeks.)

3. To prepare the pork, melt the butter with the oil in a Dutch oven over medium heat. Season the pork with salt and pepper, add it to the pan a few pieces at a time, and brown the pork on all sides, removing the pork as it browns. When all the pork has been browned, return it to the pan and add the onion, carrot, celery, and sage. Sauté for about 5 minutes, until the vegetables begin to soften.

4. Add the tomatoes and simmer for 5 minutes to reduce the liquid. Add the wine and simmer for another 5 minutes. Add the chicken and beef broths, cover, and simmer for 45 minutes, until the pork is tender. Stir in the parsley, garlic, and orange and lemon zests. Let cool, then spoon the pork over the polenta in the casserole dish. Cover and refrigerate for up to 3 days or freeze for up to 6 weeks.

1. Defrost the casserole in the refrigerator overnight, if necessary.

2. Preheat the oven to 350°F. Allow the casserole to come to room temperature for about 30 minutes.

3. Bake the casserole for 45 to 50 minutes, until the stew is bubbling. Serve hot.

Braised Pork with Apples and Cider

THIS IS A GREAT DISH TO SERVE TO COMPANY, a one-pot meal that is packed with flavor and offers comforting satisfaction. When my husband and I visited Normandy, we were surprised that there were no vineyards; the treasure there is apples in every conceivable form. We loved the apple cider, apple tarts, and the dishes cooked with apples. This is my rendition of a typical Norman pork dish, with my apologies to your French grandmother! SERVES 6 TO 8

½ cup Dijon mustard

½ cup plus ⅔ cup firmly packed light brown sugar

One 4-pound rolled boneless pork loin roast

3 tablespoons olive oil

1 large onion, thinly sliced

1½ teaspoons dried thyme

1½ cups apple cider

2 beef bouillon cubes

¼ cup (½ stick) unsalted butter

4 large apples, peeled, cored, and sliced into 8 wedges (I like to use Gala or another sweet apple—Granny Smiths are too tart)

3 tablespoons cornstarch

3 tablespoons water

½ cup heavy cream (optional, but it really rounds out the flavor) -

1 pound wide egg noodles, cooked according to the package directions and tossed with 2 tablespoons unsalted butter

Make It Now

1. Preheat the oven to 350°F. Place a long piece of waxed paper or aluminum foil on a cutting board and spread the mustard on it, the length of the roast. Sprinkle with ½ cup brown sugar, and lay the roast on top of the mixture, turning the roast to coat it completely. (This is messy work, but the results are great!)

2. Heat the oil in a 5- to 7-quart Dutch oven over medium-high heat. Brown the meat on all sides, being careful to turn it often so that it doesn't burn. Add the onion and thyme and stir to coat with the mixture in the bottom of the pan. Lift the meat and slide some of the onion underneath the roast. Add the cider and bouillon cubes and stir. Bring the cider to a boil, cover the pan, and bake for 45 minutes.

3. While the pork is baking, prepare the apples. Melt the butter in a large skillet over medium heat. Add the apples and sauté for 4 to 5 minutes, until the apples begin to soften and color. Add the remaining ⅔ cup brown sugar and cook for another 5 minutes, until the apples have rendered some juice and are beginning to soften, but are not mushy. Remove from the heat and add to the pork. Return the pan to the oven and simmer the pork and apples together for 30 minutes.

4. Remove the pork from the sauce, place on a cutting board or plate, and cover with aluminum foil.

5. To finish the sauce, skim off any fat that has accumulated on the surface of the sauce and bring the sauce to a boil.

Combine the cornstarch and water in a small bowl, and stir into the boiling sauce, whisking until the sauce returns to a boil and thickens. Add the cream and stir until the mixture returns to a boil. Cool the sauce.

6. Remove the string from the roast and slice the meat thinly. Place the noodles in a 9 x 13-inch baking dish and arrange the meat on top of the noodles. Top with some of the apples and sauce. Cover the casserole with plastic wrap or aluminum foil and store any extra sauce in an airtight container. Refrigerate for up to 3 days or freeze for up to 2 months.

Bake It Later

1. Defrost the pork and apples and extra sauce overnight in the refrigerator, if necessary.

2. Preheat the oven to 350°F. Allow the pork to come to room temperature for 30 minutes. Reheat the extra sauce over low heat.

3. Bake the casserole, covered, for 30 minutes. Uncover and bake for an additional 20 minutes, until the sauce is bubbling and the casserole is heated through. If you uncover the casserole and it appears dry (the noodles may have absorbed some of the sauce), ladle some of the warmed extra sauce over the casserole and continue baking. Serve with additional sauce on the side.

VARIATION

This recipe also works well with pears instead of apples, but they should be *rock hard*, which is how you will find them in the store most of the time. Substitute pear nectar for the cider, and don't sauté the pears in the butter for more than about 5 minutes total.

Braised Pork with Caramelized Sauerkraut

WHEN I THINK OF THIS MEAL, I think of cold New England winters and opening the back door of my mom's house to have the aroma of pork, apples, and sauerkraut meet me. This is warming, stick-to-your-ribs food that should be served with mashed potatoes and apple sauce. The pork will literally fall apart, and it melts into the mustard- and brown sugar–flavored sauerkraut and apples. A food processor will make short work of slicing the onions and apples. SERVES 6 TO 8

2 tablespoons olive oil

8 center-cut pork chops, cut ¾ to 1 inch thick

Salt and freshly ground black pepper to taste

2 tablespoons unsalted butter

3 large onions, thinly sliced

2 large Granny Smith apples, peeled, cored, and thinly sliced

¾ cup firmly packed light brown sugar

¼ cup Dijon mustard

4 cups fresh sauerkraut *or* three 15.5-ounce cans sauerkraut, drained

1½ cups beef broth

½ cup chicken broth

Make It Now

1. Heat the oil in a 4- to 5-quart Dutch oven over medium heat. Sprinkle the chops with salt and pepper, add the meat to the pan and brown on both sides. When the meat is browned, remove it from the pan and set aside.

2. Melt the butter in the pan, add the onions and apples, and sauté until the onions begin to turn translucent and golden, 10 to 12 minutes. Return the meat to the pan and add the brown sugar, mustard, sauerkraut, beef broth, and chicken broth and bring to a boil. Decrease the heat and simmer, uncovered, for 20 minutes. Let cool, then cover and refrigerate for up to 24 hours or freeze for up to 6 weeks.

Bake It Later

1. Defrost the pork in the refrigerator overnight, if necessary.

2. Preheat the oven to 350°F. Allow the pork to come to room temperature for about 30 minutes.

3. Bake the pork, covered, for 45 minutes, until tender. Drain off any excess liquid from the sauerkraut and serve immediately.

Not-Your-Mother's Scalloped Potato and Ham Gratin

IF I HAD TO GUESS, I'd say the scalloped ham and potato casseroles you've had have been filled with strange sauce that may have separated in baking, not-so-well-cooked potatoes, and a less-than-spectacular cheesy topping. Well, I have found a way to make this casserole a winner in your house. Fortunately, you can have a few stashed in the freezer for those occasions when your family begs you to make it again. The potatoes are precooked in cream and milk to help thicken the sauce, and then the potatoes take on the flavors of the ham, onions, and other seasonings to give you a dish that will work every time, without fail. SERVES 6

2 cups heavy cream (see Diva Notes)

2 cups whole milk

1½ teaspoons salt

1 teaspoon Tabasco sauce

1 clove garlic, minced

1 tablespoon Dijon mustard

½ teaspoon chopped fresh thyme (optional)

5 medium-size red or Yukon gold potatoes, sliced ¼ inch thick

1 large yellow onion, thinly sliced

½ pound ham, thinly sliced

2 cups finely shredded Gruyère cheese

1 cup fresh bread crumbs (see Diva Notes)

2 tablespoons unsalted butter, melted

Make It Now

1. Coat the inside of a 9 x 13-inch casserole dish with non-stick cooking spray. Combine the cream, milk, salt, Tabasco sauce, garlic, mustard, and thyme in a large skillet or Dutch oven over high heat and bring to a boil. Add the potatoes, onion, and ham, and cook for 7 to 8 minutes, until the potatoes are tender but still hold their shape. You should be able to pierce them with the sharp tip of a knife and get a bit of resistance. Transfer the mixture to the prepared dish.

2. In a small bowl, combine the cheese, bread crumbs, and butter, tossing to coat the crumbs with the butter. Sprinkle the mixture evenly over the top of the potatoes.

3. Let cool, then cover and refrigerate for up to 3 days or freeze for up to 2 months.

Bake It Later

1. Defrost the casserole in the refrigerator overnight, if necessary.

2. Preheat the oven to 350°F. Allow the casserole to come to room temperature for about 30 minutes.

3. Bake the casserole, covered, for 30 minutes. Uncover and bake for an additional 20 minutes, until the casserole is bubbling and the cheese is golden brown. Allow to rest for at least 15 minutes before serving hot.

VARIATION

The choice of cheese is strictly up to you. Gruyère has a nutty flavor and will give you a European flavor, but cheddar is also an awesome choice with ham.

Diva Notes

Lowering the fat in this recipe will not work: half-and-half tends to separate when baked, and the heavy cream actually helps to protect the integrity of the sauce.

———

The easiest way to make fresh bread crumbs is to take a day-old baguette and run it through the food processor. Store the crumbs in your freezer so you can make the crunchy toppings for all of your casseroles; they will keep indefinitely.

Pot-Roasted Lamb with White Beans

THIS MATCH-UP OF LAMB, ROSEMARY, AND WHITE BEANS is a warming meal to serve on a cold night, and it takes only a few minutes to put it together and get it ready for the refrigerator or freezer. Pot-roasted lamb shoulder will become meltingly tender, and the white beans will become creamy and help to thicken the sauce. SERVES 6

2 tablespoons olive oil

3 pounds boneless lamb shoulder, cut into 1-inch chunks

2 teaspoons salt

1 teaspoon freshly ground black pepper

3 garlic cloves, minced

1 cup finely chopped onion

1 cup finely chopped celery

1 cup finely chopped carrot

1 tablespoon finely chopped fresh rosemary

1/2 cup red wine

2 cups beef broth

2 cups chicken broth

Two 15.5-ounce cans small white beans, rinsed and drained

1/4 cup finely chopped fresh flat-leaf parsley

Make It Now

1. Heat the oil in a 4- to 5-quart Dutch oven over medium heat. Sprinkle the lamb with the salt and pepper, add it to the pan a few pieces at a time, and cook until browned on all sides, removing the meat from the pan as it browns. After all the lamb has been browned, return the meat to the pan and add the garlic, onion, celery, carrot, and rosemary. Sauté until the vegetables begin to soften and the onions are translucent, 6 to 8 minutes. Add the wine, bring to a boil, and boil for 1 minute. Add the beef broth, chicken broth, beans, and parsley and simmer for 20 minutes. Let cool, then cover and refrigerate for up to 3 days or freeze for up to 6 weeks.

Bake It Later

1. Defrost the casserole in the refrigerator overnight, if necessary. Remove any fat that has accumulated on the surface of the casserole.

2. Preheat the oven to 350°F. Allow the casserole to come to room temperature for about 30 minutes.

3. Bake the casserole, covered, for 45 minutes. Uncover and bake for an additional 30 minutes, until the lamb is tender and the sauce is thickened. Serve immediately.

Stuffed Leg of Lamb

PREPARING A LEG OF LAMB can sometimes seem like a daunting task, but with the butterflied legs on the market now, you can bypass the bone and stuff the meat with a myriad of flavorful ingredients. To tie the roast, I recommend the new silicone food loops or silicone stretch cooking bands. They will stay on, you won't need to search for kitchen twine, and you can reuse them after washing in the dishwasher. The stuffing for this leg of lamb is a favorite of mine, with spinach and feta cheese as the stars. When you slice the lamb, you will have a beautiful green and white spiral inside. Serve this with your favorite wine reduction sauce or make a pan sauce from the juices in the pan, deglazing with wine and broth. SERVES 6

One 4-pound butterflied leg of lamb

1 teaspoon salt, plus more to sprinkle on the lamb

½ teaspoon freshly ground black pepper, plus more to sprinkle on the lamb

2 tablespoons olive oil

2 cloves garlic, minced

Two 10-ounce packages fresh baby spinach

½ cup dried bread crumbs

1 cup crumbled feta cheese

Make It Now

1. Lay the lamb on a flat surface with the fat side down. Sprinkle the surface of the meat with salt and pepper.

2. Heat the oil in a large sauté pan over medium heat. Add the garlic and sauté for about 1 minute, until it is fragrant. Add the spinach, 1 teaspoon salt, and ½ teaspoon pepper and sauté until the spinach is wilted, 4 to 6 minutes. Transfer to a bowl to cool slightly. Add the bread crumbs and cheese, stirring to blend.

3. Spread the cooled spinach mixture over the lamb. Roll up the lamb, tucking in the sides. Secure with kitchen twine, silicone cooking bands, or silicone food loops. Transfer to a large zipper-top plastic freezer bag and refrigerate for up to 2 days or freeze for up to 1 month.

1. Defrost the lamb in the refrigerator overnight, if necessary.

2. Preheat the oven to 400°F. Place the meat in a roasting pan and allow to come to room temperature for 20 minutes.

3. Roast the lamb for 15 minutes. Decrease the oven temperature to 325°F and roast for another 45 minutes, until an instant-read thermometer inserted into the thickest part of the meat registers 145°F. Remove the meat from the oven and allow to rest for 15 minutes. When the meat has rested, it should register 155°F, which is medium for lamb. Slice and serve hot.

Mom's Old-Fashioned Meat Loaf

THIS IS THE QUINTESSENTIAL COMFORTING MEAT LOAF of your childhood, with a bit of onion, celery, and ketchup, covered with a brown sugar and ketchup glaze and bacon that cooks along with it for a smoky flavor. SERVES 6

1 tablespoon unsalted butter

1 cup finely chopped yellow onion

1/2 cup finely chopped celery

1 teaspoon dried thyme

2 slices white bread, crusts removed

1/4 cup milk

1/2 cup ketchup

1 tablespoon Worcestershire sauce

1 teaspoon salt

1/2 teaspoon freshly ground black pepper

2 large eggs

1/4 cup chopped fresh flat-leaf parsley

1 pound ground beef (85 percent lean chuck is a great choice for flavor)

1 pound lean ground pork

Make It Now

1. Melt the butter in a small sauté pan over medium heat. Add the onion, celery, and thyme and sauté for about 3 minutes, until the vegetables are softened. Transfer to a large mixing bowl and let cool.

2. Tear the bread into small pieces and place in a small bowl. Pour the milk over the bread and allow the bread to soak up the milk.

3. Add the ketchup, Worcestershire sauce, salt, pepper, eggs, parsley, and milk and bread mixture to the bowl with the vegetables. Stir to blend and break up the eggs.

4. Crumble the beef and pork into the bowl, and stir until the ingredients are well distributed throughout the meat (you may want to use your hands for this).

5. Shape the meat loaf into a 9-inch-long by 5-inch-wide loaf shape (about 3 inches high). Place on the center of a large piece of heavy-duty aluminum foil and wrap tightly. Slide the wrapped meat loaf into a large zipper-top plastic freezer bag and seal. Refrigerate for up to 24 hours or freeze for up to 1 month.

Diva Note

If you have a meat loaf pan with a perforated bottom, it's a great thing to use, but I don't recommend packing the meat loaf into a conventional loaf pan, as it will steam rather than bake, so it won't be as crispy, and it will swim in its own grease. It is a better idea to shape the meat loaf freeform and bake it on a lined sheet pan, which gives you a quick cleanup, too!

Meat Loaves and Meatballs

Meatballs are nothing more than smaller versions of meat loaf, and it's up to you to decide which to make. Any of these three recipes make excellent meatballs as well as meat loaf. For each meat loaf recipe that you make, you will get ten to twelve 2-inch round meatballs. The meatballs can be cooked on a baking sheet at the same temperature as the meat loaf for 30 to 35 minutes, until they are cooked through.

Meat loaf or meatballs make a great weeknight dinner or weekend comfort food when paired with mashed potatoes, gravy or sauce, and vegetables on the side, to say nothing of the glories of the meat loaf sandwich, which screams for recognition the next day layered between a favorite bread and topped with the condiments of your choice.

---

2 cups ketchup

½ cup firmly packed light brown sugar

2 tablespoons Worcestershire sauce

1 tablespoon Dijon mustard

6 slices bacon

Bake It Later

1. Defrost the meat loaf in the refrigerator overnight, if necessary.

2. Preheat the oven to 350°F. Line a baking sheet with aluminum foil, parchment paper, or a silicone baking liner. Unwrap the meat loaf and arrange it in the center of the baking sheet. Allow the meat to come to room temperature for 20 minutes.

3. In a small saucepan over low heat, heat the ketchup, brown sugar, Worcestershire sauce, and mustard together. Spoon about half of the mixture over the meat loaf, reserving the rest. Lay the bacon over the top of the meat loaf. Bake the meatloaf for 55 to 60 minutes, until the bacon is cooked and the meat loaf registers 170°F on an instant-read thermometer. Allow to rest for 15 minutes. Rewarm the reserved sauce. Slice the meat loaf with a serrated knife and serve, with the reserved warmed sauce on the side.

Pacific Rim Meat Loaf

THIS ASIAN SPIN ON MEAT LOAF will give you a terrific change of pace, and everyone will be all smiles when they bite into it. Flavored with soy, pork, shrimp, and sesame oil, the meat loaf is also an awesome appetizer when shaped into small meatballs and served with the sauce for dipping at a grazing party. SERVES 6

2 tablespoons vegetable oil

2 cloves garlic, minced

1 teaspoon minced fresh ginger

3 green onions (white and tender green parts), finely chopped

1/2 cup finely chopped celery

One 4-ounce can water chestnuts, drained and finely chopped

10 shiitake mushrooms, stems removed and caps coarsely chopped

2 tablespoons soy sauce

1 tablespoon cornstarch

1/2 teaspoon sugar

1 tablespoon mirin (rice wine)

1 teaspoon toasted sesame oil

1 tablespoon hoisin sauce

1 large egg, beaten

1/2 cup panko crumbs or dried bread crumbs

1/2 pound bean sprouts, finely chopped

3/4 pound raw shrimp, peeled, deveined and finely chopped

1 1/2 pounds lean ground pork

Make It Now

1. Heat the oil in a large sauté pan or wok over medium-high heat. Add the garlic and ginger and sauté until fragrant, about 1 minute, being careful not to brown the garlic. Add the green onions, celery, water chestnuts, and mushrooms, and stir-fry until the liquid in the pan has evaporated and the mushrooms begin to color. Remove from the pan to a large mixing bowl and let cool.

2. In a separate bowl, stir together the soy sauce, cornstarch, sugar, mirin, sesame oil, and hoisin sauce. Stir the mixture into the cooled vegetables.

3. Stir in the egg, panko, bean sprouts, shrimp, and pork and continue to stir until blended.

4. Shape the mixture into a 9-inch-long by 5-inch-wide loaf. Place in the center of a large piece of heavy-duty aluminum foil and wrap tightly. Place the wrapped meat loaf in a large zipper-top plastic freezer bag. Refrigerate for up to 24 hours or freeze for up to 1 month.

1 clove garlic, minced

1/2 cup apricot preserves

1/2 cup ketchup

2 teaspoons Dijon mustard

1/4 cup rice vinegar

1/2 teaspoon chili oil

1. Defrost the meat loaf in the refrigerator overnight, if necessary.

2. Preheat the oven to 350°F. Line a baking sheet with aluminum foil, parchment paper, or a silicone baking liner. Arrange the meat loaf in the center of the pan. Allow the meat loaf to come to room temperature for 20 minutes.

3. Combine the garlic, apricot preserves, ketchup, mustard, vinegar, and chili oil in a small saucepan and bring to a simmer. Spoon about one-third of the sauce over the meat loaf, keeping the rest warm. Bake the meat loaf for 50 to 60 minutes, until an instant-read thermometer inserted into the center registers 170°F. Allow to rest for at least 15 minutes before slicing and serving with the warm sauce.

Mediterranean Gyro-Style Meat Loaf

A GYRO IS A COMBINATION OF LAMB, BEEF, AND SPICES that is roasted on a spit—essentially a Mediterranean twist on meat loaf. This one is highly spiced, and when served tucked into pita bread with lettuce, tomato, and a traditional yogurt sauce called tzatziki, it's heaven! Leftovers make great appetizer bites, cut into cubes, skewered with cherry tomatoes, and served with a tzatziki dip.

SERVES 6

1½ pounds lean ground lamb

½ pound lean ground beef

2 garlic cloves, minced

1 cup finely chopped yellow onion

2 teaspoons dried oregano

1 teaspoon dried rosemary, crushed

2 slices bread, crusts removed and torn into pieces

¼ cup milk

2 teaspoons salt

1 teaspoon freshly ground black pepper

Grated zest of 1 lemon

2 teaspoons freshly squeezed lemon juice

2 large eggs, beaten

Tzatziki Sauce, for serving (recipe follows)

Make It Now

1. In a large mixing bowl, combine the lamb, beef, garlic, onion, oregano, and rosemary.

2. Place the bread in a small bowl, add the milk, and let soak until the bread absorbs it all. Add the bread to the mixing bowl, along with the salt, pepper, lemon zest, lemon juice, and eggs.

3. Blend the mixture until it is thoroughly combined. Shape the meat into a 9-inch-long by 5-inch-wide loaf. Place in the center of a large piece of heavy-duty aluminum foil and wrap tightly. Place the wrapped meat loaf in a large zipper-top plastic freezer bag and refrigerate for up to 24 hours or freeze for up to 1 month.

Bake It Later

1. Defrost the meat loaf in the refrigerator overnight, if necessary.

2. Preheat the oven to 350°F. Line a baking sheet with aluminum foil, parchment paper, or a silicone baking liner. Place the meat loaf on the baking sheet and allow to come to room temperature for 20 minutes.

3. Bake for 50 to 60 minutes, until the meat loaf registers 170°F on an instant-read thermometer. Let rest for 15 minutes before slicing and serving with the Tzatziki Sauce on the side.

Tzatziki Sauce

A DELICIOUS CUCUMBER AND YOGURT SAUCE, this is also terrific to serve with pita chips or as a slather on sandwiches. Try adding ½ cup crumbled feta cheese to it for a bit more pizzazz. MAKES ABOUT 2½ CUPS

1½ cups plain yogurt, preferably Greek style

1 clove garlic, minced

1 cup peeled and finely chopped European cucumber

½ teaspoon salt

2 tablespoons finely chopped fresh dill

1 teaspoon distilled white vinegar

Pinch of freshly ground white or black pepper

In a bowl, stir together all the ingredients. Cover and refrigerate for at least 2 hours or for up to 4 days. Stir before serving.

The Main Dish
Poultry

Chicken is on American dinner tables an average of three nights a week. Turkey—cutlets, tenderloins, or ground—is widely available as well. In an effort to make this lean protein more exciting, I've created some chicken and turkey dishes with terrific flavors from around the world for make-ahead meals that your family will love. There are meals for weeknight dinners, like oven-barbecued chicken or chicken chili casserole, and then there are more formal meals that you might enjoy with company, like stuffed chicken breasts with crab and Boursin cheese or chicken Florentine, all waiting in your refrigerator or freezer for a quick warming in the oven. I've even got a formula for great chicken casseroles that incorporate starch (potatoes, noodles, or rice), sauce, poultry, and vegetables, in case you get stuck and need to whip up a quick dinner with leftovers. Simple, delicious, and all done ahead, these dishes will become the staples of your repertoire.

The Main Dish: Poultry

Old-Fashioned Barbecued Chicken, Diva Style

I LOVE BARBECUE-SAUCED CHICKEN. But because many people find it impossible to grill chicken year-round or consider it more trouble than it's worth, I came up with a wonderful way to oven-bake chicken with a sticky barbecue sauce even when there is snow on the ground. By using boneless chicken, it becomes a meal that can be on the table in 30 minutes. SERVES 6

2 tablespoons vegetable oil, plus more as needed

8 boneless chicken breast halves

1½ teaspoons salt, plus more as needed

1 teaspoon freshly ground black pepper, plus more as needed

½ cup chopped onion

1 clove garlic, minced

1 cup ketchup

1 cup tomato sauce

¼ cup pure maple syrup

2 tablespoons Dijon mustard

2 tablespoons Worcestershire sauce

1 teaspoon hot sauce of your choice, plus more as needed

Make It Now

1. Heat the oil in a large ovenproof pan over medium heat. Sprinkle the chicken with the salt and pepper. Sauté the chicken until it is browned on both sides; it may not be cooked through at this point, which is fine. Remove the chicken to a dish, and add the onion to the pan. If there isn't enough oil left in the pan, add a tablespoon or two. Sauté the onion until golden brown, about 5 minutes. Add the garlic and sauté another 1 minute.

2. Decrease the heat to medium-low, and slowly add the ketchup, tomato sauce, maple syrup, mustard, Worcestershire sauce, and hot sauce, scraping up any loose bits on the bottom of the pan. Simmer the sauce for 5 minutes. Taste for seasoning and add salt, pepper, or additional hot sauce, if desired. Let the sauce cool, then return the chicken to the pan. Cover and refrigerate for 3 days or freeze for up to 1 month.

Bake It Later

1. Defrost the chicken in the refrigerator overnight, if necessary.

2. Preheat the oven to 325°F. Let the chicken come to room temperature for 20 minutes.

3. Bake the chicken for 20 minutes, until cooked through, basting twice with the sauce during the baking time. Serve hot, cold, or at room temperature.

Panko-Parmesan Oven-Fried Chicken

FRIED CHICKEN IS A GUILTY PLEASURE. But if I can bake chicken that comes close to the crispy, crackly chicken of a roadside diner without having to deep-fry it, and it comes out moist and juicy, I think it's a winner. Using boneless chicken cuts down on the cooking time and ensures that the chicken will cook evenly in the oven. Your family will love this dish. Try some of the variations if you are feeling the need for a change of pace. This dish is terrific topped with a field green salad dressed with vinaigrette. SERVES 6

8 boneless chicken breast halves

1 teaspoon salt

½ teaspoon Tabasco sauce or your favorite hot sauce

½ cup (1 stick) unsalted butter, melted

½ cup olive oil

2 cups panko crumbs
(see Diva Note)

1 cup freshly grated Parmesan cheese

Make It Now

1. Season the chicken with the salt and Tabasco sauce. Line a baking sheet with aluminum foil, parchment paper, or a silicone baking liner.

2. In a shallow, wide bowl, combine the butter and oil, stirring to blend. In another shallow bowl, combine the panko and Parmesan cheese.

3. Dip the chicken pieces into the butter mixture, and then dredge in the crumbs, pressing the crumbs into the chicken. Lay the breasts on the prepared baking sheet. Drizzle the chicken evenly with the remaining butter mixture. Cover with heavy-duty plastic wrap and refrigerate for up to 2 days or freeze for up to 1 month. (When the chicken is frozen, transfer it to zipper-top plastic bags, separating each piece with plastic wrap.)

Diva Note

Panko crumbs, which give this chicken its crackly coating, are Japanese bread crumbs and are available in larger supermarkets. If you can't find them, substitute plain dried bread crumbs.

1. Defrost the chicken overnight in the refrigerator, if necessary.

2. Preheat the oven to 400°F. If necessary, transfer the chicken to a baking sheet that has been lined with aluminum foil, parchment paper, or a silicone baking liner. Let the chicken come to room temperature for 20 minutes.

3. Bake the chicken for 20 to 25 minutes, until golden brown and cooked through. Remove from the oven and serve hot, warm, or at room temperature.

VARIATIONS

Chicken Breasts Olé!

Substitute 2 cups crushed tortilla chips combined with ½ teaspoon ground cumin for the panko crumbs.

Tropical Chicken Breasts

Substitute 1 cup shredded unsweetened coconut for the Parmesan cheese and add ¼ cup finely chopped macadamia nuts to the panko crumbs. Omit the salt and add 1 tablespoon soy sauce to the butter and oil mixture.

Provençal Oven-Fried Chicken

Reduce the olive oil to ¼ cup, add ¼ cup Dijon mustard to the butter and oil mixture, and add 1 tablespoon herbes de Provence to the panko crumb mixture.

Curried Chicken Rice Casserole

CURRIED CHICKEN WAS CONSIDERED EXOTIC FARE IN THE '50S, when casserole cooking was in its heyday. Hostesses would serve the chicken over rice with condiments on the side, including raisins, chutney, shredded coconut, sliced bananas, and peanuts. This dish combines them all in a delicious casserole with the rice on the bottom and the curry on the top; a simple, yet elegant take on the classic. You can also make the rice separately and freeze it for up to a month, if you'd like to serve it with another meal. SERVES 8

CONDIMENT RICE

2 cups chicken broth

1 cup basmati rice

¼ cup golden raisins

¼ cup crushed banana chips

2 tablespoons Major Grey's chutney (see Diva Note)

2 tablespoons unsweetened shredded coconut

CURRIED CHICKEN

¼ cup (½ stick) unsalted butter

½ cup finely chopped sweet onion, such as Vidalia

½ cup finely chopped apple (peeling is optional)

1 teaspoon curry powder

¼ cup unbleached all-purpose flour

2 cups chicken broth

1 cup whole milk

4 cups chopped cooked chicken (bite-size pieces)

Salt and freshly ground black pepper to taste

Make It Now

1. To make the rice, bring the broth to a boil in a medium-size saucepan. Add the rice, raisins, banana chips, chutney, and coconut. Simmer for 20 minutes, until the rice is tender and the liquid is absorbed. Remove from the heat and allow to cool completely.

2. Coat the inside of a 9 x 13-inch baking dish with nonstick cooking spray. Spread the rice in the pan in an even layer.

3. To make the chicken, melt the butter in a large sauté pan over medium heat. Add the onion and apple and sauté until the onion begins to soften, 3 to 4 minutes. Add the curry powder and flour and stir until bubbles form on the surface. Whisk for 2 minutes, cooking the flour and curry powder. Gradually add the broth, bringing the sauce to a boil. Add the milk and chicken and simmer for 10 minutes. Season with salt and pepper. Spread the mixture over the rice and let cool. Cover and refrigerate for up to 3 days or freeze for up to 1 month.

Chopped roasted and salted peanuts for garnish (optional)

Bake It Later

1. Defrost the casserole in the refrigerator overnight, if necessary.

2. Preheat the oven to 350°F. Allow the casserole to come to room temperature for about 30 minutes.

3. Bake the casserole, covered, for 20 minutes. Uncover and bake for an additional 15 minutes, or until the casserole is bubbling and the top is beginning to brown. Garnish the top of the casserole with the chopped peanuts, if desired.

VARIATION

This dish is also delicious with a combination of chicken and cooked, peeled, and deveined shrimp. Or use that leftover Thanksgiving turkey for a great do-ahead dinner!

Diva Note

Chutney is to Indian cooking what salsa is to Latino cooking; a sweet and spicy sauce to complement dishes. Major Grey and Bengal Club chutneys are two types that are made for Western tastes and are not as hot as many of the Indian chutneys. Each region in India has its own type of chutney, and they are generally spicier than most of us are used to. For the rice in this dish, I recommend the Major Grey variety; it is readily available and complements the curried chicken.

Chicken Chili Casserole

THIS LIGHTENED-UP CHILI loaded with black beans, corn, and chicken will become a weeknight favorite, especially for nights when you want a comforting stick-to-your-ribs entrée that doesn't require a lot of fuss. Serve the chili family style in a casserole dish, or serve it in six individual gratin dishes. SERVES 6

¼ cup vegetable oil

½ cup finely chopped onion

1 clove garlic, minced

1 teaspoon chili powder

½ teaspoon ground cumin

½ teaspoon dried oregano

3 tablespoons cornmeal

2½ cups chicken broth

1 cup tomato sauce

4 cups cooked chopped or shredded chicken

2 cups fresh or defrosted frozen corn

One 15.5-ounce can black beans, rinsed and drained

1½ teaspoons salt

½ teaspoon freshly ground black pepper

3 cups tortilla chips (6 to 8 ounces)

1½ cups finely shredded mild cheddar cheese

½ cup finely shredded Monterey Jack cheese

Make It Now

1. Heat the oil in a large stockpot or Dutch oven over medium heat. Add the onion, garlic, chili powder, cumin, and oregano and sauté for 3 minutes, until the garlic is fragrant. Add the cornmeal and stir until it is incorporated into the vegetables, about 2 minutes. Slowly add the broth and tomato sauce and bring the mixture to a boil. Simmer for 10 minutes.

2. Add the chicken, corn, black beans, salt, and pepper. Simmer, uncovered, for 30 minutes, stirring frequently to prevent sticking.

3. Coat the inside of a 9 x 13-inch with nonstick cooking spray. Line the baking dish with enough tortilla chips to cover the bottom. Spoon the chili over the chips, top with the remaining chips, sprinkle with the cheddar and Monterey Jack cheeses, and let cool. Cover and refrigerate for up to 2 days or freeze for up to 1 month.

Bake It Later

1. Defrost the casserole in the refrigerator overnight, if necessary.

2. Preheat the oven to 350°F. Allow the casserole to come to room temperature for about 30 minutes.

3. Bake the casserole, covered, for 20 minutes. Uncover and bake for an additional 20 minutes, until the cheese has melted and the casserole is bubbling. Serve immediately.

VARIATION

Fill individual gratin dishes with about 1 cup of chili per serving. Bake for 10 minutes covered. Uncover and bake for an additional 15 to 20 minutes.

Chicken, Mushroom, and Rice Casserole

THIS COMFY DISH IS A MODERNIZED VERSION OF A '50S CLASSIC, and one that soothes after a long day at the office. Filled with shiitake and cremini mushrooms, chicken, and white and wild rice, and topped with a crunchy almond topping, it's perfect with a fruit or vegetable salad on the side.

SERVES 6

1 1/2 cups cooked wild rice

1 1/2 cups cooked white rice

1/2 cup (1 stick) unsalted butter

2 cloves garlic, minced

1/2 pound shiitake mushrooms, stems removed and caps sliced 1/2 inch thick

1/2 pound cremini mushrooms, sliced 1/2 inch thick

1/4 cup unbleached all-purpose flour

2 cups chicken broth

2 to 3 tablespoons soy sauce (see Diva Note)

1 cup whole milk

5 dashes of Tabasco sauce

3 cups diced cooked chicken

1/4 cup finely chopped fresh flat-leaf parsley

1/2 cup sliced almonds (optional)

Make It Now

1. Coat the inside of a 2-quart casserole dish with nonstick cooking spray. Combine the wild and white rices and spread the mixture in the casserole dish.

2. Melt 1/4 cup of the butter in a large sauté pan over medium heat. Add the garlic and sauté for 1 minute, until it is fragrant. Add the shiitake and cremini mushrooms and sauté until their liquid has evaporated and they begin to color a bit, 8 to 10 minutes. Add the remaining 1/4 cup butter, stir in the flour, and cook the flour for 3 minutes, until it bubbles. Slowly add the broth, soy sauce, milk, and Tabasco sauce and bring the mixture to a boil. Add the chicken and parsley and stir to combine.

3. Pour the mixture over the rice, let cool, and top with the almonds, if desired. Cover and refrigerate for up to 3 days or freeze for up to 1 month.

Diva Note

The amount of soy sauce to use will depend upon the brand; some are saltier than others. I recommend that you taste the sauce first and use your own judgment, adding a teaspoon at a time until you reach the desired flavor. I used Kikkoman when making this recipe.

4 green onions (white and tender green parts), finely chopped

1. Defrost the casserole in the refrigerator overnight, if necessary.

2. Preheat the oven to 350°F. Allow the casserole to come to room temperature for about 30 minutes.

3. Bake the casserole, covered, for 20 minutes. Uncover and bake for an additional 15 minutes, until the almonds are golden brown and the casserole is bubbling. Sprinkle with the green onions and serve hot.

Chicken Cacciatore

WHEN I PICTURE CHICKEN CACCIATORE, or chicken hunter's style, I picture something entirely different from the Italian-American version drowning in tomato sauce. The version I grew up with had no tomatoes at all (see Chicken Balsamico with Roasted Potatoes, page 179). I decided that there had to be a better way to make this classic Italian-American dish with lively flavor and a sauce that would make it sing (preferably a Maria Callas aria!). What resulted from my experimentation is a delicious casserole with polenta on the bottom and a savory stew of chicken, herbed tomatoes, and mushrooms on top that can be waiting in the freezer for you to defrost and bake. What's not to love about that? SERVES 6

POLENTA

4 cups water

1 teaspoon salt

1 cup instant polenta

3 tablespoons unsalted butter, softened

1/2 cup freshly grated Parmesan cheese

CHICKEN

1/2 cup olive oil

8 chicken thighs, bones and skin removed, *or* one 2 1/2-pound chicken, cut into 8 pieces (see Diva Note)

1 pound cremini mushrooms, quartered

4 cloves garlic, cut in half

One 28-ounce can diced tomatoes, drained

1 teaspoon salt

1/2 teaspoon freshly ground black pepper

2 teaspoons finely chopped fresh rosemary

1/2 cup chopped fresh flat-leaf parsley

Make It Now

1. Coat the inside of a 9 x 13-inch casserole dish with non-stick cooking spray. To make the polenta, bring the water and salt to a boil in a large saucepan. Add the polenta, whisking until it is smooth. Cook the polenta, stirring it with a wooden spoon, for about 15 minutes. Remove it from the heat, and stir in the butter and Parmesan. Spread the polenta into the prepared baking dish and set aside.

2. To make the chicken, heat 1/4 cup of the oil in a large sauté pan. Add the chicken, in batches if necessary, and sauté, browning it evenly on both sides. Remove to a plate. Add the remaining 1/4 cup oil to the pan, add the mushrooms, and sauté until their liquid evaporates and they begin to color. Add the garlic to the pan and sauté another minute, until it becomes fragrant. Add the tomatoes, salt, pepper, and rosemary. Simmer for 5 minutes. Return the chicken to the sauté pan and cook for another 10 minutes. Add the parsley. Pour the chicken mixture over the polenta and let cool. Cover and refrigerate for up to 2 days or freeze for up to 1 month.

1. Defrost the casserole in the refrigerator overnight, if necessary.

2. Preheat the oven to 350°F. Allow the casserole to come to room temperature for about 30 minutes.

3. Bake the casserole for 35 to 45 minutes for boneless chicken thighs, or 45 to 55 minutes for chicken parts with bones. Serve hot.

Diva Note

In general, I prefer using boneless chicken breasts and thighs because they cook faster and are easier to eat. If you prefer using bone-in chicken parts, feel free, but remember that you'll need to increase the cooking time by 15 to 20 minutes.

Old-Fashioned Chicken Pot Pie

MY SON, RYAN, LOVES CHICKEN POT PIE. Simple, homey, and comforting, my version is filled with vegetables and chicken and topped with a puff pastry crust. You can prepare this in a large casserole dish for a family-style dinner or in individual ramekins for a company presentation. I serve this with cranberry sauce or sautéed apples on the side. SERVES 6

3½ cups chicken broth

3 medium-size red potatoes, peeled and cut into ½-inch cubes

4 medium-size carrots, cut into ½-inch cubes

¼ cup (½ stick) unsalted butter

2 teaspoons finely chopped fresh thyme, *or* 1 teaspoon dried thyme

¼ cup unbleached all-purpose flour, plus more for rolling out pastry

½ cup heavy cream (see Diva Notes)

6 cups diced cooked chicken (½-inch pieces)

1½ cups fresh or defrosted frozen corn

1 cup fresh or defrosted frozen petite peas

1 sheet frozen puff pastry, defrosted (see Diva Notes)

Make It Now

1. Bring the chicken broth to a boil in a large pot. Add the potatoes and carrots and cook for 5 minutes, until the vegetables begin to soften slightly; they will not be tender, but they will cook further in the oven. Drain the vegetables, reserving the chicken broth.

2. Melt the butter in a large saucepan over medium heat. Whisk in the thyme and flour and cook until white bubbles form on the surface. Continue to cook the mixture for 2 to 3 minutes, until smooth and thick. Gradually add 2½ cups of the reserved broth and bring the mixture to a boil. Add the cream. If the sauce is too thick, thin with more of the reserved broth. Bring the mixture to a boil. Add the potatoes, carrots, chicken, corn, and peas. Cool the filling and pour it into a 9 x 13-inch casserole dish.

3. On a lightly floured work surface, roll out the puff pastry to a 11 x 15-inch rectangle. Place the pastry over the casserole dish, roll the edges under, and seal with the tines of a fork or a pastry crimper. Cover and refrigerate for up to 2 days or freeze for up to 1 month.

1. Defrost the casserole in the refrigerator overnight, if necessary.

2. Preheat the oven to 400°F. Allow the casserole to come to room temperature for 15 minutes.

3. Slash a few vent holes into the top of the pastry crust. Bake the pot pie for 25 minutes, until the pastry is puffed and golden and the filling is bubbling. Serve immediately.

Diva Notes

If you would like a lower-fat pot pie, substitute ½ cup of the reserved broth for the cream.

If you would like to bake this in individual ramekins, you will need ⅔ to ¾ cup filling per ramekin. Cut the pastry 1 inch larger than the rim of your ramekins (in some cases this may necessitate using both sheets of puff pastry that come in the package), and bake for 15 to 20 minutes, until puffed and golden.

Chicken, Sun-Dried Tomato, and Artichoke Bake

NOTHING COULD BE SIMPLER THAN THIS SAVORY CHICKEN DISH, and it goes together in a snap, too. Chicken breasts bake in a creamy mascarpone and herb sauce with the flavor of sun-dried tomatoes, artichokes, and Parmesan cheese. Serve this with orzo or another pasta for your next dinner party. SERVES 6

¼ cup olive oil

8 boneless chicken breast halves

1½ teaspoons salt

½ teaspoon freshly ground black pepper

Two 8-ounce jars marinated artichoke hearts, drained, marinade reserved, and artichokes cut into quarters

2 cups mascarpone cheese

½ cup sun-dried tomatoes packed in oil, drained and thinly sliced

⅔ cup freshly grated Parmesan cheese

½ cup pine nuts

Make It Now

1. Coat the inside of a 9 x 13-inch baking dish with nonstick cooking spray.

2. Heat the oil in a large sauté pan over medium heat. Sprinkle the chicken with the salt and pepper, add the chicken to the pan, and sauté until the chicken is browned on both sides. Remove from the pan and arrange in the baking dish. Scatter the artichokes around the chicken.

3. In a medium-size bowl, mix together the mascarpone cheese, ¼ to ⅓ cup of the reserved artichoke marinade, the sun-dried tomatoes, and ⅓ cup of the Parmesan. Spread the mixture over the chicken. Sprinkle with the remaining ⅓ cup Parmesan cheese and the pine nuts. Cover and refrigerate for up to 2 days or freeze for up to 2 weeks.

Bake It Later

1. Defrost the casserole in the refrigerator overnight, if necessary.

2. Preheat the oven to 350°F. Allow the casserole to come to room temperature for about 30 minutes.

3. Bake the chicken, covered, for 20 minutes. Uncover and bake for an additional 15 minutes, until the casserole is bubbling and the cheese is golden brown. Serve hot.

Diva Note

If you would like to bake the chicken over a bed of cooked pasta, double the amount of mascarpone sauce. Cook the pasta according to the package directions and stir half the sauce into the cooked pasta. Spread the pasta in the prepared pan, and then top with the chicken and remaining sauce and freeze as directed. The pasta will absorb a lot of moisture, so make sure to double the sauce if you are baking these together. Also, increase the baking time by about 10 minutes.

Chicken Florentine Casserole

SIMPLE YET ELEGANT, this layered casserole is the perfect dish for a special occasion, with its brightly colored spinach and cheesy chicken topping. This preparation also works well with seafood (see page 208) or leftover turkey. SERVES 6

½ cup (1 stick) unsalted butter

½ cup finely chopped shallots

1 pound fresh baby spinach *or* one 16-ounce package frozen spinach, defrosted and squeezed dry

¼ teaspoon ground nutmeg

Salt and freshly ground black pepper to taste

6 boneless chicken breast halves

¼ cup unbleached all-purpose flour

1½ cups chicken broth

1 cup heavy cream

¼ cup cream sherry

½ cup finely shredded Swiss cheese

½ cup freshly grated Parmesan cheese

Make It Now

1. Coat the inside of a 9 x 13-inch casserole dish with non-stick cooking spray. Melt 3 tablespoons of the butter in a large skillet over medium heat. Add the shallots and cook, stirring, until softened, about 3 minutes. Add the spinach and nutmeg and cook, stirring, until the spinach is wilted and cooked through, another 3 minutes. Season with salt and pepper, transfer to the prepared baking dish, and let cool.

2. Clean out the skillet with a paper towel. Melt the remaining 5 tablespoons butter over medium heat. Sprinkle the chicken with salt and pepper, add to the skillet, and sauté for 3 minutes on each side, until the pieces begin to turn golden brown. Transfer the chicken to the baking dish on top of the spinach.

3. Whisk the flour into the butter in the pan and cook until white bubbles form on the surface. Cook the mixture for 2 to 3 minutes, until smooth and thick. Slowly add the broth, whisking until the sauce comes to a boil. Add the cream and sherry. Pour the sauce over the chicken in the baking dish.

4. Allow the casserole to cool. Sprinkle the top with the Swiss and Parmesan cheeses. Cover and refrigerate for up to 2 days or freeze for up to 6 weeks.

Bake It Later

1. Defrost the casserole in the refrigerator overnight, if necessary.

2. Preheat the oven to 350°F. Allow the casserole to come to room temperature for about 30 minutes.

3. Bake the casserole for 35 to 40 minutes, until the sauce is bubbling and the cheeses are melted and golden brown. Serve hot.

Rita's Creamy Chicken-Stuffed Peppers

MY MOM WAS AN INCREDIBLE COOK, and consequently she was very critical of restaurants, especially Italian restaurants, since she was first-generation Italian. One of her favorite places to eat near Boston was a little hole-in-the-wall restaurant in Charlestown called Rita's, and when we visited her, she would want to go there for lunch or dinner. She would call ahead to find out if their delicious stuffed peppers were on the menu, and if they weren't, we'd wait another day until they were! This version comes very close to the original, and I love remembering how much my mom enjoyed the meals at this family-style Italian restaurant. SERVES 4 TO 6

4 cups Quick Marinara Sauce
(page 246)

¼ cup (½ stick) unsalted butter

½ cup finely chopped sweet onion,
such as Vidalia

2 cups finely chopped cooked
chicken

1 cup ricotta cheese

½ cup finely minced ham

½ cup freshly grated Parmesan
cheese

1¼ cups heavy cream

¼ cup finely chopped fresh flat-leaf
parsley

Salt and freshly ground black pepper
to taste

6 large red bell peppers, tops cut off
and reserved, seeds removed

Make It Now

1. Pour the marinara sauce into an ovenproof casserole dish that will hold the peppers comfortably, so they don't wobble.

2. Melt the butter in a large skillet over medium heat. Add the onion and sauté until the onion begins to turn translucent, about 3 minutes. Reduce the heat to medium-low and add the chicken, ricotta, ham, Parmesan, and cream. Simmer the mixture for 10 minutes, until the sauce is reduced by half. Stir in the parsley and season with salt and pepper. Let the filling cool.

3. Stuff the peppers with the filling and arrange them on the sauce in the dish. Cover the peppers with the reserved tops. Cover with plastic wrap and refrigerate for up to 3 days or freeze for up to 1 month.

Bake It Later

1. Defrost the peppers in the refrigerator overnight, if necessary.

2. Preheat the oven to 350°F. Allow the peppers to come to room temperature for about 30 minutes.

3. Bake the peppers for 45 to 50 minutes, until the filling is bubbling and the peppers are softened. Serve immediately.

Chicken Balsamico with Roasted Potatoes

MY GRANDMOTHER'S CHICKEN CACCIATORE, or chicken hunter's style, is made in the style of Umbria, the green heart of Italy and home of St. Francis of Assisi. Many were the times I would stand by the stove and watch her make this peasant dish and marvel at the flavor she coaxed out of the simple ingredients. The addition of the potatoes, which she would cook separately, and the use of balsamic vinegar rather than red wine vinegar, are my contributions to this classic dish. SERVES 6

¼ cup olive oil

6 slices bacon, cut into ½-inch pieces

8 boneless chicken thighs (skin left on)

Freshly ground black pepper to taste

2 tablespoons dried rosemary, crumbled

4 cloves garlic, sliced

½ cup balsamic vinegar

½ cup chicken broth

8 small red potatoes, quartered

Make It Now

1. Heat the oil in a large Dutch oven over medium heat. Add the bacon and fry until it begins to get crispy, 10 to 12 minutes. Add the chicken and sprinkle with the pepper, rosemary, and garlic. Sauté until the chicken is golden brown on all sides, 12 to 15 minutes.

2. Stir in the vinegar and allow it to boil for 1 minute. Add the broth, scraping up any bits that are stuck to the bottom of the pan. Cover and simmer the chicken for 10 minutes. Remove from the heat and let cool. Cover and refrigerate for up to 2 days or freeze for up to 1 month.

Bake It Later

1. Defrost the chicken in the refrigerator overnight, if necessary.

2. Preheat the oven to 350°F. Allow the casserole to come to room temperature for about 30 minutes.

3. Add the potatoes to the chicken and turn to mix them into the sauce. Cover the Dutch oven and bake for 35 minutes, turning the chicken and potatoes twice during the cooking time. Remove from the oven and serve immediately.

Tarragon Chicken Bake

THIS MOUTHWATERING RENDITION of an old favorite is a bit of France, with a zing from Dijon mustard and a delightful crispy crumb coating on top. Terrific for a quick holiday or company dinner, it can be made weeks in advance, then defrosted and baked to be ready when you are. I love to bake this with egg noodles on the bottom, so that all I have to do for my party is toss the salad and heat up the casserole. SERVES 6

1 pound wide egg noodles, cooked according to package directions

1/4 cup (1/2 stick) unsalted butter

1/4 cup olive oil

6 boneless, skinless chicken breast halves

Salt and freshly ground black pepper to taste

2 cloves garlic, minced

1/2 cup finely chopped shallot or onion

1 pound cremini or white mushrooms, thinly sliced

1/4 cup unbleached all-purpose flour

2 1/2 cups chicken broth

1/4 cup Dijon mustard

1 cup heavy cream

1 tablespoon finely chopped fresh tarragon

Make It Now

1. Coat the inside of a 9 x 13-inch baking dish with nonstick cooking spray. Spread the noodles in an even layer in the bottom of the dish.

2. Melt 1 tablespoon of the butter with the oil in a large sauté pan over medium heat. Sprinkle the chicken with salt and pepper. Add the chicken and sauté for 3 minutes on each side, until golden and almost cooked through. Remove to a plate to cool.

3. Melt the remaining 3 tablespoons butter in the sauté pan, add the garlic and shallot, and sauté for 3 minutes, until softened. Add the mushrooms and sauté until they begin to color, 7 to 9 minutes. Sprinkle the mushrooms with the flour and cook for 3 minutes. Slowly add the chicken broth, scraping up any bits that may be stuck to the bottom of the pan, and bring the sauce to a boil. Add the mustard, cream, and tarragon, and simmer for 5 minutes. Let the sauce cool.

4. Arrange the chicken over the noodles in the prepared pan and pour the sauce over all. Cover and refrigerate for up to 2 days or freeze for up to 6 weeks.

1 tablespoon finely chopped fresh tarragon

1½ cups fresh bread crumbs

2 tablespoons pure olive oil

1 tablespoon Dijon mustard

Bake It Later

1. Defrost the casserole in the refrigerator overnight, if necessary.

2. Preheat the oven to 350°F. Allow the casserole to come to room temperature for about 30 minutes.

3. In a small bowl, combine the tarragon, bread crumbs, oil, and mustard and mix until the crumbs are evenly moistened. Spread over the chicken in the casserole dish and bake for 35 to 40 minutes, until the topping is golden brown and the sauce is bubbling. Serve immediately.

Diva Note

But Diva, you might ask, can I freeze mushrooms? For this dish the answer is a resounding yes, because you have cooked the liquid out of the mushrooms first, so they will not weep into the creamy sauce and the sauce won't separate when you reheat it. Sautéing the mushrooms until they begin to color is the secret here.

Bistro Chicken Casserole

I LOVE DISHES THAT HAVE A FEW INGREDIENTS, offer deep flavors, and can be made ahead of time; this is one of them. It reminds me of the classic French dish coq au vin, but with a lot less cooking time, and it can be hidden away in the freezer. When you're ready, it turns your kitchen into a French bistro for the night, sending the aromas of wine and thyme through your home. Crusty bread for dipping into the luscious sauce is essential! SERVES 6

¼ cup olive oil

8 boneless chicken thighs (skin left on)

Salt and freshly ground black pepper to taste

4 shallots, quartered

3 cloves garlic, minced

2 teaspoons dried thyme

1 pound cremini mushrooms, quartered

1 cup Burgundy

2 cups chicken broth

¼ cup (½ stick) unsalted butter

¼ cup unbleached all-purpose flour

Make It Now

1. Heat the oil in a large Dutch oven over medium-high heat. Sprinkle the chicken with salt and pepper, add the chicken to the pot, and sauté on both sides, until the chicken is golden brown, 12 to 15 minutes. Remove the chicken to a plate. Add the shallots, garlic, and thyme to the Dutch oven. Sauté until the garlic is fragrant and the shallots are softened, 3 to 5 minutes. Add the mushrooms and cook for 5 minutes, until they begin to color.

2. Return the chicken to the pan, pour in the wine and broth, and bring the sauce to a boil. Simmer for 15 minutes. In a small bowl, stir together the butter and flour until it forms a paste. Gradually add some of the flour mixture to the bubbling casserole, and stir until the sauce thickens. If you would like to serve this in an oven-to-table casserole dish, transfer it to the serving dish now; otherwise, it can be reheated in the oven in the Dutch oven. Let cool, then cover and refrigerate for up to 4 days or freeze for up to 6 weeks.

8 slices French bread, toasted on both sides

¼ cup finely chopped fresh flat-leaf parsley

1 cup finely shredded imported Swiss cheese, such as Gruyère or Emmentaler

½ cup freshly grated Parmesan cheese

1. Defrost the casserole in the refrigerator overnight, if necessary.

2. Preheat the oven to 350°F. Allow the casserole to come to room temperature for about 30 minutes.

3. Lay the bread on top of the casserole. In a small bowl, combine the parsley, Swiss cheese, and Parmesan cheese. Sprinkle the mixture on top of the bread, and bake the casserole for 35 to 40 minutes, until the cheeses are melted and golden brown and the casserole is bubbling. Serve immediately.

Asparagus, Black Forest Ham, and Gruyère–Stuffed Chicken Breasts with Dilled Velouté

STUFFED CHICKEN BREASTS are the quintessential elegant chicken entrée, with their crispy crusts and savory, tempting fillings. This is a better version of chicken cordon bleu, incorporating asparagus and topped with a creamy dill sauce. It's a knockout! SERVES 6

6 boneless, skinless chicken breast halves

Salt and freshly ground black pepper to taste

18 asparagus stalks, tough ends trimmed and stalks peeled

1/4 pound Black Forest ham, julienned

1 1/2 cups coarsely shredded Gruyère cheese

1/2 cup (1 stick) unsalted butter

1/2 cup olive oil

1 teaspoon Old Bay seasoning

2 cups dried bread crumbs or panko crumbs, *or* a mixture of 1 cup panko and 1 cup dried bread crumbs

Make It Now

1. Cover a flat surface with plastic wrap and place a chicken breast with the flat side (where the skin would have been) down in the center of the plastic wrap. Cover with a second sheet of plastic wrap and pound the chicken with a meat pounder or the bottom of a flat-bottomed wine bottle until it is a uniform thickness, about 1/2 inch. Season the chicken with salt and pepper on both sides. Repeat with the remaining chicken breasts.

2. Blanch the asparagus in boiling salted water for 2 minutes, then shock in ice water to retain their color. Drain and thoroughly pat dry. Lay 3 asparagus stalks widthwise in the center of each chicken breast. Trim the asparagus stalks, keeping the tips intact, so that they fit when the chicken is rolled up. Combine the ham and cheese in a small bowl, and top the asparagus with a scant 1/4 cup of the mixture.

3. Roll up the cutlets from the V-shaped end, folding in the sides to make a nice compact package. Place the chicken seam side down on a baking sheet. Refrigerate for at least 1 hour to firm the chicken and the filling.

4. Melt the butter with the oil and Old Bay seasoning and let cool slightly. Dip each rolled chicken breast into the

butter mixture, then roll it in the bread crumbs. Place the chicken in a 9 x 13-inch baking dish and drizzle with any remaining butter mixture. Cover and refrigerate for up to 2 days or freeze for up to 1 month.

3 to 4 cups Dilled Velouté
(page 186)

Bake It Later

1. Defrost the chicken in the refrigerator overnight, if necessary.

2. Preheat the oven to 350°F. Allow the chicken to come to room temperature for 20 minutes.

3. Pour 1 cup of sauce around the chicken in the baking dish. Warm the remaining sauce on the stovetop. Bake the chicken for 25 to 30 minutes, until it is cooked through (160°F on an instant-read thermometer) and the crumbs are golden brown.

4. Remove from the oven and allow to rest for 5 to 10 minutes. Slice each chicken breast into rounds with a serrated knife and serve in a pool of sauce on a plate or platter. Serve any additional sauce warm in a fondue pot or a small slow cooker.

Dilled Velouté

THIS DELECTABLE SAUCE is a beautiful lemony color flecked with bright green dill. It can be used to accompany any number of dishes, especially chicken, seafood, or vegetables. MAKES 3½ CUPS

¼ cup (½ stick) unsalted butter

3 tablespoons unbleached all-purpose flour

2½ cups chicken broth

1 cup heavy cream

2 tablespoons chopped fresh dill

Grated zest of 1 lemon

1 teaspoon salt

½ teaspoon freshly ground black pepper

Melt the butter in a medium-size saucepan over medium heat. Whisk in the flour until bubbles appear on the surface. Continue to cook the flour, whisking constantly, for 3 minutes. Slowly add the broth, whisking and bringing the mixture to a boil. Add the cream, dill, lemon zest, salt, and pepper, and simmer for 5 minutes. Remove from the heat and use immediately, or let cool, cover, and refrigerate for up to 3 days or freeze for up to 6 weeks. Defrost and bring to room temperature before proceeding.

Green Chile, Monterey Jack, and Chorizo–Stuffed Chicken Breasts with Salsa Verde

THE SOUTHWESTERN-INSPIRED SPICY FILLING in this dish is cooled by a versatile, creamy herbed sauce. Serve this with Spanish- or Mexican-style rice. SERVES 6

6 boneless, skinless chicken breast halves

Salt and freshly ground black pepper to taste

6 canned green chiles, slit lengthwise, rinsed, and drained

6 pieces of Monterey Jack cheese, 1/2 inch wide by 4 inches long

1 cup Mexican chorizo sausage (about 1/3 pound), crumbled, cooked, and drained

1/2 cup (1 stick) unsalted butter

1/2 cup olive oil

1/4 teaspoon ground cumin

1/8 teaspoon chili powder

2 cups dried bread crumbs or panko crumbs, *or* a mixture of 1 cup panko and 1 cup dried bread crumbs, *or* one 11-ounce bag plain tortilla chips, crushed

Make It Now

1. Cover a flat surface with plastic wrap and place a chicken breast with the flat side (where the skin would have been) down in the center of the plastic wrap. Cover with a second sheet of plastic wrap and pound the chicken with a meat pounder or the bottom of a flat-bottomed wine bottle until it is a uniform thickness, about 1/2 inch. Season the chicken with salt and pepper on both sides. Repeat with the remaining chicken breasts.

2. Stuff the chiles with the cheese, wrapping the chiles so that the cheese is enclosed. Place a chile in the center of each chicken breast and sprinkle 2 tablespoons of the chorizo onto each chile.

3. Roll up the chicken breasts from the V-shaped end, folding in the sides to make a nice compact package. Place the chicken seam side down on a baking sheet. Refrigerate for at least 1 hour to firm the chicken and the filling.

4. Melt the butter with the oil, cumin, and chili powder and let cool slightly. Dip each rolled chicken breast in the butter mixture, then roll it in the bread crumbs. Place in a 9 x 13-inch baking dish and drizzle with any remaining butter mixture. Cover and refrigerate for up to 2 days or freeze for up to 1 month.

3 to 4 cups Salsa Verde (page 88)

Bake It Later

1. Defrost the chicken in the refrigerator overnight, if necessary.

2. Preheat the oven to 350°F. Allow the chicken to come to room temperature for 20 minutes.

3. Pour 1 cup sauce around the chicken in the baking dish. Warm the remaining sauce on the stovetop. Bake the chicken for 25 to 30 minutes, until it is cooked through (160°F on an instant-read thermometer) and the crumbs are golden brown.

4. Remove from the oven and allow to rest for 5 to 10 minutes. Slice each chicken breast into rounds with a serrated knife and serve in a pool of sauce on a plate or platter. Serve any additional sauce warm in a fondue pot or in a small slow cooker.

Gorgonzola, Apple, and Bacon-Stuffed Chicken Breasts with Blue Cider Sauce

CHICKEN IS A GREAT HOST, able to absorb strong flavors and become a backdrop for tangy blue cheese, apples, and bacon in this fabulous entrée. SERVES 6

6 boneless, skinless chicken breast halves

Salt and freshly ground black pepper to taste

2 tablespoons unsalted butter

2 large apples, finely diced

1 tablespoon light brown sugar

One 3-ounce package cream cheese, softened

1 cup crumbled Gorgonzola cheese

6 strips bacon, cooked crisp, drained, and crumbled

½ cup (1 stick) unsalted butter

½ cup olive oil

1 teaspoon Old Bay seasoning

2 cups dried bread crumbs or panko crumbs, *or* a mixture of 1 cup panko and 1 cup dried bread crumbs

Make It Now

1. Cover a flat surface with plastic wrap and place a chicken breast with the flat side (where the skin would have been) down in the center of the plastic wrap. Cover with a second sheet of plastic wrap and pound the chicken with a meat pounder or the bottom of a flat-bottomed wine bottle until it is a uniform thickness, about ½ inch. Season the chicken with salt and pepper on both sides. Repeat with remaining chicken breasts.

2. Melt the butter in a small skillet over medium heat. Add the apples and brown sugar and sauté until the apples are caramelized and have turned a nice golden brown, 7 to 10 minutes. Transfer the apples to a bowl and let cool. Stir in the cream cheese, Gorgonzola, and bacon, and form into a log that is 6 inches long and 1½ to 2 inches wide. Wrap in plastic wrap and freeze until firm, about 15 minutes (or up to 2 months).

3. Cut the log into 6 pieces, and place 1 piece in the center of each chicken breast. Roll up the chicken breasts from the V-shaped end, folding in the sides to make a nice compact package. Place the chicken seam side down on a baking sheet. Refrigerate for at least 1 hour to firm the chicken and the filling.

4. Melt the butter with the oil and Old Bay seasoning and let cool slightly. Dip each rolled chicken breast into the butter mixture, then roll it in the bread crumbs. Place in a 9 x 13-inch baking dish and drizzle with any remaining butter mixture. Cover and refrigerate for up to 2 days or freeze for up to 1 month.

3 to 4 cups Blue Cider Sauce
(recipe follows)

Bake It Later

1. Defrost the chicken in the refrigerator overnight, if necessary.

2. Preheat the oven to 350°F. Allow the chicken to come to room temperature for 20 minutes.

3. Pour 1 cup sauce around the chicken in the baking dish. Warm the remaining sauce on the stovetop. Bake the chicken for 25 to 30 minutes, until it is cooked through (160°F on an instant-read thermometer) and the crumbs are golden brown.

4. Remove from the oven and allow to rest for 5 to 10 minutes. Slice each chicken breast into rounds with a serrated knife and serve in a pool of sauce on a plate or platter. Serve any additional sauce warm in a fondue pot or in a small slow cooker.

Blue Cider Sauce

I KNOW THE COMBINATION of blue cheese and cider may sound strange, but trust me; you won't regret making this recipe. It will give the chicken extra personality.
MAKES 2½ TO 3 CUPS

2 tablespoons unsalted butter

2 tablespoons unbleached all-purpose flour

½ cup apple cider

2 cups heavy cream

1 cup finely crumbled Gorgonzola cheese

¼ teaspoon freshly ground black pepper

Melt the butter in a 2-quart saucepan over medium heat. Add the flour and whisk until bubbles form on the surface. Continue to whisk the sauce for 2 minutes, then add the cider and cream. Bring the sauce to a boil, whisking constantly. Remove from the heat and add the cheese and black pepper, stirring to thoroughly combine. Serve warm.

Tuscan Stuffed Chicken Breasts

THIS ELEGANT ENTRÉE IS SO DELICIOUS, I don't even know where to start to describe it. The chicken is stuffed with spinach and fresh mozzarella, then rolled in prosciutto, sautéed, and baked in a brandied tomato cream sauce that is a perfect balance of flavors. Serve this entrée over orzo, and you will have a dinner that will garner a standing ovation. SERVES 6 TO 8

8 boneless, skinless chicken breast halves

Salt and freshly ground black pepper to taste

8 thin slices prosciutto

6 tablespoons (¾ stick) unsalted butter

2 cloves garlic, minced

Two 10-ounce packages fresh baby spinach

⅛ teaspoon freshly grated nutmeg

⅛ teaspoon freshly ground black pepper, plus more to taste

8 ounces fresh mozzarella cheese, cut into ½-inch pieces

¼ cup freshly grated Parmesan cheese

½ cup olive oil

½ cup finely chopped shallots

1 pound cremini mushrooms, sliced

¼ cup brandy

One 14.5-ounce can diced tomatoes, drained

1½ cups heavy cream

Make It Now

1. Cover a flat surface with plastic wrap and place a chicken breast with the flat side (where the skin would have been) down in the center of the plastic wrap. Cover with a second sheet of plastic wrap and pound the chicken with a meat pounder or the bottom of a flat-bottomed wine bottle until it is a uniform thickness, about ½ inch. Season the chicken with salt and pepper on both sides. Repeat with remaining chicken breasts.

2. Lay the pieces of prosciutto on a cutting board, and then lay a chicken breast over each piece. Refrigerate while making the filling.

3. Melt 2 tablespoons of the butter in a sauté pan over medium heat. Add the garlic, swirling in the pan for about 1 minute, until the garlic becomes fragrant. Add the spinach and cook, stirring with tongs, until the spinach is wilted, 2 to 3 minutes. Season with the nutmeg and pepper, then transfer to a mixing bowl and allow to cool. Add the mozzarella and Parmesan cheeses to the bowl and stir well.

4. Spread about 2 tablespoons of the stuffing mixture on each chicken breast. Roll up the chicken breasts from the short side, folding in the sides, and tucking the ends under. Secure the ends and prosciutto "cover" with toothpicks. Cover and refrigerate for at least 1 hour.

5. Melt the remaining 4 tablespoons butter with the oil in a large skillet. When the foam from the butter subsides,

add the chicken breasts and sauté until all sides are browned. Remove the chicken from the pan and arrange in a 9 x 13-inch baking dish.

6. Discard all but 2 tablespoons of the oil mixture in the pan, add the shallots, and sauté until they are soft, about 2 minutes. Add the mushrooms and sauté until they begin to color and their liquid evaporates, 12 to 15 minutes. Remove the pan from the heat, and add the brandy. Return to the heat and bring the mixture to a boil, stirring. Add the tomatoes, return the mixture to a boil, and simmer for 5 minutes to reduce the juices and concentrate the flavors. Add the cream and simmer for another 5 minutes to thicken the sauce. Season with salt and pepper. Let the sauce cool.

7. Pour the sauce over the chicken breasts in the casserole dish. Cover and refrigerate for up to 2 days or freeze for up to 1 month.

Bake It Later

1. Defrost the chicken in the refrigerator overnight, if necessary.

2. Preheat the oven to 325°F. Allow the chicken to come to room temperature for 20 minutes.

3. Bake the casserole, covered, for 25 minutes. Uncover and bake for an additional 10 to 15 minutes, until the sauce is bubbling and the chicken is cooked through (160°F on an instant-read thermometer). Serve immediately.

All-Purpose Formula for
Poultry Casseroles to Serve 6

Sometimes we just need a formula to get us through, and this one works very well for recycling leftovers or helping you to make a casserole to keep on hand for your family when you need it. Remember that making extra rice, pasta, or mashed potatoes can help you prepare another very special meal, with just a few additional ingredients. You will need 4 cups of the white sauce with pasta or rice, and 3 cups of the sauce with potatoes.

   3 cups cooked rice, pasta, or leftover mashed potatoes
   3 to 4 cups Diva White Sauce (recipe follows)
   3 cups cooked chicken or turkey
   1 1/2 cups chopped cooked vegetables of your choice
   1 cup fresh bread crumbs, crushed potato chips, crushed tortilla chips, or crushed buttery crackers
   1/2 to 1 cup grated or shredded cheese of your choice
   3 tablespoons melted butter, olive oil, or a combination

Make It Now

1. Coat the inside of a 3-quart casserole or 9 x 13-inch baking dish with nonstick cooking spray. If using rice or pasta, stir 1 cup of the sauce into the rice or pasta and spread in the casserole dish. If using potatoes, press the potatoes evenly into the casserole dish.

2. Combine the remaining 3 cups sauce with the chicken and the vegetables. Pour the mixture over the ingredients in the baking dish. Toss together the bread crumbs, cheese, and melted butter and sprinkle them evenly over the top. Cover and refrigerate for up to 2 days or freeze for up to 6 weeks.

Bake It Later

1. Defrost the casserole in the refrigerator overnight, if necessary.

2. Preheat the oven to 350°F. Allow the casserole to come to room temperature for about 30 minutes.

3. Bake the casserole for 30 minutes, or until it is bubbling and the crumb topping is golden brown and the cheese is melted. Serve immediately.

Formula for Diva White Sauce

White sauce (or French béchamel) is basically a flour- and fat-thickened sauce using milk as the liquid. The formula is simple, and the results will get you on your way to a great dish. But

I've found recently that more flavor is derived from using some broth as part of the liquid; this intensifies the sauce's flavor and also gives you a lower-fat sauce. The French call this type of sauce velouté; I call it a Diva trick!

- The fat can be unsalted butter or vegetable or olive oil (extra-virgin olive oil will overpower the sauce).

- The flour should be unbleached all-purpose flour; no Wondra or instant blending, as this type of flour isn't meant to be cooked in a roux.

- The liquid can be broth, whole or 2 percent milk, or heavy cream. For savory sauces I don't recommend nonfat half-and-half (too much sugar) or evaporated skim milk.

- If you want to make a cheesy sauce, make sure to remove the sauce from the heat before adding the cheese to taste; otherwise, the sauce can become grainy. Finely shredded or grated cheeses will melt more quickly than coarsely grated cheeses.

FAT	FLOUR	LIQUID	YIELD/CONSISTENCY
2 tablespoons	2 tablespoons	1 cup	1¼ cups/thick
¼ cup	¼ cup	2 cups	2½ cups/thick
2 tablespoons	2 tablespoons	1½ cups	1¾ cups/medium
¼ cup	¼ cup	3 cups	3½ cups/medium
2 tablespoons	2 tablespoons	2 cups	2¼ cups/thin
¼ cup	¼ cup	4 cups	4½ cups/thin

To make a white sauce, melt the fat in a saucepan over medium heat. Add the flour and, with a sauce whisk, whisk until bubbles form on the surface. After the bubbles begin to form, cook the roux for 2 to 3 minutes. This will cook the flour so that you won't taste it in your finished sauce, and so that the fat and flour will form a bond and not separate when you reheat the sauce. Slowly add the liquid, whisking constantly. (The liquid can be cold, hot, or at room temperature—the warmer it is, the faster the sauce will come to a boil.) Bring the sauce to a boil; otherwise, it will not thicken. Boil for 1 minute, whisking constantly. Then taste for seasoning and add salt and pepper, if desired. If you are making a cheese sauce, Tabasco or another hot sauce is a good substitute for pepper; it brings out the flavor in the cheese. Most chefs recommend seasoning with white pepper for aesthetic reasons, but I find that my cooking students buy white pepper, use it once, and then when they need it again, it's lost its potency. So either white or black pepper is fine here.

King Ranch Turkey Casserole

NO COOKBOOK ABOUT MAKE-AHEAD DINNERS would be complete without one version of this classic Southwestern potluck dish. Layers of tortillas, turkey, chiles, cheese, and creamy sauce *have* to sit overnight in the refrigerator for the tortillas to melt into the sauce. Then the whole thing goes into the oven and becomes a creamy mélange that will have your guests asking for both the recipe and a doggie bag! Remember that casseroles were created to recycle leftovers, so use up that leftover roast turkey in this dish. The classic old-school version of this casserole is in my book *The Soup Mix Gourmet* (The Harvard Common Press, 2001), using canned cream of chicken soup, but this sauce is even more delectable, using some ground chipotle chile powder and fresh cilantro to punch up the flavor. SERVES 8

½ cup vegetable oil

1 cup finely chopped sweet onion, such as Vidalia

1 clove garlic, minced

¼ cup canned roasted green chiles, rinsed, drained, and finely chopped

1 teaspoon ground chipotle chile powder

½ cup unbleached all-purpose flour

2 cups chicken broth

½ cup mild salsa

1½ cups whole milk

½ cup finely chopped fresh cilantro, plus more for garnish

Salt and freshly ground black pepper to taste

Twelve 6-inch white corn or yellow corn tortillas, torn into pieces

4 cups shredded or diced cooked turkey

1½ cups sour cream, plus more for garnish

2 cups finely shredded mild cheddar cheese

2 cups finely shredded Monterey Jack cheese

Make It Now

1. Coat the inside of a 2½-inch deep, 9 x 13-inch baking dish with nonstick cooking spray.

2. Heat the oil in a large saucepan over medium heat. Add the onion, garlic, and chiles, and sauté for 3 minutes, until the onion and garlic are fragrant. Add the chipotle chile powder and sauté another minute. Whisk in the flour and cook for about 3 minutes, still whisking, being careful not to burn the chile powder. Gradually add the chicken broth, whisking until the mixture comes to a boil. Stir in the salsa and milk and simmer for 5 minutes. Remove from the heat, add the cilantro, and season with salt and pepper. Let cool slightly.

3. Spread about one-quarter of the sauce in the prepared baking dish. Top with one-third of the tortilla pieces to form a ragged layer.

4. In a large bowl, combine the turkey, sour cream, 1 cup of the cheddar cheese, and 1 cup of the Monterey Jack cheese. Spread one-half of the turkey mixture over the tortillas. Repeat the sauce-tortilla-turkey layering. Top with half of the remaining sauce and another layer of tortillas. Pour the remaining sauce over the tortillas and cover with the remaining 1 cup cheddar and

1 cup Monterey Jack cheese. Cover and refrigerate for up to 2 days, or freeze for up to 1 month.

Bake It Later

1. Defrost the casserole in the refrigerator overnight, if necessary.

2. Preheat the oven to 350°F. Allow the casserole to come to room temperature for about 30 minutes.

3. Bake the casserole, covered, for 30 minutes. Uncover and bake for another 20 minutes, until the cheese is melted and the casserole is bubbling. Allow the casserole to rest for a few minutes before serving hot.

Turkey Vegetable Pie with Thyme Biscuit Crust

THIS SPIN ON TURKEY POT PIE uses delicate thyme-flavored biscuits to top a saucy turkey and colorful vegetable combination. The sauce for this pie tends to be thin, because biscuits or any breadlike topping tend to absorb a lot of the sauce, so you will have a filling that goes in a bit thin, but thickens as the biscuits bake. Feel free to substitute your favorite vegetables in this pie, but you'll need to precook any harder root vegetables before putting them into the filling. Remember that these biscuits can top any of your favorite stews—beef, chicken, pork, or turkey—so try them on other dishes as well. SERVES 6

FILLING

3½ cups chicken broth

2 medium-size sweet potatoes, peeled and cut into ½-inch cubes

½ cup (1 stick) unsalted butter

½ cup finely chopped sweet onion, such as Vidalia

½ cup chopped fennel (about ½ bulb)

¼ cup unbleached all-purpose flour

2 small zucchini, ends trimmed and cut into ½-inch cubes

2 small yellow squash, ends trimmed and cut into ½-inch cubes

3 cups cooked chopped or shredded turkey or chicken

½ cup heavy cream (optional)

Make It Now

1. To make the filling, bring the broth to a boil in a large saucepan. Add the sweet potatoes and cook for 5 minutes, until the potatoes give a bit when pierced with the tip of a sharp knife. Drain the potatoes and reserve the broth.

2. Heat the butter in a large saucepan over medium heat. Add the onion and fennel and sauté, stirring, for about 3 minutes, until the onion is fragrant and beginning to soften. Add the flour, stir until it is incorporated, and continue to cook for 3 minutes. Gradually add 2½ cups of the reserved broth, and bring to a boil. Add the sweet potatoes, zucchini, yellow squash, and turkey, and simmer for 10 minutes. Add the cream, if using. Pour the mixture into a 9 x 13-inch baking dish, 3-quart casserole dish, or 6 individual ramekins. Cover and refrigerate for up to 2 days or freeze for up to 2 months.

3. To make the biscuits, combine the flour, baking powder, thyme, and salt in a large mixing bowl. Cut up the shortening and toss it together with the flour until the mixture resembles crumbs. Gradually blend in some milk, a few tablespoons at a time, stirring with a fork; stop adding

BISCUITS

2 cups unbleached all-purpose flour, plus more for flouring the board

1 tablespoon baking powder

2 tablespoons finely chopped fresh thyme or your favorite herb (chives, dill, sage, and marjoram all work well)

½ teaspoon salt

⅓ cup vegetable shortening

About ¾ cup milk

milk when the mixture comes together. Turn the dough out onto a floured board and knead it 4 to 5 times, until the dough begins to form into a cohesive mass. Pat the dough into a circle, then roll it out ½ inch thick. Cut into 1½-inch biscuits and place on a baking sheet. Cover and refrigerate the dough for up to 3 days or freeze for up to 2 months.

Bake It Later

1. Defrost the casserole and the biscuits in the refrigerator overnight, if necessary.

2. Preheat the oven to 375°F. Allow the casserole and biscuits to come to room temperature for about 30 minutes.

3. Press your finger into the center of each biscuit to make an indentation so that the sides are higher than the centers; this will prevent the biscuits from sinking into the filling. Place the biscuits on top of the filling. Bake the pot pie in a casserole or baking dish for 20 to 25 minutes, or in individual ramekins for 15 to 17 minutes, until the biscuits are browned and the pie is bubbling. Serve immediately.

VARIATION

Top the turkey mixture with puff pastry, pie crust, or mashed potatoes instead of the biscuits.

Turkey Meat Loaf with Rosemary–Cranberry Sauce Glaze

I LOVE MEAT LOAF, and I am always in search of new variations on the theme. This meat loaf actually tastes like a Thanksgiving dinner in one dish, with packaged stuffing cubes in the meat, along with a delicious rosemary–cranberry sauce glaze. Sometimes turkey meat loaf can be dry, but I've added a little mayonnaise to the mix to help keep it moist. The cranberry sauce can be frozen ahead of time, or you can make it the same day you put together the meat loaf and freeze them both together. The sauce is also terrific with pork. SERVES 6

MEAT LOAF

2 tablespoons unsalted butter

½ cup finely chopped onion

½ cup finely chopped celery

1 teaspoon dried thyme

½ teaspoon dried sage, crumbled

2 pounds ground turkey

½ cup mayonnaise

2 cups prepared stuffing cubes (Pepperidge Farm is a good brand)

1½ teaspoons salt

½ teaspoon freshly ground black pepper

1 large egg

ROSEMARY CRANBERRY SAUCE

½ cup chopped onion

2 tablespoons chopped fresh rosemary

Two 16-ounce cans whole-berry cranberry sauce

Grated zest of 1 lemon

Make It Now

1. To make the meat loaf, melt the butter in a medium-size sauté pan over medium heat. Add the onion, celery, thyme, and sage and sauté until the onion is translucent, about 5 minutes. Transfer the mixture to a large bowl and let cool slightly.

2. Add the turkey, mayonnaise, stuffing cubes, salt, pepper, and egg to the bowl, and stir until the mixture is blended. Line a 9-inch loaf pan with plastic wrap and pack the mixture into the loaf pan. Cover and refrigerate for up to 2 days or freeze for up to 2 months. (If you are in need of your loaf pan before you bake this, allow the meat loaf to freeze until firm, then pop it out of the loaf pan and store it in a large zipper-top plastic bag. If you are refrigerating it, allow it to firm up in the fridge for about 5 hours, then pop it out of the pan, using the plastic wrap to help, and arrange it in a baking dish that is large enough to hold it. Cover with plastic wrap and refrigerate until ready to bake.)

3. To make the cranberry sauce, combine the onion, rosemary, cranberry sauce, and lemon zest in a medium-size saucepan, bring to a boil, and boil for 3 minutes. Remove from the heat and let cool. Transfer to an airtight container and refrigerate for up to 2 weeks or freeze for up to 2 months.

1. Defrost the meat loaf and the sauce in the refrigerator overnight, if necessary.

2. Preheat the oven to 350°F. Allow the meat loaf and sauce to come to room temperature for about 30 minutes. Remove the meat loaf from the loaf pan. Be sure to remove the plastic wrap from the meat loaf.

3. Transfer the meat loaf to a baking dish with 1-inch sides. Pour the cranberry sauce over the meat loaf, reserving any if you would like to serve some on the side. Bake for 45 to 55 minutes, until the meat loaf is cooked through (170°F on an instant-read thermometer). Allow the loaf to rest for 10 minutes before cutting with a serrated knife into ½-inch-thick slices.

The Main Dish
Seafood

Seafood is good for you, and it's a terrific make-ahead entrée. Whether you choose fish fillets, shrimp, crab, or lobster, they can all be made into amazing do-ahead dishes for you to serve to family and friends. If you are hesitant to cook seafood at home (and you know who you are), start with a mild, firm fish, like halibut. You can serve fish fillets in a variety of ways, and they will never let you down because baking fish is a no-brainer, estimating 10 minutes of cooking time for each inch of thickness. Most fillets will come with the skin taken off for you, but if not, it's simple enough to remove it after the fish is cooked.

Shrimp come in sizes from small or "cocktail" up to super colossal, but the names are not really as important as the numbers that appear on the package or near the shrimp at the fish store. If the numbers are 36/40, that means that these are medium-size shrimp and that there will be 36 to 40 in a pound. That's how the labeling works, and you should be aware of this when trying to save money—medium-size shrimp are bite-size when cooked, so use those for casseroles, and you'll have dishes bursting with shrimp. If you want to make a statement, colossal or super colossal, with fewer than 12 to 15 per pound, are gigantic and gorgeous, and you'll only need 3 to 4 per person. Shrimp often come with the shell on, and it's easy enough to peel and devein them yourself, but you can also buy them peeled and deveined, or you can buy the "easy peel" variety, which has been de-veined by a slit down the back that helps the peel to just slip right off. Most shrimp are frozen right on the boats, unless you live in an area where the shrimp are caught and sold when the boats come in. I always buy my shrimp frozen so I can control how it is defrosted (overnight in my refrigerator) and how I cook it. Ask for frozen shrimp in the size that you want; it's a good bet that the fishmonger has a huge stash in the back. Double-bag the shrimp in zipper-top plastic bags and store in the freezer.

Lump crabmeat comes pasteurized in refrigerated cans, which means that it is fresh but will have a long shelf life. You can buy cooked crabmeat in bulk in some areas of the country, and king crab legs, which are usually frozen and then defrosted, are more widely available these days at your local fish market. Because the seafood is already cooked, you just have to add it to your seafood dishes.

Scallops come in two varieties: bay scallops are the tiny, penny-size scallops with a delicate flavor and short cooking time, while sea scallops are larger and take longer to cook. Both have their advantages, but I have to say that I am partial to bay scallops for their sweet, nutty flavor. Scallops should come "dry pack," without being soaked in a preservative solution. This solution will retard any caramelization that you would have when browning the scallops, and the scallops will leach out a lot of liquid when cooked, changing the flavor and texture of sauces.

Clams and mussels are not really appropriate for do-ahead cooking, but you can prepare a sauce for mussels marinara weeks ahead of time and have it ready in the freezer. Or you can make lemon-parsley-garlic butter sauce for clams and freeze that until you are ready to make the clams. Canned clams are terrific for make-ahead casseroles.

When preparing seafood dishes ahead of time, I generally do not freeze them; this is more a matter of personal taste rather than food science. Seafood certainly can be frozen in casseroles, but in many cases its texture just doesn't seem the same to me after defrosting, which is why I shy away from making a seafood dish and freezing it. In each recipe in this chapter, I indicate if it's possible to freeze a dish.

The Main Dish: Seafood

Mediterranean Halibut with Tomatoes, Feta, and Mint

THIS GORGEOUS DISH OOZES PERSONALITY. From the oven-roasted topping to the slightly minty flavor and the salty feta, it's a terrific weeknight dinner, but it's also great to serve to friends for an informal get-together. With a side of orzo, some crusty bread, and a dry, crisp white wine, you've got yourself a ticket to a taverna in the Greek isles. I recommend halibut here, but you can use any firm, thick-fleshed fish. SERVES 6

Two 14.5-ounce cans diced tomatoes, drained

1/2 cup chopped onion

2 cloves garlic, minced

2 tablespoons finely chopped fresh mint

1 1/2 teaspoons salt

1/2 teaspoon freshly ground black pepper

1/2 cup olive oil

2 pounds halibut fillets

Make It Now

1. Preheat the oven to 400°F. Line a baking sheet with aluminum foil or a silicone baking liner.

2. In a large mixing bowl, combine the tomatoes, onion, garlic, mint, salt, and pepper with 5 tablespoons of the olive oil. Pour the tomato mixture onto the baking sheet and bake for 15 minutes, until the tomatoes are fragrant and most of the liquid has evaporated. Cool to room temperature, transfer to an airtight container, and refrigerate for up to 2 days or freeze for up to 1 month.

3. Pour the remaining 3 tablespoons olive oil into a 9 x 13-inch baking dish and turn the halibut in the oil, coating the fish. (At this point, you may cover and refrigerate for up to 8 hours.)

8 ounces feta cheese, crumbled

1 tablespoon finely chopped fresh mint

Bake It Later

1. Defrost the tomatoes in the refrigerator overnight, if necessary.

2. Preheat the oven to 350°F. Allow the tomatoes and the fish to come to room temperature for 20 minutes.

3. Pour the tomatoes over the fish and top with the feta cheese. Bake for 15 to 20 minutes, until the cheese is melted and the fish is cooked through. Sprinkle with the mint and serve hot.

Not-Your-Mom's Fish Sticks

MANY OF MY STUDENTS are always looking for ways to serve fish to their family without ending up with a full-scale rebellion on their hands. This basic recipe will help to take the fear out of trying new things because it's foolproof. Halibut strips are breaded with a savory cheesy coating and bake in less than 10 minutes. I defy your finicky eaters to dislike them! You can even use frozen halibut; just make sure to defrost it and use the same technique. SERVES 4

1 pound halibut fillets

½ cup olive oil

1 tablespoon Old Bay seasoning

2 cups cheddar or Parmesan cheese–flavored crackers (such as Goldfish), crushed into crumbs in the food processor

Make It Now

1. Line a baking sheet with aluminum foil, parchment paper, or a silicone baking liner. Remove any skin from the halibut and cut the halibut into ¼-inch-thick slices, widthwise.

2. In a shallow dish, combine the oil and 2 teaspoons of the Old Bay seasoning. In another shallow dish, combine the remaining 1 teaspoon Old Bay with the cracker crumbs.

3. Dip the fish strips into the oil a couple at a time, coating on all sides, then dredge in the cracker mixture, coating on all sides. Lay the strips on the baking sheet, and continue until all the fish strips are coated. Drizzle any remaining oil over the fish strips. Cover and refrigerate for at least 4 hours, or overnight.

Bake It Later

1. Preheat the oven to 400°F. Allow the fish on the baking sheet to come to room temperature for about 15 minutes.

2. Bake the fish for 5 to 7 minutes, until the coating is golden brown and the fish is cooked through. Remove from the oven, let rest for 5 minutes, and serve hot.

10-Minute Baked Halibut with Garlic-Butter Sauce

HALIBUT IS MY FAVORITE FISH. It is mild and firm, it is simple to prepare with spectacular results, and it takes well to any seasonings that strike your fancy. This dish is very simple; the fillets are coated with an olive-oil glaze, then baked with a lemon-garlic butter sauce—what's not to love? I will sometimes roast vegetables alongside the fish, such as asparagus, broccoli, or mushrooms.

SERVES 6

1/4 cup olive oil

1 tablespoon Old Bay seasoning

1 1/2 pounds halibut fillets

1/2 cup (1 stick) unsalted butter

3 cloves garlic, minced

2 tablespoons freshly squeezed lemon juice

1 teaspoon grated lemon zest

1 tablespoon finely chopped herbs of your choice (optional; see Diva Note)

Make It Now

1. In a small bowl, mix together the olive oil and Old Bay seasoning. Brush the halibut with the mixture, then arrange the fillets in a single layer in an ovenproof baking dish. Cover and refrigerate for up to 24 hours.

2. Melt the butter in a small sauté pan or saucepan over low heat. Add the garlic and sauté until the garlic is fragrant, about 5 minutes, being careful not to burn the garlic. Remove from the heat and add the lemon juice, lemon zest, and herbs, if using. Store the butter in the refrigerator until you are ready to bake the fish.

Diva Note

Although I love to chop up herbs and add them to the garlic butter, sometimes when fresh herbs in the market aren't looking great, I will leave them out. My favorites for this dish are dill, oregano, tarragon, marjoram, chervil, and rosemary. Basil doesn't do well in the oven, so if you would like a hint of basil, finely chop it and sprinkle it over the fish after it's baked.

1. Preheat the oven to 400°F. Allow the fish to come to room temperature for about 15 minutes. Melt the garlic butter and pour it over the fish.

2. Bake the fish for 10 minutes, basting once with the sauce. The fish is done when it is opaque all the way through when slashed in the thickest part or an instant-read thermometer registers 165°F. Serve the fish with the garlic butter spooned over each portion.

Seafood Florentine

THIS LUXURIOUS CASSEROLE is comprised of a layer of spinach topped with a creamy seafood sauce, then baked in the oven with a cheesy topping. It is sophisticated, luscious, and simple to assemble. Although it has several parts, they can all be done ahead of time, and you can probably get the whole thing made in less than an hour. The choices for seafood are up to you; I love to use a combination of crab and shrimp, and if my pocketbook is really full, I add scallops to the mix. But the versions using salmon or halibut are equally delicious, and the salmon is particularly pretty. You can find seafood stock in the prepared soup section of most supermarkets—my favorite is the lobster stock by Superior Touch Better Than Bouillon. SERVES 10 TO 12

3/4 cup (1 1/2 sticks) unsalted butter

2 pounds fresh baby spinach *or* two 16-ounce packages frozen spinach, defrosted and squeezed dry

1 1/2 teaspoons salt

1 teaspoon freshly ground black pepper

1/4 teaspoon ground nutmeg

2 pounds mixed fish and/or shellfish (see Diva Note)

1/4 cup dry white wine or dry vermouth

1/4 cup unbleached all-purpose flour

1 cup seafood stock, milk, or bottled clam juice

1 1/2 cups milk

2 tablespoons cream sherry (optional)

1 cup finely shredded imported Swiss cheese, such as Gruyère or Emmentaler

Make It Now

1. Melt 1/4 cup of the butter in a medium-size skillet over medium heat. Add the spinach, salt, pepper, and nutmeg and cook, stirring, until the spinach is wilted and cooked through and all the liquid in the pan has evaporated, 5 to 7 minutes. Transfer to a 9 x 13-inch baking dish. (At this point, you may cool, cover, and refrigerate overnight.)

2. Clean out the skillet, melt another 1/4 cup of the butter, add the seafood and wine, and cook for 3 to 5 minutes. Shrimp should begin to turn pink, while fish and scallops will begin to turn opaque. Transfer the contents of the pan to a colander set over a bowl and drain, reserving any juices.

3. Melt the remaining 1/4 cup butter in a large saucepan over medium heat. Add the flour and whisk until white bubbles form on the surface. Cook, whisking constantly, for 2 to 3 minutes longer. Gradually add the liquid from the sautéed seafood and the seafood stock, stirring until the mixture begins to boil. Add the milk, remove from the heat, add the sherry, if using, and the Swiss cheese, and stir until the cheese is melted. Add the seafood and stir to combine. Pour the seafood mixture over the spinach in the baking dish. Let cool, then cover and refrigerate for up to 2 days.

½ cup freshly grated
Parmesan cheese

Bake It Later

1. Preheat the oven to 350°F. Allow the casserole to come to room temperature for about 15 minutes.

2. Sprinkle the casserole with the grated Parmesan and bake until the sauce is bubbling and the cheese begins to turn golden, 30 to 40 minutes. Serve immediately.

Diva Note

If you want to prepare this with shellfish, I suggest including scallops, peeled and deveined shrimp, crabmeat, and/or lobster. If you want to prepare it with fish, use salmon and/or halibut fillets, cutting them into 1-inch pieces.

Dilly Salmon Cakes

A NEW TWIST ON BAKED FISH CAKES, these salmon cakes are delicious with their buttery dill baste, the addition of chopped artichoke hearts to give them some character, and their crispy coating of panko crumbs. Again, you can freeze these, but I prefer to make them a day or two ahead before baking. Mini versions of these cakes are terrific for small tapas; form them into 1- to 1½-inch cakes and bake them for half the time. Serve these with a dilled mayonnaise, and you will win raves from family and friends. SERVES 6

2 tablespoons unsalted butter

1 clove garlic, minced

1 tablespoon finely chopped sweet onion, such as Vidalia

One 15.5-ounce can artichoke hearts, coarsely chopped

2 cups flaked cooked salmon (see Diva Note)

2 teaspoons Dijon mustard

½ teaspoon Old Bay seasoning

2 teaspoons freshly squeezed lemon juice

2 tablespoons mayonnaise, plus more as needed

1 teaspoon finely chopped fresh flat-leaf parsley

1 large egg

1 cup panko crumbs or dried bread crumbs

Make It Now

1. Melt the butter in a small sauté pan over medium heat. Add the garlic, onion, and artichoke hearts and sauté until the onion and garlic are fragrant and the artichoke liquid has evaporated, 8 to 10 minutes. Transfer the mixture to a large bowl and allow to cool slightly.

2. Add the salmon to the bowl, along with the mustard, Old Bay seasoning, lemon juice, mayonnaise, parsley, egg, and ½ cup of the panko crumbs. Gently mix everything together. If the mixture seems dry, add a teaspoon or two more mayonnaise. Form the mixture into 6 cakes about 3 inches in diameter. Coat one side of the cakes with the remaining panko.

3. Line a baking sheet or 9 x 13-inch baking dish with aluminum foil, parchment paper, or a silicone baking liner. Lay the cakes, panko side up, in the pan, cover, and refrigerate for up to 2 days. Or place them on a baking sheet, freeze until firm, then transfer to a zipper-top plastic bag, separating the cakes with parchment paper or plastic wrap. Freeze the cakes for up to 4 weeks.

Diva Note

This is a great dish to make when you have leftover grilled or poached salmon. I don't recommend canned salmon at all. It has a distinctively "off" flavor and it will not taste nearly as good as freshly cooked salmon.

Poaching Salmon in the Microwave

To poach your salmon in the microwave, place 1 pound salmon, 1 teaspoon Old Bay seasoning, and ¼ cup white wine or water in a microwavable dish. Cover with microwavable plastic wrap, cut a few vent holes, and cook for 7 to 8 minutes. Allow the salmon to rest for 5 minutes, then remove the skin and dark underlayer of fat from the salmon. Refrigerate for up to 3 days before using in your favorite recipes.

½ cup (1 stick) unsalted butter, melted

½ cup finely chopped fresh dill

Bake It Later

1. Defrost the salmon cakes in the refrigerator overnight, if necessary.

2. Preheat the oven to 400°F. Allow the salmon cakes to come to room temperature for about 15 minutes. Mix the butter and dill together in a small bowl.

3. Brush the cakes with the butter mixture and bake for 8 minutes. Brush again and bake for another 7 to 8 minutes, until the cakes are golden brown and the internal temperature registers 165°F on an instant-read thermometer. (There is no need to turn them.) Serve hot.

Shiitake-Sesame Salmon Cakes

ANOTHER GREAT IDEA WITH AN ASIAN FLAIR, these cakes are filled with shiitake mushrooms and green onions, flavored with soy sauce and sesame oil, and then coated with panko and sesame seeds. They are delicious served on a bed of sautéed bok choy or with an Asian slaw. I'm not fond of these frozen, as I think the mushrooms lose something in the freezing process, and they aren't quite as flavorful. Serve these with wasabi-spiked mayonnaise. SERVES 6

2 teaspoons vegetable oil

1 clove garlic, minced

½ teaspoon freshly grated ginger

8 ounces shiitake mushrooms, stems removed and caps finely chopped

3 green onions (white and tender green parts), finely chopped

2 cups flaked cooked salmon

1 tablespoon soy sauce

1 teaspoon toasted sesame oil

1 large egg

1 tablespoon mayonnaise, plus more as needed

¼ cup sesame seeds

1 cup panko crumbs

Make It Now

1. Heat the oil in a small skillet over medium heat. Add the garlic and ginger and swirl over the heat for 30 seconds. Add the mushrooms and cook until the mushroom liquid has evaporated and the mushrooms have begun to color, about 6 minutes. Remove from the pan, transfer to a large mixing bowl, add the green onions, and allow to cool slightly.

2. Add the salmon to the bowl along with the soy sauce, sesame oil, egg, mayonnaise, 2 tablespoons of the sesame seeds, and ½ cup of the panko, stirring gently until blended. If the mixture seems too dry, add more mayonnaise, a teaspoon at a time.

3. Line a sheet pan or 9 x 13-inch baking dish with aluminum foil, parchment paper, or a silicone baking liner. In a shallow dish, combine the remaining 2 tablespoons sesame seeds and ½ cup panko. Form the salmon mixture into 6 cakes about 3 inches in diameter. Dip one side into the panko-sesame mixture. Lay the cakes, panko side up, on the prepared sheet pan. Cover and refrigerate for up to 2 days.

½ cup (1 stick) unsalted butter, melted

2 tablespoons soy sauce

Bake It Later

1. Preheat the oven to 400°F. Allow the salmon cakes to come to room temperature for about 15 minutes.

2. Combine the butter and soy sauce in a small bowl, stirring to blend. Brush the cakes with the butter mixture and bake for 7 to 8 minutes. Brush the cakes again and bake for an additional 7 to 8 minutes, until golden brown and the temperature registers 165°F on an instant-read thermometer. (There is no need to turn the cakes.) Remove from the oven and serve hot.

Wasabi-Miso Salmon

THIS DISH MAY SOUND LIKE IT'S GOING TO BE SPICY HOT, but the wasabi is really a nice counterpoint to the rich, flavorful salmon, and you can back off on the wasabi if you are not into it. You can find white miso and wasabi powder in the Asian section of your supermarket, and both will keep well when sealed in an airtight container. The marinade works well with any firm fish fillets. This dish is so easy that you'll have plenty of energy left over to make a few creative side dishes. SERVES 4

Four 4- to 5-ounce salmon fillets, skin removed (see Diva Note)

2 teaspoons water

2 tablespoons rice vinegar

2 tablespoons mirin (rice wine) or dry sherry

1 tablespoon sugar

2 teaspoons soy sauce

1/2 cup white miso

1/2 to 1 teaspoon wasabi powder

Make It Now

1. Arrange the salmon in a single layer in a 9 x 13-inch glass baking dish. In a small bowl, combine the water, rice vinegar, mirin, sugar, soy sauce, white miso, and wasabi powder with a whisk until blended. Pour over the salmon. Cover and refrigerate for up to 24 hours.

Diva Note

If the fishmonger doesn't remove the skin when you buy the fish, there is no need to panic. Don't remove the skin until after you have cooked the salmon, and then it will slip right off.

¼ cup sesame seeds

6 green onions (white and tender green parts), sliced on the diagonal

Bake It Later

1. Preheat the oven to 400°F. Line a baking sheet with aluminum foil or a silicone baking liner.

2. Drain the marinade from the fish, discarding the marinade, and place the fish on the baking sheet. Sprinkle the sesame seeds over the fillets. Bake for 10 minutes, or until the fish is cooked through. Remove from the oven, sprinkle with the green onions, and serve hot.

VARIATIONS

Wasabi-Miso Shrimp

Substitute 1½ pounds shrimp (or try 1½ pounds scallops) for the salmon and marinate for about 3 hours. Bake for 3 to 5 minutes.

Wasabi-Miso Chicken

Substitute 1 whole chicken, cut up, with skin on, or 6 boneless, skinless chicken breast halves for the salmon. If the chicken is boneless, bake for 15 minutes; bake bone-in chicken for 35 to 40 minutes.

Baked Salmon and Spinach Casserole

THIS BEAUTIFUL DISH, with its bright pink salmon and deep green spinach interspersed with noodles, is really a dressed-up version of that old standby, tuna noodle casserole, but with loads more panache. The casserole is terrific served as a weeknight dinner or a take-along to a potluck, or you can dress it up for company with a dynamite salad and some nice soft rolls. One of its more stellar qualities is that it freezes well, so you can make two casseroles and freeze one for another time.

SERVES 6

1 1/2 pounds salmon fillets

1 1/4 teaspoons Old Bay seasoning

1/3 cup dry white wine

1/4 cup (1/2 stick) unsalted butter

1/4 cup finely chopped shallots (see Diva Note)

1/4 cup unbleached all-purpose flour

2 1/2 cups milk

1/2 cup white wine

1 cup finely shredded Swiss cheese

1/2 cup finely chopped fresh dill

Two 10-ounce packages fresh baby spinach, blanched and squeezed dry, or one 16-ounce package frozen chopped spinach, defrosted and squeezed dry

1/2 pound medium-width egg noodles, cooked according to package directions

Make It Now

1. Place the salmon in a single layer in a microwave-safe dish. Sprinkle with the Old Bay seasoning and wine. Cover with microwave-safe plastic wrap, cut a few vent holes in the wrap, and microwave for 10 minutes. Allow the salmon to rest for 5 minutes. Remove the skin and dark under-layer of fat from the salmon. When the salmon is cool, flake it into a large bowl.

2. Melt the butter in a medium-size saucepan over medium heat. Add the shallots and swirl the pan to coat the shallots. Sauté for 2 to 3 minutes until fragrant. Sprinkle with the flour, and cook, whisking, for 3 minutes. Slowly add the milk, whisking constantly, then add the wine and bring the sauce to a boil. Remove the pan from the heat, stir in the Swiss cheese and dill, and continue stirring until the cheese is melted.

3. Combine the salmon, spinach, and noodles in a large mixing bowl. Stir in the sauce, being careful not to break up the salmon, but coating all of the noodles.

4. Coat the inside of a 3-quart casserole dish or 9 x 13-inch baking dish with nonstick cooking spray. Pour the noodle mixture into the pan, cover, and refrigerate for up to 2 days or freeze for up to 1 month.

1 cup fresh bread crumbs

½ cup finely shredded Swiss cheese

2 tablespoons unsalted butter, melted

Bake It Later

1. Defrost the casserole in the refrigerator overnight, if necessary.

2. Preheat the oven to 350°F. Allow the casserole to come to room temperature for 30 minutes.

3. In a small bowl, stir together the bread crumbs, Swiss cheese, and butter until moistened. Top the casserole with the bread crumbs. Bake for 30 minutes, until the topping is golden brown and the casserole is bubbling. Serve hot.

Diva Note

No shallots? No problem. Substitute red onion or sweet onion, such as Vidalia. Shallots have a more garlicky onion flavor, and I love them for dishes where I want to get a bit more oomph in the sauce, but a red onion or sweet onion will also do the trick.

Steamed Fish Packets with Six Variations

STEAMING FISH IN THE OVEN IS A TERRIFIC WAY to serve a moist and flavorful entrée any night of the week, but it's especially nice to serve to company, because each guest has his or her own little packet or "present" to open at the table. The French call this dish *poisson en papillote*. The packets can be made up the night before, then popped into the oven 10 minutes before serving. I think that's better than a 30-minute meal! Remember that the vegetables should be on the soft side (no root veggies here) so that they can steam along with the fish and be ready at the same time. Since this is a basic formula, use your own favorite seafood, herbs, spices, and vegetables. The variations that follow will get you started. SERVES 4

Four 4- to 5-ounce halibut, salmon, or other firm-fleshed fish fillets, skin removed

½ cup olive oil

1½ teaspoons Old Bay seasoning or seafood seasoning of your choice

2 tablespoons finely chopped fresh herbs of your choice

1 to 1½ cups finely sliced vegetables of your choice

⅓ to ½ cup finely shredded or crumbled cheese of your choice

Make It Now

1. Cut 4 pieces of parchment paper or heavy-duty aluminum foil 2½ times the size of your fish fillets. Place a fillet in the center of each piece. Brush each fillet with 2 tablespoons of the oil, and sprinkle with one-quarter of the Old Bay seasoning and one-quarter of the herbs.

2. Divide the vegetables into 4 equal portions and lay 1 portion over each fillet. Divide the cheese into 4 equal portions and sprinkle 1 portion over each fillet. Fold the parchment over each fish fillet and make a package, sealing the edges by folding them over securely. Place the packets on a baking sheet and refrigerate for up to 24 hours.

Bake It Later

1. Preheat the oven to 400°F. Allow the packets to come to room temperature for 15 minutes.

2. Make two small slits in the top of each packet for steam to escape. Bake for 15 minutes, until the fish is cooked through and the vegetables are softened. Remove from the oven and allow to rest for 5 minutes before serving hot. Open the packets carefully, because there will be hot steam.

Here are some great combos to get your creative juices flowing. Feel free to try others to suit your taste.

alla Pizzaiola

Divide among the packets: 2 tablespoons finely chopped fresh oregano, ⅓ cup diced tomato, ⅓ cup thinly sliced fennel, ⅓ cup thinly sliced sweet onion, such as Vidalia, and ½ cup finely shredded mozzarella cheese.

Pesce Parmigiano

Divide among the packets: 2 tablespoons finely chopped fresh oregano or marjoram, ½ cup thinly sliced sun-dried tomatoes, ⅓ cup finely chopped onion, ⅓ cup finely chopped prosciutto, and ⅓ cup freshly grated Parmigiano-Reggiano.

Dillicious

Divide among the packets: 2 tablespoons finely chopped fresh dill; ½ cup asparagus tips, sliced in half; ½ cup finely chopped shallots; and ½ cup julienned havarti cheese with dill.

Veracruz

Divide among the packets: 2 tablespoons finely chopped fresh cilantro, ⅓ cup finely chopped sweet onion, such as Vidalia, ⅓ cup finely chopped tomato, ⅓ cup finely chopped roasted chiles, and ½ cup finely shredded Monterey Jack cheese.

Fajita Style

Divide among the packets: 2 tablespoons finely chopped fresh cilantro, ½ cup finely chopped sweet onion, such as Vidalia, ½ cup finely chopped red bell pepper, ½ cup finely chopped yellow bell pepper, and ½ cup finely chopped tomato.

Mediterranean

Divide among the packets: 2 tablespoons finely chopped fresh flat-leaf parsley, ½ cup thinly sliced lemon, ½ cup thinly sliced zucchini, ½ cup thinly sliced red onion, and ½ cup crumbled feta cheese.

Macadamia-Crusted Sea Bass

THIS TROPICAL DISH WITH A PACIFIC RIM FLAVOR is the perfect entrée to serve with steamed rice, some stir-fried veggies, and maybe a nice tropical fruit salsa on the side. SERVES 4

Four 4- to 5-ounce sea bass fillets, skin removed

1 teaspoon freshly squeezed orange juice

1 teaspoon freshly squeezed lime juice

2 tablespoons hoisin sauce

2 green onions (white and tender green parts), finely chopped

1 teaspoon honey

1 teaspoon dry sherry

1 teaspoon soy sauce

1 cup ground macadamia nuts (use a food processor or nut grinder)

2 tablespoons sesame seeds

Make It Now

1. Arrange the fillets in one layer in a rimmed glass dish. In a small mixing bowl, combine the orange juice, lime juice, hoisin sauce, green onions, honey, sherry, and soy sauce, whisking until blended.

2. Pour the marinade over the fish and turn the fish in the marinade. Cover and refrigerate for up to 24 hours.

Bake It Later

1. Preheat the oven to 400°F. Line a baking sheet with aluminum foil, parchment paper, or a silicone baking liner.

2. Combine the macadamia nuts and sesame seeds on a flat plate. Remove the fish from the marinade and discard the marinade. Dredge the fish in the nut mixture until thoroughly coated. Place the fillets on the prepared baking sheet. Bake for 15 to 20 minutes, until an instant-read thermometer inserted into the fish registers 165°F and the inside of the fish is opaque. Serve hot.

Sea Bass Tagine

TAGINES ARE BOTH THE VESSELS used for baking a traditional Moroccan dish and the dishes that are prepared in them. The vessel resembles a volcano, with a round flat bottom where the food is placed and a conical top with a large vent hole. A Dutch oven can be used in place of a tagine, so you can make this dish in any covered ovenproof casserole dish that you have. Sea bass, with its unique protein structure, works beautifully here without overcooking; it absorbs the spices in this dish and yet the flavor of the fish shines through. If you have a tagine or a nice buffet pan, serve this as a family-style dinner with couscous or steamed rice. Preserved lemons are essential for authentic Moroccan tagines, but most of us don't have time to preserve lemons, so I've improvised here with a bit of lemon zest and juice, and I think it works well. SERVES 6

2 pounds sea bass fillets

1/2 cup olive oil

1/2 teaspoon ground cumin

1 teaspoon sweet paprika

1/2 teaspoon ground coriander

1/8 teaspoon ground cinnamon

1/2 teaspoon ground ginger

6 dashes of Tabasco or other hot sauce

1/2 teaspoon freshly grated lemon zest

1/4 cup finely chopped shallot

2 cloves garlic, minced

1/4 cup finely chopped fresh cilantro

1/4 cup finely chopped fresh flat-leaf parsley

2 tablespoons freshly squeezed lemon juice

2 cups Greek olives, pitted and halved

Make It Now

1. Place the fish in the cooking vessel, in a single layer. In a small bowl, stir together the oil, cumin, paprika, coriander, cinnamon, ginger, Tabasco, and lemon zest. Pour the mixture over the fish and turn to coat the fish in the oil and spices.

2. Sprinkle the fish with the shallot, garlic, cilantro, parsley, and lemon juice and arrange the olives around the fish. Cover the baking dish and refrigerate overnight.

Bake It Later

1. Preheat the oven to 350°F. Bring the fish to room temperature for about 30 minutes.

2. Bake the fish, covered, for 45 minutes, basting the fish with the pan juices several times during cooking. Allow to rest for 5 to 10 minutes, then serve the fish topped with some of the pan juices and the olives.

Pacific Rim Fish Fillets

HERE'S AN EASY WEEKNIGHT DINNER. Brush the miso-soy-lime glaze on the fish the day before, then bake it the next day. I recommend a thick-fleshed fish like halibut, salmon, sea bass, or cod for this simple dinner. Serve over Asian slaw with steamed rice. SERVES 4

2 tablespoons white miso

1/2 cup soy sauce

1/4 teaspoon Tabasco or other hot sauce

1/4 cup freshly squeezed lime juice

2 cloves garlic, minced

2 tablespoons mirin (rice wine) or seasoned rice vinegar

2 tablespoons honey

Four 4- to 5-ounce firm-fleshed fish fillets (salmon, halibut, mahi mahi, cod, or sea bass all work well here)

1/2 to 3/4 cup sesame seeds

1/4 cup toasted sesame oil

Make It Now

1. In a small bowl, stir together the miso, soy sauce, Tabasco sauce, lime juice, garlic, mirin, and honey, whisking to blend.

2. Lay the fish in a 9 x 13-inch glass baking dish and pour the marinade over the fish. Refrigerate for at least 4 hours, or up to 24 hours.

Bake It Later

1. Preheat the oven to 400°F. Line a baking sheet with aluminum foil, parchment paper, or a silicone baking liner.

2. Remove the fish from the marinade, discarding the marinade. Lay the fish on the baking sheet. Press some of the sesame seeds on top of each fillet. Bake for 10 minutes, or until the fish is cooked through and the seeds are golden brown. Drizzle a bit of sesame oil over each fillet before serving hot.

Baked Stuffed Fillet of Sole with Crabmeat and Creamy Corn and Lobster Sauce

THIS IS MY "GO TO" SEAFOOD ENTRÉE for a nice dinner with company. Simple to prepare, it can be made and refrigerated the day before, then popped into a hot oven for less than 10 minutes before serving with a luxurious corn and lobster stock sauce. The result is an elegant entrée that needs nothing more than a bit of sautéed spinach or a mixed green salad and some nice rolls to set it off. If you would like to substitute your favorite shellfish in the stuffing, finely chopped shrimp, lobster, or clams work here. SERVES 4

½ cup (1 stick) unsalted butter

1 clove garlic, minced

4 ounces lump crabmeat

1 teaspoon brandy

2 tablespoons mayonnaise, plus more as needed

1 teaspoon freshly squeezed lemon juice

1 teaspoon chopped fresh tarragon

1 tablespoon finely chopped fresh chives

1 cup fresh bread crumbs

8 sole fillets (about 1 pound)

2 teaspoons Old Bay seasoning

Make It Now

1. Melt the butter in a small sauté pan over medium-high heat. Add the garlic and sauté for about 45 seconds, until it is fragrant. Add the crabmeat and swirl in the butter to coat thoroughly and heat through, about 2 minutes. Remove the pan from the heat and add the brandy. Return the pan to the stovetop for about 1 minute, stirring, to blend. Transfer the mixture to a medium-size bowl and allow to cool slightly.

2. Add the mayonnaise, lemon juice, tarragon, chives, and bread crumbs to the crab mixture and stir gently to mix. If the mixture seems too dry, add additional mayonnaise, 1 teaspoon at a time. (The stuffing can be covered and refrigerated for up to 2 days or frozen for up to 1 month.)

3. Coat the inside of a 9 x 13-inch baking dish with nonstick cooking spray. Lay the sole on a cutting board, sprinkle each piece on both sides with some of the Old Bay seasoning, and top with a tablespoon or two of the stuffing. Since some pieces will be larger than others, you will need to adjust the size of the mound of stuffing for each piece. Roll up the sole around the filling and place seam side down in the prepared pan. Repeat with the remaining pieces of sole. Cover and refrigerate for up to 2 days or freeze for up to 1 month.

½ cup white wine or dry vermouth

4 cups Creamy Corn and Lobster Sauce (recipe follows), heated

1. Defrost the sole in the refrigerator overnight, if necessary.

2. Preheat the oven to 350°F. Allow the sole to come to room temperature for about 20 minutes.

3. Pour the wine into the baking dish and bake the fish for 15 to 18 minutes, until the sole is cooked through and begins to turn opaque. Drain off any excess liquid from the pan and add to the sauce to thin it, if you'd like. Serve the fish with the corn and lobster sauce.

Creamy Corn and Lobster Sauce

THIS REMARKABLY SIMPLE SAUCE is a perfect accompaniment to serve with any grilled or baked seafood. It's also lovely when you add cooked lobster, crab, or shrimp to it and serve it over toast points or in puff pastry shells. Make sure to use a lobster stock for this—seafood stock will not be nearly as luxurious. MAKES 4 CUPS

¼ cup (½ stick) unsalted butter

¼ cup unbleached all-purpose flour

1½ cups lobster stock

2 cups fresh or defrosted frozen white corn

1 tablespoon brandy

½ cup heavy cream

Salt and freshly ground black pepper to taste

Melt the butter in a small saucepan over medium heat. Add the flour, whisking until small white bubbles form on the surface. Cook for 2 minutes, whisking constantly. Slowly add the lobster stock, whisking, and continue to cook until the mixture comes to a boil. Add the corn, brandy, and cream and heat through. Season with salt and pepper. Serve immediately, or cool to room temperature, cover, and refrigerate for up to 3 days. Reheat over low heat before serving.

Baked Maryland Crab Cakes

A MARYLAND SPECIALTY, crab cakes are either fried, broiled, or baked. I think this method of baking them with a flavored butter baste really gives them an awesome flavor. Most locals complain about "filler" in crab cakes, but you need a bit of filler (bread or cracker crumbs) to help hold them together without the aid of a ring mold, which is way too much work! Although you can freeze these, I prefer to make them and refrigerate them a day before I serve them. If you would like to make mini-cakes, shape them into 1- to 1½-inch cakes and bake them for half the time. SERVES 6

1 large egg

¼ cup mayonnaise

1 tablespoon Old Bay seasoning

1 teaspoon Worcestershire sauce

1 teaspoon Dijon mustard

½ cup crushed buttery cracker crumbs (such as Ritz)

1 pound lump crabmeat, picked over for shells and cartilage

½ cup (1 stick) unsalted butter, melted

Make It Now

1. In a large mixing bowl, stir together the egg, mayonnaise, 2½ teaspoons of the Old Bay seasoning, ½ teaspoon of the Worcestershire sauce, the mustard, and the cracker crumbs until combined. Carefully fold in the crab, being careful not to break up the lumps too much.

2. Line a baking sheet or 9 x 13-inch baking dish with aluminum foil, parchment paper, or a silicone baking liner. Form the crab mixture into 6 balls and flatten into cakes about 3 inches wide. Place the cakes on the prepared pan, cover, and refrigerate for up to 24 hours. If you decide to freeze these, place them on a baking sheet and freeze until firm, then transfer to a zipper-top plastic bag, separating them with parchment paper or plastic wrap. Freeze the cakes for up to 4 weeks.

3. Stir the remaining ½ teaspoon Old Bay seasoning and ½ teaspoon Worcestershire sauce into the melted butter, and refrigerate or freeze until you are ready to bake the cakes.

Bake It Later

1. Defrost the crab cakes in the refrigerator overnight, if necessary.

2. Preheat the oven to 375°F. Allow the cakes to come to room temperature for 20 minutes. Rewarm the seasoned butter in a small saucepan or the microwave.

3. Brush the top of each cake with some of the seasoned butter. Bake for 12 minutes, brush the cakes again, and bake for another 10 to 12 minutes, until golden brown. (There is no need to turn the cakes.) Serve hot.

Crab Casserole

BACK IN THE HEYDAY OF CASSEROLE COOKERY in the '50s, '60s, and '70s, you might have eaten a crab casserole and been really sorry you'd tried it because the cook had used canned crab, which can be stringy and fishy tasting. Now, with the advent of pasteurized crabmeat, you can buy refrigerated lump crab that actually tastes like crab. This casserole combines crab with rice in a creamy, cheesy mushroom sauce for a delicious dinner that just needs a veggie or salad on the side. You can feel free to substitute cooked chicken, turkey, or other seafood for the crab if you would like.

SERVES 6

½ cup (1 stick) unsalted butter

¼ cup finely chopped sweet onion, such as Vidalia

½ pound sliced white mushrooms

⅓ cup unbleached all-purpose flour

1 teaspoon Old Bay seasoning

3 cups milk

1 tablespoon cream sherry

1 teaspoon Worcestershire sauce

1½ cups finely shredded imported Swiss cheese, such as Gruyère

1 pound lump crabmeat, picked over for shells and cartilage

Salt and freshly ground black pepper to taste

2 cups cooked rice

Make It Now

1. Melt the butter in a medium-size sauté pan over medium heat. Add the onion and sauté for 2 minutes, until the onion is softened. Add the mushrooms and sauté until the mushroom liquid is absorbed and the mushrooms begin to color, 5 to 7 minutes.

2. Sprinkle the flour and Old Bay seasoning over the vegetables and cook, stirring to cook the flour, for about 2 minutes. Slowly add the milk, scraping up any bits stuck to the bottom of the pan, and bring the sauce to a boil. Add the sherry and Worcestershire sauce, and stir to blend.

3. Remove the pan from the heat and add the cheese a little at a time, stirring until all the cheese is melted. Fold in the crabmeat, being careful not to break up the lumps. Season with salt and pepper.

4. Coat the bottom of a 2-quart casserole dish with nonstick cooking spray. Stir about 1 cup of the crab mixture into the rice, and line the bottom of the casserole with the rice. Top with the remaining crab mixture. Cover and refrigerate for up to 3 days.

Diva Note

This casserole cooks well and looks lovely served in 6 individual gratin dishes or deep ceramic scallop shells. Bake for about 15 minutes, until the topping is golden brown and the sauce is bubbling.

1 cup crushed buttery cracker crumbs (such as Ritz)

½ cup freshly grated Parmesan cheese

1 tablespoon finely chopped fresh flat-leaf parsley

2 tablespoons pure olive oil

Bake It Later

1. Preheat the oven to 350°F. Allow the casserole to come to room temperature for 20 to 30 minutes.

2. In a small bowl, stir together the cracker crumbs, Parmesan cheese, and parsley. Toss with the oil until moist. Sprinkle the crumbs over the casserole and bake the casserole for 25 to 30 minutes, until bubbling and the topping is golden brown. Allow to rest for 5 minutes before serving hot.

Scallop Pie with Parmesan-Herb Puff Pastry Crust

THIS CREAMY SEAFOOD PIE can be served in individual gratin dishes, or you can serve it in a large casserole dish. The creamy filling is reminiscent of the classic coquilles St. Jacques, laced with mushrooms, sherry, and tiny bay scallops. A puff pastry crown rolled in Parmesan and herbs gives added flavor and complements the filling. SERVES 6

6 tablespoons (^{3}/$_4$ stick) unsalted butter

8 ounces white mushrooms, sliced

8 ounces bay scallops or quartered sea scallops

3 tablespoons cream or dry sherry

^{1}/$_4$ cup unbleached all-purpose flour

1^1/$_2$ cups seafood stock, lobster stock, or bottled clam juice

1^1/$_2$ cups heavy cream

Salt and freshly ground black pepper to taste

1 cup finely grated Parmesan cheese

^{1}/$_4$ cup finely chopped fresh thyme

2 tablespoons finely chopped fresh chives

1 or 2 frozen puff pastry sheets (depending on which pan size you choose), defrosted

Make It Now

1. Melt 3 tablespoons of the butter in a medium-size sauté pan over medium heat. Add the mushrooms and sauté for 5 to 6 minutes, until the mushroom liquid has evaporated. Add the scallops and sauté for 1 minute. Add the sherry and toss with the mushrooms and scallops. Drain in a colander set over a bowl, reserving the liquid that drains out.

2. Melt the remaining 3 tablespoons butter in the same pan and add the flour, whisking until white bubbles form on the surface. Whisk constantly for 2 to 3 minutes, then slowly add the stock and the reserved mushroom and scallop liquid and bring the mixture to a boil. Add the cream and return the scallops and mushrooms to the pan. Remove from the heat and season with salt and pepper.

3. In a small bowl, combine the cheese, thyme, and chives. Sprinkle the mixture on a pastry board and roll out 1 sheet of puff pastry, using the cheese mixture as you would flour. If you are using a 9 x 13-inch casserole dish, roll one sheet of the pastry into an 11 x 15-inch rectangle. If you are using gratin dishes, roll the pastry into a 14- to 15-inch square and cut into quarters; you will need both pastry sheets for this presentation.

4. Pour the scallop mixture into a baking dish or dishes, then cover with the puff pastry, crimping the outside

edges in a decorative pattern using the tines of a fork or a pastry crimper. Cover and refrigerate for up to 8 hours.

1 large egg, beaten with 2 tablespoons milk, cream, or water

Bake It Later

1. Preheat the oven to 400°F. Allow the casserole to come to room temperature for 20 to 30 minutes.

2. Brush the pastry with the egg wash, and make a few small slits in the pastry to allow steam to escape. Bake the casserole for 20 to 25 minutes, until the crust is golden brown and the filling is bubbling. Allow to rest for 5 minutes before serving hot.

Pesto Scallops

THIS SIMPLE BUT SOPHISTICATED DISH is a winner any night of the week, and it makes a great company dinner as well. You can prepare your side dish while you are preheating the oven—it's that simple. I like to serve this with orzo, or on top of polenta with a bit of Parmesan cheese mixed into it.

SERVES 4

16 to 20 sea scallops

²/₃ cup prepared basil pesto

1 tablespoon olive oil

Make It Now

1. Wash the scallops and pat them dry with paper towels. Place them in an ovenproof skillet.

2. Stir the pesto and oil together, and top each scallop with some of the pesto. Cover and refrigerate the skillet and any remaining pesto for up to 24 hours.

¹/₄ cup freshly grated Parmigiano-Reggiano cheese

2 tablespoons balsamic vinegar

2 tablespoons heavy cream

Bake It Later

1. Preheat the oven to 400°F. Bring the skillet to room temperature for about 20 minutes.

2. Sprinkle the cheese over the scallops. Bake for 7 to 10 minutes, until the cheese has melted and the pesto is bubbling in the pan. Remove from the oven and plate the scallops, serving 4 per person.

3. Heat the skillet over medium-high heat. Deglaze the pan with the balsamic vinegar and add any remaining pesto and the heavy cream, scraping up the browned bits on the bottom of the pan. Drizzle the sauce over the top of the scallops and serve hot.

Do-Ahead Scampi

SCAMPI **IS ACTUALLY THE ITALIAN WORD FOR "PRAWNS,"** though in America we sometimes use it to refer to large shrimp. Simple to prepare, this really is a great do-ahead dish, because you can make the sauce ahead of time, then bake everything together in the oven and serve it over pasta or rice. I love this version because it has a nice lemon flavor to complement the seafood. You can also use this sauce for fish fillets, but you will need to increase the baking time by 5 to 7 minutes.

SERVES 6

½ cup (1 stick) unsalted butter

¼ cup olive oil

6 cloves garlic, minced

Pinch of red pepper flakes

Grated zest of 1 lemon

3 tablespoons freshly squeezed lemon juice

2 tablespoons finely chopped fresh oregano

1 tablespoon finely chopped fresh flat-leaf parsley

Make It Now

1. Melt the butter with the oil in a large sauté pan over medium heat. Add the garlic and red pepper and sauté for 3 to 4 minutes, until the garlic is fragrant. Remove from the heat and add the lemon zest, lemon juice, oregano, and parsley. Let cool, then transfer to an airtight container and refrigerate for up to 3 days or freeze for up to 1 month.

¼ cup olive oil

2 pounds large shrimp, peeled and deveined

1 cup panko crumbs (optional)

Bake It Later

1. Defrost the sauce in the refrigerator overnight, if necessary.

2. Preheat the oven to 375°F. Rewarm the sauce in the microwave until it is liquid.

3. Pour the olive oil into a large ovenproof baking dish. Turn the shrimp in the oil, and pour all but ¼ cup of the sauce over the shrimp. In a small bowl, toss the remaining sauce with the panko crumbs until they are moist. Sprinkle the crumbs over the shrimp. Bake for 15 minutes, until the shrimp have turned pink and the butter is bubbling. Spoon some of the butter over the top of the shrimp and serve hot.

Creamy Boursin Baked Stuffed Shrimp

THIS ELEGANT DISH CAN BE READY AND WAITING in the fridge for a quick heating in the oven, and then you have a four-star meal for family or friends. Creamy Boursin cheese and smoky ham are a dynamite combination with the shrimp, and the Boursin will ooze a bit, to give you a little bit of a pan sauce when it mixes with the wine in the baking dish. Serve this with steamed or grilled veggies on the side and a salad of mixed greens and orange or grapefruit wedges. SERVES 6

24 jumbo or colossal shrimp, peeled, deveined, and butterflied (see Diva Note)

One 5.2-ounce package Boursin cheese

1/4 cup finely diced Black Forest ham

1 1/2 cups fresh bread crumbs

Make It Now

1. Lay the shrimp in a large baking dish that will hold them comfortably in a single layer. Depending upon the size of shrimp you choose, you may need 2 pans.

2. In a small bowl, stir together the Boursin, ham, and bread crumbs until blended. Spread 1 to 2 tablespoons of the mixture on top of each shrimp, mounding slightly. Cover and refrigerate for up to 2 days.

1 cup panko crumbs

1/4 cup (1/2 stick) unsalted butter, melted

1/2 cup white wine or dry vermouth

Bake It Later

1. Preheat the oven to 350°F. Allow the baking dish to come to room temperature for about 15 minutes.

2. Sprinkle the panko crumbs evenly over the top of the shrimp and drizzle with the butter. Pour the wine into the bottom of the pan. Bake for 15 to 17 minutes, until the filling is golden brown and bubbling. Divide the shrimp among 6 plates, then stir the wine and any residual melted Boursin together in the pan, and drizzle over the top of each shrimp. Serve hot.

Diva Note

To butterfly a shrimp, after removing the back vein, slit the shrimp almost all the way through, so that they will lay flat in the pan.

On the
Side

I could make a meal entirely from side dishes. At a potluck dinner, I'm often eating the side dishes and bypassing the main courses. Possibilities just seem endless with sides—there's so much more you can do than just serving boiled or mashed potatoes or a green salad.

Side dishes make any meal special, with the colors, flavors, and textures that complement various main courses. This chapter will help you take the ordinary vegetable into the extraordinary realm, with a variety of internationally flavored corn casseroles, eggplant rollatini, gratins, and even curried fruit. Naturally, they can all be made up ahead of time, then popped into a hot oven when you're good and ready.

On the Side

Oven-Roasted Corn on the Cob

THIS SIMPLE RECIPE IS A TERRIFIC WAY to serve corn on the cob to a crowd. The corn is coated with a seasoned paste, then wrapped in foil. It can be refrigerated for up to 2 days, then roasted and served. If you would like to take the corn to a potluck, roast it ahead of time, then transport it in the foil packages. You can rewarm it on a grill or in a 325°F oven for 10 minutes. SERVES 10

10 ears of corn, husks and silk removed

²/₃ cup freshly grated Parmesan cheese

¹/₃ cup mayonnaise

¹/₄ cup finely chopped fresh flat-leaf parsley (see Diva Note)

5 cloves garlic, mashed

2 teaspoons sugar

1 teaspoon freshly squeezed lemon juice

³/₄ teaspoon cayenne pepper

Make It Now

1. Cut 10 squares of aluminum foil 1½ times the size of the corn. Place each ear of corn in the center of a piece of aluminum foil.

2. In a small bowl, stir together the Parmesan, mayonnaise, parsley, garlic, sugar, lemon juice, and cayenne until it forms a thick paste.

3. Rub 2 tablespoons of the paste over each piece of corn, and then seal the corn in the foil. Store in zipper-top plastic bags in the refrigerator for up to 2 days or in the freezer for up to 1 month.

Bake It Later

1. Defrost the corn overnight in the refrigerator, if necessary.

2. Preheat the oven to 400°F. Place the corn on a baking sheet and allow to come to room temperature for about 30 minutes.

3. Bake the corn for 10 minutes, turn the corn over, and bake for another 10 minutes. Serve hot, in the foil.

Diva Note

You can add other herbs to the seasoned coating to give your corn a different flavor. Try chopped fresh tarragon, dill, basil, or thyme.

Chipotle Cheddar Corn Casserole
with Variations

THE SMOKY FLAVOR OF CHIPOTLE CHILE balanced by the sweetness of corn makes this dish almost addictive. Just when your taste buds think they're too warm, your brain says, I want more of that! If you don't like your food too spicy, you may want to use half of the chile pepper. SERVES 4 TO 6

2 tablespoons unsalted butter

1/4 cup finely chopped sweet onion, such as Vidalia

1 chipotle chile in adobo sauce, finely chopped

2 tablespoons unbleached all-purpose flour

2 1/4 cups whole milk

2 teaspoons sugar

One 16-ounce bag frozen white corn, defrosted

1/2 to 3/4 cup finely shredded mild cheddar cheese

Make It Now

1. Coat the inside of a 9-inch square baking dish with non-stick cooking spray. Melt the butter in a medium-size saucepan over medium heat. Add the onion and chipotle and sauté for about 2 minutes, until the onion begins to soften.

2. Add the flour, and whisk until white bubbles form on the vegetables. Cook the flour for about 2 minutes, being careful not to burn the chipotle. Gradually add the milk and sugar and bring to a boil, whisking constantly.

3. Add the corn, and stir to blend. Pour the mixture into the prepared dish and sprinkle the cheese over the top. Cool, cover, and refrigerate for up to 2 days or freeze for up to 1 month.

Bake It Later

1. Defrost the casserole in the refrigerator overnight, if necessary.

2. Preheat the oven to 350°F. Allow the casserole to come to room temperature for about 30 minutes.

3. Bake for 30 minutes, until the casserole is bubbling and the cheese is golden brown. Serve hot.

Parmesan-Crusted Corn Casserole with Sun-Dried Tomatoes

Substitute ¼ cup finely chopped sun-dried tomatoes for the chipotle chile and freshly grated Parmesan for the cheddar.

Green Chile Corn Casserole

Substitute one 4-ounce can chopped green chiles, rinsed and drained, for the chipotle, and substitute pepper Jack cheese for the cheddar.

Creamy Herbed Corn Casserole

Omit the chipotle chile and add 2 teaspoons chopped fresh tarragon to the onion while sautéing. Substitute either shredded Gruyère or sliced Brie cheese for the cheddar.

Broccoli au Gratin

ONE OF OUR PRESIDENTS famously had a disdain for broccoli. Even though there was a French chef at the White House, the president was probably remembering steam-table cafeteria broccoli rather than its more appealing blanched, steamed, or roasted preparations. Broccoli au gratin will, I guarantee, convert even the fussiest eater into a broccoli aficionado. Who can resist the delicious flavor of bright green broccoli enfolded in a sharp cheddary sauce with a crispy bread crumb topping? Since the broccoli will bake in the oven, make sure to undercook it when you blanch it; it should have quite a bit of resistance when pierced with the sharp tip of a knife. I've lightened up the cream sauce a bit with chicken broth, but you can certainly substitute additional milk for the broth if you wish. SERVES 6

2 pounds broccoli, cut into small florets

Salt and freshly ground black pepper to taste

5 tablespoons unsalted butter

3 tablespoons unbleached all-purpose flour

1 cup chicken broth

1 cup milk

2 cups finely shredded sharp cheddar cheese

6 dashes of Tabasco sauce (see Diva Note)

1 cup fresh bread crumbs

Make It Now

1. Bring a large pot of salted water to a boil. Add the broccoli and cook for 3 minutes. Drain the broccoli in a colander and sprinkle it with salt and pepper, shaking the broccoli to distribute the seasoning evenly. Leave the broccoli in the colander, as it will weep a bit of moisture once it's been salted.

2. Melt 3 tablespoons of the butter in a large saucepan over medium heat. Add the flour, whisking until smooth. When white bubbles form on the surface, continue to whisk for another 2 minutes. Gradually add the broth and milk and bring to a boil. Remove the pan from the stovetop and add 1½ cups of the cheese and the Tabasco, stirring until the cheese is melted and blended.

3. Spread the broccoli in a 9-inch square baking dish and pour the cheese sauce over the broccoli. Melt the remaining 2 tablespoons butter and toss with the bread crumbs and remaining ½ cup cheese. Sprinkle over the top of the casserole. Cover and refrigerate for up to 2 days or freeze for up to 1 month.

Gratins

Strictly speaking, anything "au gratin" means it is covered with bread crumbs, and sometimes butter and/or cheese, and baked to a golden brown on the top. Usually the vegetables are precooked and then covered with the topping, which works just fine for our make-ahead strategy. My favorites are cauliflower, potatoes, and broccoli au gratin, but you can use this formula for your favorite vegetables with great success. I love cheese sauce, so my recipes provide more than you need if you aren't as cheese-crazed as I am. Freeze any extra sauce, then defrost in the microwave and serve over your favorite cooked vegetables. In addition to the two recipes that follow, look for other gratins on pages 147, 252, and 253.

Bake It Later

1. Defrost the casserole in the refrigerator overnight, if necessary.

2. Preheat the oven to 350°F. Allow the casserole to come to room temperature for about 30 minutes.

3. Bake the broccoli for 25 to 30 minutes, until the casserole is bubbling and the topping is golden brown. Remove from the oven and serve immediately.

Diva Note

Why the Tabasco? you might ask. Well, Tabasco sauce brings out the flavor of cheeses, and I recommend it in place of pepper in cheesy dishes because it complements the flavors.

Cauliflower au Gratin

THIS SIMPLE GRATIN USES MILD MONTEREY JACK mixed with Gruyère for a sublimely smooth and delicious sauce with a hint of Dijon mustard. I think it works beautifully with the cauliflower; of course, if you'd prefer to use the cheddar cheese sauce from the Broccoli au Gratin (page 240), that is fine, too. SERVES 6

One 2½- to 3-pound cauliflower, cut into small florets

Salt and freshly ground black pepper to taste

¼ cup (½ stick) unsalted butter

3 tablespoons unbleached all-purpose flour

2 cups milk

1 tablespoon Dijon mustard

1 cup finely shredded Monterey Jack cheese

1 cup finely shredded Gruyère or other imported Swiss cheese

6 dashes of Tabasco sauce

1 cup fresh bread crumbs

Make it Now

1. Bring a large pot of salted water to a boil. Add the cauliflower and boil the florets for 2 minutes. Drain in a colander and sprinkle with salt and pepper, gently tossing the cauliflower to distribute the salt and pepper evenly. Set the cauliflower aside in the colander.

2. Coat the inside of a 9-inch square baking dish with nonstick cooking spray. Spread the cauliflower in the dish evenly.

3. Melt 3 tablespoons of the butter in a medium-size saucepan over medium heat. Add the flour, whisking until smooth. When the flour begins to form white bubbles, whisk constantly for at least another 2 minutes. Add the milk and mustard, and continue whisking until the mixture comes to a boil. Remove from the heat and add the Monterey Jack, ½ cup of the Gruyère cheese, and the Tabasco sauce, stirring until the cheese is melted. Pour the sauce over the cauliflower in the baking dish.

4. Melt the remaining 1 tablespoon butter and toss with the bread crumbs and remaining ½ cup Gruyère. Sprinkle over the top of the cheese sauce. Cover and refrigerate for up to 2 days or freeze for up to 1 month.

1. Defrost the casserole in the refrigerator overnight, if necessary.

2. Preheat the oven to 350°F. Allow the casserole to come to room temperature for about 30 minutes.

3. Bake for 25 to 30 minutes, until the cheese sauce is bubbling and the topping is golden brown. Serve immediately.

VARIATION

Fennel au Gratin

Substitute fennel for the cauliflower. Trim the root ends, tougher stalks, and wispy fronds from 4 fennel bulbs. Slice the bulbs on the diagonal into ½-inch-thick slices (no need to cook the fennel) and lay the slices in the prepared baking dish. Add the sauce and topping and bake the fennel for 15 minutes, until bubbling. Freezing Fennel au Gratin before baking is not recommended, but it will keep in the refrigerator for up to 2 days before baking.

Creamy Green Bean Bake with Crumb Topping

THIS CREAMY GREEN BEAN CASSEROLE is nothing like its cousin with the cream-of-mushroom-soup sauce and canned-fried-onion-ring topping. This green bean make-ahead dish has a sour cream sauce and is topped with a bubbling blanket of Swiss cheese and crunchy panko crumbs. Serve this with grilled or roasted meats, poultry, or seafood. SERVES 6

1 pound green beans or a combination of yellow and green beans, ends trimmed

6 tablespoons unsalted butter

¼ cup unbleached all-purpose flour

1 teaspoon salt

½ teaspoon freshly ground black pepper

2 teaspoons sugar

2 cups sour cream (do not use low-fat)

2 cups finely shredded Swiss cheese

½ cup panko crumbs or dried bread crumbs

Make It Now

1. Bring a large pot of salted water to a boil and blanch the beans for 2 minutes. Drain and set aside.

2. Coat the inside of a 9- to 10-inch square baking dish with nonstick cooking spray and set aside.

3. Melt 4 tablespoons of the butter in a large saucepan over medium heat. Stir in the flour, salt, pepper, and sugar, stirring until the mixture bubbles. Lower the heat, stir in the sour cream, and whisk until the mixture has thickened. Fold in the cooked beans and toss to coat.

4. Spread the beans in the prepared baking dish, and sprinkle evenly with the cheese. Melt the remaining 2 tablespoons butter, blend with the panko, and sprinkle the top of the casserole with the crumbs. Cover and refrigerate for up to 2 days.

Bake It Later

1. Preheat the oven to 350°F. Allow the casserole to come to room temperature for about 30 minutes.

2. Bake the beans for 20 to 25 minutes, until the sauce is bubbling and the crumbs are golden brown. Serve immediately.

Eggplant Rollatini

ROLLED EGGPLANT STUFFED WITH A CHEESY BREAD CRUMB FILLING and topped with a delicious tomato sauce makes an excellent side dish with grilled or roasted meats, poultry, or seafood. Or you can double the recipe and serve it as a main course. It can be served hot or at room temperature, giving you another versatile dish that can be taken from freezer to oven or covered grill. Since the eggplant is broiled rather than fried, it's not nearly the production that eggplant Parmesan is.

SERVES 4 TO 6

1 large purple eggplant, ends removed and cut lengthwise in ½-inch slices

1 cup olive oil

2 teaspoons salt

1 teaspoon freshly ground black pepper

2 cups Quick Marinara Sauce (page 246)

2 cups fresh bread crumbs

2 cloves garlic, minced

2 tablespoons finely chopped fresh basil

2 tablespoons finely chopped fresh flat-leaf parsley

¾ cup freshly grated Parmesan cheese

1 large egg

One 8-ounce ball fresh mozzarella cheese

Make It Now

1. Preheat the broiler for 10 minutes. Line a baking sheet with aluminum foil and place the eggplant slices on the baking sheet.

2. In a small bowl, combine the oil, salt, and pepper. Brush the slices with the oil and broil on one side for 5 to 7 minutes, until the eggplant begins to turn golden brown. Turn the slices over, brush again with the oil, and broil until browned. Set aside to cool. (At this point, you may refrigerate for up to 2 days.)

3. Spread 1 cup of the marinara sauce in a baking dish. Depending upon your eggplant, you may need a 9 x 13-inch dish (for more than 8 slices of eggplant) or a 9- to 10-inch baking dish (for 8 or fewer slices).

4. In a small bowl, combine the bread crumbs, garlic, basil, parsley, ½ cup of the Parmesan cheese, and the egg, stirring to combine. Cut the mozzarella cheese into quarters. Dice one-quarter of the mozzarella into tiny pieces and add to the bread crumb mixture. Drizzle in some of the leftover olive oil mixture if the bread crumb mixture seems dry.

5. Lay an eggplant slice on a flat surface and place 1 to 2 tablespoons of the filling in the center of the slice. Roll up the eggplant and place seam side down on the marinara sauce in the prepared dish. Continue to stuff and roll the slices and place them in the dish. Cover

with some of the remaining marinara sauce. Cut the remaining 3 mozzarella quarters into ¼-inch-thick slices and distribute them evenly over the rolls. Sprinkle with the remaining ¼ cup Parmesan. Cover and refrigerate for up to 2 days or freeze for up to 1 month. Refrigerate or freeze any remaining sauce.

Fresh basil leaves for garnish (optional)

Bake It Later

1. Defrost the eggplant in the refrigerator overnight, if necessary.

2. Preheat the oven to 350°F. Allow the eggplant to come to room temperature for about 30 minutes.

3. Bake the eggplant for 35 to 40 minutes, until the cheese is melted and begins to turn golden brown. Serve hot, warm, or at room temperature garnished with the basil, if desired.

Quick Marinara Sauce

A PLAIN AND SIMPLE SAUCE to use for pasta, roasted or grilled meats, or vegetables, this marinara can be jazzed up with your favorite additions: try fresh or dried mushrooms; black olives and capers; fresh Italian herbs; or cooked sausage, meatballs, Italian tuna, clams, or shrimp. MAKES ABOUT 3 CUPS

2 tablespoons olive oil

½ cup finely chopped sweet onion, such as Vidalia

2 cloves garlic, minced

One 32-ounce can crushed tomatoes (do not drain)

1½ teaspoons salt

½ teaspoon freshly ground black pepper

1 teaspoon sugar

1. Heat the oil in a medium-size saucepan over medium heat. Add the onion and garlic and sauté, stirring, until the onion begins to turn translucent, about 3 minutes.

2. Add the tomatoes, salt, pepper, and sugar, and simmer, uncovered, stirring occasionally, until the sauce is reduced and thickened, 30 to 45 minutes. Use immediately, or let cool and refrigerate for up to 4 days or freeze for up to 3 months.

Plentiful Potatoes

I've never met a potato I didn't like. Sometimes I feel like Bubba in the movie *Forrest Gump*, extolling the gloriously different ways to prepare potatoes: fried, baked, stuffed, au gratin, Delmonico, O'Brien. . . . I could go on and on and on! For our make-ahead purposes, potatoes are an ideal side dish, and most can be refrigerated or frozen so that you have them on hand for unexpected emergencies.

Peeling potatoes or leaving the skins on is a personal choice most of the time, but if the potatoes have a greenish tinge on the skin, you will need to remove that. It is a toxin that is caused by exposure to light, and it can make you sick if you eat it. Once it's peeled off, though, there's no problem with eating the rest of the potato. If the skins of your potatoes aren't really nice looking, and have lots of black spots, I would advise you to peel those as well.

There are lots of varieties of potatoes to choose from, and a little information on them might be helpful. I've recommended particular types of potatoes for the best results in each dish, because some perform better than others in certain preparations.

- **High-starch potatoes:** These are generally russet Burbank, also called baking potatoes, Idaho potatoes, or simply russet potatoes. They are terrific baked, stuffed, mashed, or fried.

- **Lower-starch potatoes:** Red, Yukon gold, and white creamer potatoes, as well as any potatoes labeled "new" potatoes, are used primarily in dishes where they will need to absorb liquids, like gratins, but they are delicious when roasted as well. They can also be boiled, for mashed potatoes and for potato salads.

- **Sweet potatoes:** In your grocery store they may be labeled as "yams," but a true yam is yellow in color and is native to Asia and Africa, and we seldom see true yams in this country unless at a specialty store. Sweet potatoes have orange-colored flesh and a high sugar content. They are delicious roasted or baked, and they can be mashed after baking.

Baked Stuffed Spuds Six Ways

ALTHOUGH YOU HAVE TO BAKE THE POTATOES before they can be made into stuffed spuds, the beauty of these potatoes is that they can be frozen, so if you need an emergency "dress-up" side dish for a dinner, this is it! Otherwise, the potatoes can be kept refrigerated for up to 24 hours. This recipe is easily doubled or tripled for larger groups, and I urge you to try the variations. SERVES 4

5 large russet baking potatoes, pricked with the point of a sharp knife in several places

Olive oil

¼ cup (½ stick) unsalted butter, melted

About ½ cup milk, warmed

1½ teaspoons salt

½ teaspoon freshly ground black pepper

Diva Note

You will notice that the recipe calls for five potatoes to serve four people. Sometimes when you've baked the potatoes, you will find that one of the potatoes may not be good all the way through, with a brown spot or tough area. The fifth potato is your insurance for making these potato halves nice and generous and may save you from having to bake more. You won't be able to tell if the potato is okay until after it's been baked, but look for potatoes with no green tinge on the skin.

Make It Now

1. Preheat the oven to 400°F. Rub the potatoes with olive oil and bake until soft when pinched with a pot holder, about 1 hour. Set aside for about 10 minutes to cool slightly.

2. With a serrated knife, cut the potatoes in half lengthwise and, using a spoon, remove the flesh to a large mixing bowl, leaving a ½-inch-thick shell. Set the shells aside.

3. Using an electric mixer, beat the potatoes with the butter and some of the warmed milk until they are fluffy. Depending on the potatoes, you may not use all the milk, but do use all the butter. Season the mashed potatoes with the salt and pepper and stuff the mixture back into the shells, mounding them slightly. Cover and refrigerate for up to 24 hours or freeze for up to 1 month.

Bake It Later

1. Defrost the potatoes in the refrigerator overnight, if necessary.

2. Preheat the oven to 350°F. Allow the potatoes to come to room temperature for about 30 minutes.

3. Bake the potatoes for 15 minutes, or until heated through and beginning to brown. Serve immediately.

Blue Heaven Stuffed Spuds

Add ½ cup crumbled blue cheese and 2 tablespoons freshly snipped chives along with the butter.

Loaded Stuffed Spuds

When you add the butter, also add ¼ cup sour cream, 1 cup finely shredded sharp cheddar cheese, 6 strips cooked crumbled bacon, and 2 green onions (white and tender green parts), finely chopped.

Chili Cheese Spuds

Melt 2 tablespoons unsalted butter in a small sauté pan over medium heat. Add ¼ cup finely chopped sweet onion and ½ teaspoon chipotle chile powder and sauté, until the onion is translucent and the chile powder is fragrant, 2 to 3 minutes. Stir into the potato mixture along with the melted butter, milk, and ½ cup finely shredded mild cheddar cheese and ½ cup finely shredded Monterey Jack cheese.

Shrimply Awesome Spuds

Melt 1 tablespoon butter in a small sauté pan over medium heat. Add 1 teaspoon Old Bay seasoning and ¼ pound medium-size raw shrimp, peeled and coarsely chopped. Sauté until the shrimp are barely pink. Stir into the mashed potato mixture along with the butter.

Pizza Spuds

Fill the potato shells halfway with the potato mixture, then top each with 1 tablespoon Oven-Roasted Tomatoes (page 98) and a ½-inch-thick slice of fresh mozzarella cheese. Cover with the remaining potato mixture and sprinkle each with 1 tablespoon freshly grated Parmesan cheese.

Diva's Do-Ahead Mashed Potatoes

EVERY YEAR I TEACH EAGER STUDENTS how to prepare a stress-free Thanksgiving dinner, and these potatoes change their lives because they can be made ahead and then refrigerated or frozen. This is the family-style version, and you can vary the cheese and add your favorite flavors to make them your own; just follow the basic recipe. SERVES 6

4 large russet baking potatoes, peeled and cut into 1-inch chunks

½ teaspoon salt

3 tablespoons unsalted butter, softened

⅓ cup freshly grated Parmesan cheese

½ cup sour cream

4 ounces cream cheese, softened

2 tablespoons chopped fresh chives (optional)

Salt and freshly ground black pepper to taste

Make It Now

1. Place the potatoes in a large saucepan with water to cover. Add the salt, bring to a boil, and boil until tender, about 15 minutes. Drain thoroughly and place in a large bowl.

2. Rub a 9-inch square baking dish with some of the butter. Sprinkle 2 tablespoons of the cheese over the butter in the dish and tilt the dish to distribute it evenly.

3. Add the sour cream, cream cheese, 2 tablespoons of the remaining butter, all but 2 tablespoons of the remaining cheese, and the chives, if using, to the potatoes. Using an electric mixer, beat the potatoes until they are smooth. Season with salt and pepper.

4. Transfer to the prepared dish, dot with any remaining butter, and sprinkle with the remaining 2 tablespoons cheese. Cover and refrigerate for up to 3 days or freeze for up to 1 month.

Bake It Later

1. Defrost the potatoes in the refrigerator overnight, if necessary.

2. Preheat the oven to 350°F. Allow the potatoes to come to room temperature for about 30 minutes.

3. Bake for 25 to 30 minutes, until puffed and golden brown. Serve hot.

Garlic-Herb Mashed Potatoes

Substitute one 5.2-ounce package Boursin cheese for the cream cheese. (You may omit the Parmesan if you like.)

Garlic Mashed Potatoes

Peel 2 or 3 cloves of garlic and add them to the potatoes while they are boiling. Drain and mash them together with the other ingredients.

More Cheesy Mashed Potatoes

Substitute shredded cheddar, Gruyère, Asiago, or provolone or crumbled blue cheese for the Parmesan.

Everything-Tastes-Better-with-Bacon Mashed Potatoes

Cook 6 strips bacon until crisp. Crumble and add to the potatoes when mashing—save a bit for garnishing the top, if you like.

Prosciutto di Parma Mashed Potatoes

Julienne 4 slices prosciutto and add to the potatoes when mashing.

Potato Gratin

SCALLOPED POTATOES—OR POTATO GRATINS—are quintessential comfort food, but sometimes they can end up partially cooked in the center, or too hard and tough on the top. With this method, your potatoes are cooked through, creamy in the center, and topped with a cheesy crunchy topping. Potato heaven doesn't get much better! SERVES 6 TO 8

6 medium-size red potatoes

½ cup finely sliced sweet onion, such as Vidalia

1 cup heavy cream

1 cup whole milk

1 teaspoon salt

6 dashes of Tabasco sauce

1½ cups finely shredded cheese (such as Gruyère, fontina, cheddar, pepper Jack, havarti with dill) or crumbled blue cheese

Make It Now

1. Using the slicing blade of a food processor, thinly slice the potatoes. Place the potatoes and onion in a large sauté pan. Add the cream, milk, salt, and Tabasco and bring to a boil. Reduce the heat to medium and simmer until the potatoes are tender, about 6 minutes. They will not be cooked through and should still hold their shape.

2. Coat the inside of a 9-inch square baking dish with non-stick cooking spray. Transfer half of the potato and onion mixture to the baking dish, along with some of the sauce, and sprinkle with ¾ cup of the cheese. Cover with the remaining potatoes and sauce and sprinkle with the remaining ¾ cup cheese. Cover and refrigerate for up to 24 hours or freeze for up to 1 month.

Bake It Later

1. Defrost the potatoes in the refrigerator overnight, if necessary.

2. Preheat the oven to 375°F. Allow the potatoes to come to room temperature for about 30 minutes.

3. Bake, covered, for 15 minutes. Uncover and bake for an additional 10 to 15 minutes, until golden brown. Allow the potatoes to rest for 10 to 15 minutes before serving hot.

Brandied Sweet Potato–Apple Gratin

FOR YEARS, I'VE TAUGHT A VERSION OF THIS DELICIOUS DISH at my Do-Ahead Thanksgiving classes, using sherry. But when testing the recipes for this book, I substituted brandy and love the combination! If you decide you just can't wait till Thanksgiving, then try these the next time you roast a ham, a chicken, or a pork loin. They are a treat at any time of year. SERVES 4

Two 15.5-ounce cans sweet potatoes, drained, or 4 large sweet potatoes, baked until soft, and peeled (see Diva Note)

1/3 cup unsalted butter, melted

1/3 cup firmly packed light brown sugar

1/3 cup dark corn syrup

1 tablespoon brandy

1 teaspoon ground cinnamon

Pinch of ground nutmeg

2 medium-size apples, peeled, cored, and sliced 1/4 inch thick

Diva Note

Some purists won't use canned sweet potatoes, but my feeling is that when you are adding so many flavors to enhance the potato, you might not taste the difference between canned and freshly baked. If you would prefer to bake your own, prick them several times with the sharp point of a knife and bake them at 400°F for 50 to 60 minutes, until the potatoes are soft when squeezed with a pot holder.

Make It Now

1. In the bowl of an electric mixer, beat together the sweet potatoes, 2 tablespoons of the butter, the brown sugar, corn syrup, brandy, cinnamon, and nutmeg at medium speed, until smooth.

2. Coat the inside of a 9-inch baking dish with nonstick cooking spray. Spread half of the sweet potato mixture in the dish. Top with a layer of apples, then the remaining sweet potato mixture. Cover the sweet potatoes with the remaining apple slices, arranging them in an artful pattern. Brush the top of the apples with the remaining butter, completely coating the apples so that they don't discolor. Cover and refrigerate for up to 4 days or freeze for up to 1 month.

Bake It Later

1. Defrost the casserole in the refrigerator overnight, if necessary.

2. Preheat the oven to 350°F. Allow the casserole to come to room temperature for about 30 minutes.

3. Bake for 30 to 40 minutes, until the apples are golden brown. Serve hot.

Baked Stuffed Chipotle-Maple Sweet Potatoes

ANOTHER WAY TO PREPARE SWEET POTATOES is to bake and stuff them; this version uses chipotle chiles to give them smoky-hot personality, sweetened with a touch of maple syrup. Try these in place of your usual potato side dish and your family will love you for it! SERVES 4

4 large sweet potatoes, pricked several times with the sharp point of a knife

½ cup (1 stick) unsalted butter

½ chipotle chile in adobo sauce, finely minced, with a bit of the adobo sauce

2 tablespoons pure maple syrup

½ teaspoon salt

About ¼ cup milk, warmed

Make It Now

1. Preheat the oven to 400°F.

2. Bake the sweet potatoes for 50 to 60 minutes, until they are soft when squeezed with an oven mitt. Set aside to cool for about 15 minutes, then cut each potato in half lengthwise with a serrated knife. Remove the flesh from the skin and place in a large bowl, leaving ¼ inch of flesh in the shell.

3. Melt the butter in a small saucepan over low heat. Add the chipotle and adobo sauce. Stir for about 3 minutes. (Heating the chipotle will develop its flavor.) Stir the chipotle butter, maple syrup, and salt into the potatoes. Using an electric mixer, beat at medium speed until smooth. Add milk until the potato puree is smooth and about the consistency of mashed potatoes, not dry, but on the wetter side.

4. Stuff the shells with the mixture, cover, and refrigerate for up to 2 days or freeze for up to 1 month.

Bake It Later

1. Defrost the potatoes in the refrigerator overnight, if necessary.

2. Preheat the oven to 350°F. Allow the sweet potatoes to come to room temperature for about 30 minutes.

3. Bake for 30 minutes, until the sweet potatoes are heated through and begin to turn golden brown on the top. Serve hot.

Spinach Soufflé

AS A CHILD, I LOVED STOUFFER'S FROZEN SPINACH SOUFFLÉ, but it took so long to cook. This souf-flé is simple to make and needs to be frozen in small ramekins for optimum effect. Bake these straight from the freezer for a delicious and light side dish. SERVES 4 TO 6

2 tablespoons unsalted butter

¼ cup unbleached all-purpose flour

1 cup milk

Salt and freshly ground black pepper to taste

½ teaspoon ground nutmeg

One 16-ounce package frozen chopped spinach, defrosted and squeezed dry

3 large eggs, separated

Pinch of cream of tartar

Make It Now

1. Coat the inside of six 4-ounce ramekins with nonstick cooking spray and set aside.

2. Melt the butter in a medium-size saucepan over medium heat. Whisk in the flour and cook until bubbles form on the surface. Whisk continually for 2 more minutes to cook the flour. Gradually add the milk, stirring until it comes to a boil. Season with salt and pepper and add the nutmeg. Add the spinach, stirring until blended. Remove from the heat, and whisk in the egg yolks, one at a time.

3. In a small bowl, beat the egg whites with the cream of tartar until stiff peaks form. Using a balloon whisk, gently fold the egg whites into the spinach mixture. Spoon the mixture into the prepared ramekins, cover, and freeze for up to 1 month.

Bake It Later

1. Preheat the oven to 375°F.

2. Bake the frozen soufflés for 25 minutes, until puffed and golden. Serve immediately.

Southern Summer Squash Casserole

SOUTHERN SQUASH CASSEROLES ARE LEGENDARY: comforting, with a rich, crispy crumb topping. These casseroles are delicious alongside everything from roasted chicken and ham to grilled meats and seafood. There are lots of variations on the theme, and I love every one. This casserole freezes very well before baking, and it can be served in a casserole dish or in six individual ramekins for a fancier presentation. SERVES 6

¼ cup (½ stick) unsalted butter

½ cup finely chopped sweet onion, such as Vidalia

8 to 9 medium-size yellow crookneck squash, ends trimmed and cut into ½-inch-thick slices (about 6 cups)

1½ teaspoons salt

½ teaspoon freshly ground black pepper

1 teaspoon sugar

1½ cups fresh bread crumbs

2 large eggs, beaten

¼ cup mayonnaise

Make It Now

1. Coat the inside of a 9-inch square baking dish or 6 individual ramekins with nonstick cooking spray. Melt 2 tablespoons of the butter in a large skillet over medium heat. Add the onion and squash and sauté until the squash is tender and the onions are translucent, about 6 minutes. Season with the salt, pepper, and sugar, and let cool in the pan.

2. In a large bowl, stir together 1 cup of the bread crumbs with the eggs and mayonnaise. Add the squash mixture and stir to combine. Turn the mixture into the prepared baking dish.

3. Melt the remaining 2 tablespoons butter and toss with the remaining ½ cup bread crumbs. Sprinkle over the top of the casserole. Cover and refrigerate for up to 2 days or freeze for up to 1 month.

Bake It Later

1. Defrost the casserole in the refrigerator overnight, if necessary.

2. Preheat the oven to 350°F. Allow the casserole to come to room temperature for about 30 minutes.

3. Bake, uncovered, for 30 to 35 minutes, until lightly golden brown. Serve hot.

Cheesy Squash Casserole

Add 1½ cups of shredded cheese to the bread crumb–butter mixture. Great choices for the cheese are cheddar, Swiss, Monterey Jack, pepper Jack, Munster, fontina, and provolone.

Herbed Squash Casserole

Add 1 teaspoon of one of the following dried herbs or combinations to the squash and onions when sautéing: thyme, basil, herbes de Provence, Italian seasoning, or chili powder.

Hot Tamale Squash Casserole

Add one 4-ounce can diced green chiles, rinsed and drained, to the squash and onions when sautéing. Use crumbled cornbread in place of the bread crumbs, and sprinkle the top with shredded Monterey Jack and cheddar cheeses. This variation is great with grilled meats for a south-of-the-border side.

Zucchini Pizzaiola

THIS SIMPLE DISH IS A GREAT WAY to use up leftover zucchini from your garden. It's best to use small zucchini, about 6 inches in length. The sautéed zucchini and onions form a crust for the tomatoes and cheese, and the whole thing can be refrigerated for a day before baking. Serve it with grilled meats, poultry, or seafood entrées or as a light luncheon entrée. SERVES 6

1/4 cup olive oil

Four 6-inch zucchini, ends trimmed and cut into 1/2-inch-thick slices

Salt and freshly ground black pepper to taste

1 small sweet onion, such as Vidalia, thinly sliced

2 medium-size tomatoes, cut into 1/4-inch-thick slices

2 teaspoons chopped fresh oregano

1/4 cup finely shredded mozzarella cheese

2 tablespoons freshly grated Parmesan cheese

Make It Now

1. Heat 2 tablespoons of the oil in a medium-size sauté pan over medium heat. Add the zucchini and sauté for a few minutes, sprinkling with salt and pepper. Add the onion, and sauté for another 4 to 5 minutes, until the vegetables begin to color. Remove from the pan and drain in a colander.

2. Coat the inside of a 9-inch pie plate with nonstick cooking spray. Arrange the zucchini and onion in the plate and top with the tomatoes. Sprinkle with the oregano, mozzarella cheese, and Parmesan cheese, and drizzle with the remaining 2 tablespoons olive oil. Cover and refrigerate for up to 24 hours.

Bake It Later

1. Preheat the oven to 375°F. Allow the zucchini to come to room temperature for about 30 minutes.

2. Bake the pie for 12 to 15 minutes, until the cheese is bubbling and golden brown. Serve warm or at room temperature.

VARIATION

Use crumbled goat cheese in place of the mozzarella and Parmesan.

Oven-Fried Zucchini

A CRISPY COATING OF PARMESAN-FLAVORED PANKO CRUMBS gives zucchini lots of personality. I like long "planks" made by slicing the zucchini lengthwise, but you can also slice it into rounds, if you prefer. SERVES 4

2 large eggs

2 tablespoons water

1 teaspoon salt

1 teaspoon freshly ground black pepper

2 cups panko crumbs

1 cup freshly grated Parmesan cheese

½ teaspoon dried oregano

½ teaspoon dried basil

3 medium-size zucchini, ends trimmed and cut lengthwise into ¼-inch-thick slices

⅓ cup olive oil

Make It Now

1. In a medium-size bowl, whisk together the eggs, water, salt, and ½ teaspoon of the pepper. In a shallow dish, stir together the panko, cheese, the remaining ½ teaspoon pepper, and the oregano and basil.

2. Line a baking sheet with aluminum foil, parchment paper, or a silicone baking liner. Dip the zucchini pieces into the egg mixture, then into the panko mixture, pressing the crumbs into the zucchini. Lay the zucchini pieces on the baking sheet, continuing until all the pieces are coated. Carefully drizzle some of the oil over each slice of zucchini (or you can use an olive oil nonstick cooking spray if you prefer). Cover and refrigerate for up to 24 hours or freeze for up to 1 month.

Bake It Later

1. Defrost the zucchini in the refrigerator overnight, if necessary.

2. Preheat the oven to 425°F. Allow the zucchini to come to room temperature for about 15 minutes.

3. Bake the zucchini for 10 to 12 minutes, until golden brown. Remove from the oven and serve warm or at room temperature.

Mrs. Fitz's Boston Baked Beans

MY GRANDMOTHER, NORA GEARY FITZ-PATRICK, came from Connemara, Ireland, to work as a cook for wealthy Boston families in the early 1900s. She soon learned that Boston baked beans were a staple in these households, not only for the domestic help, but sometimes for the upstairs residents of the house, who would sneak downstairs to the kitchen to eat a bowl. This is her recipe, with my addition of a bit of garlic and Dijon mustard to give the beans a flavor boost. Note that in true old-fashioned baked bean style, these use dried beans and bake at a low temperature for many hours.

SERVES 8 TO 10

2 cups dried small white pea beans, rinsed and picked over

4 strips bacon, cut into 2-inch dice

1 large onion, coarsely chopped

¼ cup dark molasses

2 tablespoons Dijon mustard

1 clove garlic, minced

1 bay leaf

1½ teaspoons salt

½ teaspoon freshly ground black pepper

½ teaspoon dried thyme

¼ teaspoon ground ginger

5 cups water (more may be needed toward the end of the baking time)

Make It Now

1. Coat the inside of a deep 4-quart casserole dish or bean pot with nonstick cooking spray. Combine the beans, bacon, onion, molasses, mustard, garlic, bay leaf, salt, pepper, thyme, and ginger in the bean pot. Cover and refrigerate for up to 2 days.

Bake It Later

1. Preheat the oven to 300°F. Allow the beans to come to room temperature for about 30 minutes.

2. Add the water to the bean pot, stirring up anything that might be on the bottom of the bean pot. Bake for 8 hours, stirring occasionally to prevent sticking, and adding more water if the beans seem to be too thick. Remove the bay leaf. Serve hot.

Cowboy Beans

FOR THOSE WHO LIKE A LOT OF SASS IN THEIR BEANS, Cowboy Beans are the way to go. Filled with nuggets of sausage and onion and bathed in a full-flavored tomato-based sauce, these beans are a hit at any barbecue. If you like spicy beans, try the Jimmy Dean "Bold Flavored" or other hot sausage. I love its bold spicy flavor balanced against the sweet-tasting beans. SERVES 8

12 ounces bulk pork sausage
(I like Jimmy Dean)

1½ cups chopped yellow onion

Three 32-ounce cans plain baked beans

¼ cup dark molasses

⅔ cup ketchup

2 tablespoons Worcestershire sauce

2 tablespoons Dijon mustard

½ cup firmly packed light brown sugar

Make It Now

1. Cook the sausage in a large Dutch oven over medium heat, breaking it apart and sautéing until it is no longer pink. Drain off the fat that has accumulated in the pan. Add the onion and sauté for another 3 to 4 minutes, until translucent.

2. Add the beans, molasses, ketchup, Worcestershire sauce, mustard, and brown sugar, stirring to blend. Let cool, then cover and refrigerate for up to 4 days or freeze for up to 1 month.

Bake It Later

1. Defrost the beans in the refrigerator overnight, if necessary.

2. Preheat the oven to 350°F. Allow the beans to come to room temperature for about 30 minutes.

3. Bake the beans, covered, for 30 minutes. Uncover and bake for another 20 to 30 minutes, until bubbling and heated through. Serve hot.

VARIATION

Just before you put the beans in the oven, lay 6 strips of bacon over the top of the beans.

Refried Bean Casserole

REFRIED BEANS ARE A GREAT SIDE for a Southwestern meal or to include in burritos. They can be used out of the can, you can make your own (too much work!), or you can jazz up the canned beans so that they have lots of personality. I prefer the third option, and this version can be waiting in the fridge for a quick reheating in the oven when you are ready. Feel free to use the low-fat or the fat-free beans; they all work well in this presentation. SERVES 4

2 tablespoons olive oil

½ teaspoon ground chipotle chile powder

1 teaspoon ground cumin

Two 15.5-ounce cans refried beans

¼ cup salsa of your choice

½ cup sour cream

1 cup finely shredded mild cheddar cheese

½ cup shredded Monterey Jack cheese

Make It Now

1. Coat the inside of a 9-inch square baking dish with non-stick cooking spray.

2. Heat the oil in a small sauté pan over medium heat. Add the chile powder and cumin and sauté for about 2 minutes, being careful to stir it so it doesn't burn.

3. Pour the oil into a large mixing bowl and add the refried beans, salsa, and sour cream, stirring until blended.

4. Spread half of the beans in the prepared dish and sprinkle with ½ cup of the cheddar cheese and ¼ cup of the Monterey Jack cheese. Cover with the remaining beans and sprinkle with the remaining cheeses. Cover and refrigerate for up to 3 days or freeze for up to 1 month.

Bake It Later

1. Defrost the casserole in the refrigerator overnight, if necessary.

2. Preheat the oven to 350°F. Allow the casserole to come to room temperature for 30 minutes.

3. Bake for 20 to 25 minutes, until the beans are bubbling and the cheeses are melting. Serve hot.

Curried Fruit

AN OLD STAPLE IN MY HOUSE, this mélange of fruit bubbling in a curried brown sugar glaze is just the ticket to serve alongside ham, pork, or poultry. You may use fruits canned in natural juice or in syrup, depending on your personal preference. Use the fruit as a garnish or serve it as a separate side dish. Try the sherry variation, too! SERVES 6 TO 8

½ cup (1 stick) unsalted butter

1 teaspoon curry powder

⅔ cup firmly packed dark brown sugar

One 15.5-ounce can pear halves, drained, juice reserved

One 15.5-ounce can pineapple slices, drained, juice reserved

One 16-ounce bag frozen peaches, defrosted and drained, *or* one 15.5-ounce can peaches, drained

1 cup dried apricots

Make It Now

1. Melt the butter in a small saucepan over medium heat. Add the curry powder and cook for 1 minute, until fragrant. Add the brown sugar and stir until melted. Stir in about ¼ cup of the reserved pear and pineapple juices. Set the mixture aside to cool.

2. Coat the inside of a 9 x 13-inch baking dish with nonstick cooking spray. Arrange the pears, pineapple slices, peaches, and apricots in the dish (it's all right if they aren't all laying flat). Pour the cooled syrup over the fruit. Cover and refrigerate for up to 4 days.

Bake It Later

1. Preheat the oven to 350°F. Allow the casserole to come to room temperature for about 30 minutes.

2. Bake for 35 to 40 minutes, basting the fruit with the sauce twice during the cooking time. Serve hot, warm, or at room temperature.

VARIATION

Substitute ½ teaspoon Chinese five-spice powder for the curry powder, and add 2 tablespoons sherry to the saucepan along with the fruit juices.

Caramelized Pears

THESE INCREDIBLY VERSATILE PEARS are scrumptious served warm with roasted poultry or pork. They can also be sliced after cooking and used to top salads of field greens and blue cheese. Or you can chill them, then chop them, mix them with a bit of the glaze, and serve as part of a cheese platter either before or after dinner. Or go the all-out dessert route and serve them warm, on a bed of pound cake with a topping of vanilla ice cream! Any leftovers can be frozen in an airtight container for up to 4 months.

The type of pear you decide to use will probably depend upon what is available. I have used red, Bosc, and d'Anjou pears, as well as Asian pears, and they all worked well. Red pears are my first choice for flavor and texture. Make sure that the pears aren't fully ripened and soft, so that they don't fall apart in the oven. SERVES 6

4 large, firm red pears

²/₃ cup firmly packed brown sugar (either light or dark; the darker the sugar, the more molasses flavor you will have)

½ cup (1 stick) unsalted butter, melted

1 teaspoon ground cinnamon

½ teaspoon ground ginger

¼ cup pear nectar, apple juice, or water

2 teaspoons vanilla bean paste (see Diva Note, page 112) or pure vanilla extract (optional)

Make It Now

1. Coat the inside of a 9-inch square baking dish with non-stick cooking spray. Peel, core, and slice the pears in half lengthwise. Place them cut side up in the prepared baking dish.

2. Place the sugar in a small mixing bowl and stir in the butter, cinnamon, ginger, pear nectar, and vanilla bean paste, if using, until blended. Spread the mixture evenly over the pears. Cover and refrigerate for up to 3 days.

Bake It Later

1. Preheat the oven to 375°F. Allow the casserole to come to room temperature for about 15 minutes.

2. Bake the pears for 25 to 30 minutes, basting with the sauce once during cooking. The pears should be golden brown and the glaze should be bubbling. Serve warm or at room temperature.

Five-Spice Baked Apples

BAKED APPLES ARE COMFORT FOOD OF THE FIRST ORDER, and these Asian-spiced apples are just the ticket to give a weeknight dinner a different twist. Try serving them warm, surrounding a roast as a side dish. They also make a great dessert served warm with a little goat cheese spooned into the center, or served cold paired with green tea ice cream. SERVES 6

4 large Granny Smith or Gala apples

½ cup firmly packed light brown sugar

1½ teaspoons Chinese five-spice powder

2 tablespoons sherry (dry or cream)

½ teaspoon almond extract

½ cup (1 stick) unsalted butter, melted

Make It Now

1. Coat the inside of a 9-inch square baking dish with non-stick cooking spray.

2. Peel and core the apples, and slice them in half lengthwise. Lay the apples cut side up in the prepared dish.

3. In a small bowl, combine the brown sugar, five-spice powder, sherry, almond extract, and melted butter, stirring to blend. Spread the glaze evenly over the apples. Cover and refrigerate for up to 3 days.

Bake It Later

1. Preheat the oven to 375°F. Allow the apples to come to room temperature for about 15 minutes.

2. Bake the apples for 45 to 50 minutes, basting occasionally with the glaze, until they are soft and the glaze is bubbling. Serve warm, at room temperature, or cold.

Desserts

I love a great dessert. I'm pretty fussy about my cookies, pies, crisps, tarts, cakes, and cheesecakes, so when testing these recipes, the frozen, defrosted, and baked dessert had to be as good as the original, or it didn't make the cut. When I discovered that there are many wonderful desserts that you can mix, freeze, and then bake fresh, I was delirious with sugar-rushed joy!

I didn't grow up in a home with many desserts. My mother was a phenomenal cook, but baking wasn't her thing. When I began baking, I had many disasters. Then I realized that baking is a science, and, if I altered the complex structure of a cake batter, or cookie, or pie crust, I was in for a rude surprise. So learn from my mistakes: follow the directions, and if they call for whole milk, use it; if they call for butter, don't substitute something else, because chances are it won't work. A great Diva tip is that you can mix the batter for a dessert that will be baked in a 9 x 13-inch baking dish and divide it equally between two 9-inch baking dishes and bake for 10 minutes less. That way, you can have two desserts for smaller gatherings waiting in the freezer.

As with many of the recipes in this book, there will be formulas and then variations for you to try. My feeling is that if you have one great brownie batter, you can make a ton of really delicious brownies by altering the flavorings, but not the batter itself, so have some fun and be creative with the flavors, nuts, and fruits. Fillings, frostings, and glazes also take some baked goods to the next level, so feel free to frost any of the cookies, cakes, or brownies here. And remember to have fun with these recipes—I know I did!

Desserts

Soft Ginger Molasses Cookies

THESE COOKIES ARE TERRIFIC TO MAKE AT ANY TIME OF YEAR. They are premium cookie jar material, with their cinnamon and clove scent, chewy texture, and molasses flavor. They are wonderful with a glass of milk or cup of tea, coffee, or hot chocolate. MAKES ABOUT 40 1½-INCH COOKIES

½ cup (1 stick) unsalted butter, softened

⅓ cup molasses

1 large egg

¾ cup sugar, plus 1 to 2 cups additional for rolling (optional)

3 cups unbleached all-purpose flour

1½ teaspoons ground cinnamon

½ teaspoon ground cloves

1 teaspoon ground ginger

¾ teaspoon baking soda

½ teaspoon salt

Make It Now

1. In a large bowl using an electric mixer, cream the butter, molasses, egg, and ¾ cup sugar together on low speed, scraping down the sides of the bowl until the mixture is combined. Add the flour, cinnamon, cloves, ginger, baking soda, and salt and stir to blend. (At this point, you may freeze the dough for up to 2 months.)

2. Scoop the dough into 1-inch balls and roll in 1 to 2 cups sugar, if using. Place the dough balls onto cookie sheets, cover, and freeze until firm, about 4 hours. Transfer to zipper-top plastic bags and freeze for up to 2 months.

Bake It Later

1. Defrost the dough balls in the refrigerator overnight.

2. Preheat the oven to 350°F. Line baking sheets with aluminum foil, parchment paper, or silicone baking liners.

3. Place the dough balls on the prepared sheets about 1 inch apart.

4. Bake for 12 to 14 minutes, until puffed and light brown at the edges.

5. Let cool for 5 minutes on the baking sheets, then transfer to wire racks and let cool completely. Store in an airtight container at room temperature for up to 3 days or freeze for up to 2 months.

Basic Chocolate Chip Cookies
and Their Friends

THIS RECIPE YIELDS A DELICIOUS CHEWY, soft cookie, and there are many flavor variations for you to try at the end of the recipe. And even better, the recipe easily doubles or triples.

MAKES ABOUT TWENTY-FOUR 2½-INCH COOKIES

1 cup (2 sticks) unsalted butter, softened

1 cup firmly packed light brown sugar

½ cup granulated sugar

2 large eggs

2 teaspoons pure vanilla extract

2⅓ cups unbleached all-purpose flour

1 teaspoon salt

1 teaspoon baking soda

One 12-ounce bag semisweet chocolate chips

Make It Now

1. In a large bowl using an electric mixer, cream together the butter, brown sugar, and granulated sugar at medium speed until light and fluffy, about 2 minutes.

2. Add the eggs and vanilla and beat until combined.

3. Add the flour, salt, and baking soda and beat until the flour disappears into the dough, about 1½ minutes. Stir in the chocolate chips. (At this point, you may freeze the dough for up to 2 months.)

4. Using a small scoop (about 2 tablespoons per cookie), drop balls of the dough 1½ inches apart onto baking sheets. Cover and freeze until firm, about 4 hours. Transfer to zipper-top plastic bags or airtight containers and freeze for up to 2 months.

Bake It Later

1. Defrost the dough balls overnight in the refrigerator.

2. Preheat the oven to 375°F. Line baking sheets with aluminum foil, parchment paper, or silicone baking liners.

3. Place the dough balls on the prepared baking sheets about 1½ inches apart. Wet your hands and press down on the dough to flatten a bit so they will bake evenly. Bake until golden brown on the edges but still a bit soft in the center, 12 to 14 minutes.

4. Cool on the baking sheets set on wire racks for 5 minutes. Remove the cookies from the sheets and let cool completely on the racks. Store in an airtight container at room temperature for up to 4 days or freeze for up to 2 months.

VARIATIONS

Instead of the semisweet chocolate chips, use:

- One 12-ounce package semisweet chocolate chips and 1 cup chopped pecans or walnuts

- One 12-ounce package white chocolate chips *or* 2 cups coconut and 1 cup chopped macadamia nuts

- One 12-ounce package peanut butter chips or milk chocolate chips and 1 cup chopped honey-roasted peanuts

- 1 cup peanut butter chips and 1 cup milk chocolate or semisweet chocolate chips

- One 12-ounce package mint chocolate chips

- 2 cups chopped candy bars (about 12 ounces)—try Baby Ruth, Snickers, or Nestlé Crunch Bars

- 2 cups plain or peanut M&M candies

- 2 cups chopped Reese's peanut butter cups (you can also use the Reese's chips if you like, but the chopped peanut butter cup candy is awesome)

Diva Note

When baking soft or chewy cookies, remove them from the oven when the edges begin to brown but the center is still a bit soft. Allowing the cookies to cool on the baking sheet helps them to continue to cook (the baking sheet is still hot) but keeps them from burning or overcooking.

Chocolate Drop Cookies

DEEP, DARK, AND CHOCOLATY, these cookies pack a wallop of chocolate flavor. If you would like to add other flavors to the mix, try flavored chips (Heath bar, white chocolate, mint chocolate), dried fruits (apricots and dried cherries), or your favorite nuts. See all the variations at the end of the recipe; you can divide the dough in half and make two different flavors if you wish.

MAKES ABOUT THIRTY-SIX 2½-INCH COOKIES

1½ cups (3 sticks) unsalted butter, softened

1½ cups firmly packed light brown sugar

1 cup granulated sugar

2 teaspoons pure vanilla extract or vanilla bean paste (see Diva Note, page 112)

3 large eggs

1 cup unsweetened natural cocoa powder

3 cups unbleached all-purpose flour

1½ teaspoons baking soda

1½ cups flavored chips, nuts, and/or dried fruit of your choice (see Variations)

Make It Now

1. In a large bowl using an electric mixer, cream together the butter, brown sugar, and granulated sugar at medium speed until light and fluffy. Add the vanilla and eggs, one at a time, and mix until blended after each addition. Add the cocoa, flour, baking soda, and chips, stirring until just blended. Make sure to scrape the bottom of the bowl and keep stirring if there is any unincorporated butter or sugar on the bottom. (At this point, you may freeze the dough for up to 2 months.)

2. Using a small scoop (about 2 tablespoons per cookie), drop balls of the dough 1½ inches apart onto baking sheets. Cover and freeze until firm, about 4 hours. Transfer to zipper-top plastic bags or airtight containers and freeze for up to 2 months.

Bake It Later

1. Defrost the dough balls overnight in the refrigerator.

2. Preheat the oven to 350°F. Line baking sheets with aluminum foil, parchment paper, or silicone baking liners.

3. Place the dough balls on the prepared baking sheets about 1½ inches apart. Wet your hands and press down on the dough to flatten a bit so they will bake evenly. Bake for 10 to 12 minutes. The tops will look set, but the cookies will be very soft.

4. Let cool on the sheets for 7 to 10 minutes, and then re-move the cookies to wire racks to cool. Store in an air-tight container at room temperature for up to 4 days or freeze for up to 2 months.

VARIATIONS

Here are some suggestions for add-ins to the basic recipe. How much to add is your choice, but 1½ cups total of additional ingredients will work well.

- Dried cherries and bittersweet chocolate chips or chopped chocolate

- Finely chopped dried apricots and finely chopped almonds

- Dried cranberries and chopped white chocolate or dark chocolate chips

- Peanut butter chips and chopped honey-roasted peanuts

- Milk chocolate chips and chopped pecans

- Shredded coconut and macadamia nuts

- Crushed peppermint candies and bittersweet choco-late chips, or chopped peppermint bark

Oatmeal Cookies

OATMEAL COOKIES SHOULD BE CHEWY, with a nice flavor of caramel. My favorites always have nuts and chocolate chips in them, but you can certainly play around with the formula and add dried fruits if you would like, or leave out the add-ins. I urge you to try the variation for jumble cookies, which are great with a cup of tea or coffee in the morning.

MAKES ABOUT TWENTY-FOUR 2½-INCH COOKIES

1 cup (2 sticks) unsalted butter, softened

1⅓ cups firmly packed dark brown sugar (see Diva Notes)

2 large eggs

½ teaspoon ground cinnamon (see Diva Notes)

1 teaspoon salt

1 teaspoon baking soda

1¾ cups old-fashioned rolled oats

1½ cups unbleached all-purpose flour

1 cup golden raisins or chocolate chips

1 cup chopped nuts of your choice (optional)

Make It Now

1. In a large bowl using an electric mixer, cream together the butter, sugar, and eggs at medium speed until blended. Add the cinnamon, salt, baking soda, oats, flour, raisins, and nuts, if using, beating on low speed until blended. (At this point, you may freeze the dough for up to 2 months.)

2. Using a small scoop (about 2 tablespoons per cookie), drop balls of the dough 1½ inches apart onto baking sheets. Cover and freeze until firm, about 4 hours. Transfer to zipper-top plastic bags or airtight containers and freeze for up to 2 months.

Bake It Later

1. Defrost the dough balls overnight in the refrigerator.

2. Preheat the oven to 325°F. Line baking sheets with aluminum foil, parchment paper, or silicone baking liners.

3. Place the dough balls on the prepared baking sheets about 2 inches apart. Wet your hands and press down on the dough to flatten a bit so that they will bake evenly. Bake for 15 to 17 minutes, until deep golden brown.

4. Cool on the baking sheets set on wire racks for 5 minutes. Remove the cookies from the sheets and let cool

completely on the racks. Store in an airtight container at room temperature for up to 3 days or freeze for up to 2 months.

VARIATION

Jumble Cookies

Prepare the cookies as directed, reducing the flour by ½ cup. Add the following:

½ cup dried cranberries, ½ cup finely chopped dried apricots, ½ cup finely chopped golden raisins, ½ cup shredded coconut, and ½ cup finely chopped nuts. Bake as directed.

Diva Notes

The darker the brown sugar, the more caramel flavor you will have, so that's why I've called for dark brown sugar here. It's fine to substitute light brown sugar, but you just won't get the deep caramel flavor that comes from the darker sugar.

I have begun to use Vietnamese cinnamon, which is a very potent and sweet cinnamon, like nothing I have ever tried before. If you haven't tried it, I suggest that you buy some for holiday baking; you'll never look back. I have used Spice Island and McCormick brands, which are widely available, and Penzeys Spices sells wonderful Vietnamese cinnamon online at www.penzeys.com.

Vanilla Log Cookies

THE BASIC FLAVOR HERE IS VANILLA, but you can certainly change it to suit your whim. The fun begins when you shape these into a log and roll them in nuts, flavored sugar, or crushed peppermint candies. Because you can divide the dough, try making several different kinds by rolling each log in a different coating. These can go directly from the freezer to the oven. MAKES ABOUT 60 COOKIES

1 cup (2 sticks) unsalted butter, softened

2 cups sugar

1 large egg

2 teaspoons pure vanilla extract or vanilla bean paste (see Diva Note, page 112)

2½ cups unbleached all-purpose flour

1 teaspoon baking powder

½ teaspoon salt

½ cup nuts or dried fruit

Make It Now

1. In a large bowl using an electric mixer, cream together the butter and 1 cup of the sugar. Add the egg and vanilla and beat at medium speed until the mixture is combined. Stir in the flour, baking powder, salt, and nuts.

2. Divide the dough into 2 equal portions. Roll and shape each portion into a log about 2 inches in diameter and 8 inches long. Roll each log in the remaining 1 cup sugar. Wrap each log tightly in plastic wrap and freeze for up to 2 months.

Bake It Later

1. Preheat the oven to 375°F. Line baking sheets with aluminum foil, parchment paper, or silicone baking liners.

2. Slice the logs into ¼-inch-thick rounds with a serrated knife and place on the prepared baking sheets about ½ inch apart.

3. Bake for 10 minutes, until the cookies are golden brown, rotating the cookie sheets halfway through the baking time to ensure even browning.

4. Allow the cookies to cool for 5 minutes on the baking sheets, then remove to wire racks to cool completely. Store in airtight containers at room temperature for up to 5 days or freeze for up to 2 months.

VARIATIONS, PART ONE

- Substitute ½ teaspoon almond extract for the vanilla extract and add finely chopped dried cherries to the dough.

- Substitute 1 teaspoon orange extract for the vanilla extract, add finely chopped cranberries to the dough, and roll the cookies in finely chopped pistachios instead of the sugar.

- Substitute firmly packed brown sugar for the granulated sugar in the dough, add finely chopped pecans to the dough, and roll the dough in turbinado (raw) sugar instead of granulated sugar.

- Substitute 1 teaspoon orange extract for the vanilla extract, add finely chopped macadamia nuts to the dough, and roll in shredded coconut instead of the sugar. Reduce the baking temperature to 350°F and bake for 12 to 14 minutes, making sure the coconut doesn't get too brown.

- Add 1 tablespoon instant espresso powder to the cookie dough and roll in macadamia nuts instead of the sugar.

VARIATIONS, PART TWO

Instead of granulated sugar, roll the cookies in finely chopped nuts, turbinado (raw) sugar, multicolored or chocolate sprinkles, or finely crushed peppermint candies.

Chocolate Log Cookies

FOR ALL THOSE CHOCOLATE LOVERS IN THE CROWD, here's your slice-and-bake cookie, which, like the vanilla version, can go straight from the freezer to the oven. Make sure to try different add-ins and ingredients to roll the cookies in. Most of all, have fun. Cookies should make you smile, especially when they are chocolate. MAKES ABOUT 60 COOKIES

1 cup (2 sticks) unsalted butter

1 cup chopped semisweet chocolate or chocolate chips

2 cups sugar

1 large egg

2 teaspoons pure vanilla extract or vanilla bean paste (see Diva Note, page 112) *or* 1 teaspoon instant espresso powder

2½ cups unbleached all-purpose flour

½ teaspoon baking soda

½ teaspoon salt

½ cup finely chopped nuts or dried fruit

Make It Now

1. Melt the butter with the chocolate in a medium-size saucepan over low heat, removing the pan from the stove when the chocolate is almost melted and allowing it to finish melting in the warm butter. Add 1 cup of the sugar, the egg, vanilla, flour, baking soda, and salt, stirring until the flour disappears. Stir in the nuts.

2. Divide the dough into 2 equal portions. Roll and shape each portion into a log about 2 inches in diameter and 8 inches long. Roll each log in the remaining 1 cup sugar. Wrap each log tightly in plastic wrap and freeze for up to 2 months.

Bake It Later

1. Preheat the oven to 375°F. Line baking sheets with aluminum foil, parchment paper, or silicone baking liners.

2. Slice the frozen logs into ¼-inch-thick rounds with a serrated knife and place on the prepared baking sheets about ½ inch apart.

3. Bake for 10 minutes, until the cookies are set, rotating the pans halfway through the baking time to ensure even browning. Cool for 3 minutes on the cookie sheets, then remove to wire racks to cool completely. Store in airtight containers at room temperature for up to 5 days or freeze for up to 2 months.

VARIATIONS

Great substitutes for granulated sugar when rolling chocolate log cookies include crushed peppermint candies; finely chopped pecans, hazelnuts, cashews, macadamia nuts, walnuts, peanuts, pistachios, or pine nuts; cinnamon sugar (1 cup granulated sugar plus 1 teaspoon ground cinnamon); colored sprinkles; shredded coconut; or turbinado (raw) sugar.

Brownies and Their Friends

BROWNIES ARE MY COMFORT FOOD; I like them chewy with nuts toasted into the top. Topping them with vanilla ice cream and hot fudge sauce makes me so happy! Brownies can be whatever you want them to be, and the fact that you can freeze the batter and then bake them gives you an edge for serving a decadent but simple dessert to your family and friends. The most recent trend in brownie baking is to bake them in muffin tins so that you get something akin to a brownie cupcake, but I'm a purist at heart, and that chewy corner piece in the rectangular baking dish is mine!

MAKES TWENTY-FOUR 2-INCH SQUARES

1 cup (2 sticks) unsalted butter, softened

2 cups sugar

4 large eggs

1 cup unsweetened natural cocoa powder

1 cup unbleached all-purpose flour

Make It Now

1. Coat the inside of a 9 x13-inch baking pan with nonstick cooking spray.

2. In a large bowl using an electric mixer, cream together the butter and sugar at medium speed until light and fluffy. Add the eggs one at a time, beating after each addition. The batter will look curdled, but that's okay.

3. Slowly add the cocoa powder and flour together, mixing until the flour has disappeared and the batter is stiff. Spread the batter in the pan in an even layer. Cover and refrigerate for up to 2 days or freeze for up to 2 months.

1½ cups pecan halves or chopped nuts of your choice

Bake It Later

1. Defrost the brownies in the refrigerator overnight, if necessary.

2. Preheat the oven to 350°F. Allow the brownies to come to room temperature for 30 minutes.

3. Sprinkle the nuts over the brownies and bake for 30 to 35 minutes, until a toothpick or cake tester inserted into the center comes out with a few crumbs clinging to it. Remove from the oven and allow to cool completely on a wire rack before cutting into squares. Store in an airtight container at room temperature for up to 2 days or freeze for up to 6 weeks.

- A teaspoon or two of espresso powder really deepens the flavor of the chocolate and gives these brownies a whole lot of personality. Other flavorings that can be used instead of espresso powder and will complement these brownies are 1 teaspoon peppermint extract; 2 teaspoons orange extract or 1 teaspoon orange oil; 2 teaspoons ground cinnamon; 1 tablespoon Kahlúa or other coffee-flavored liqueur; or 1 tablespoon Chambord.

- Toss in 1½ cups of your favorite semisweet chocolate, white chocolate, Heath bar, or toffee chips; M&M's (peanut or plain); or chopped flavored truffles.

- Frostings for brownies can be as varied as a chocolate glaze, a caramel drizzle, buttercream flavored with cinnamon, or German chocolate cake frosting with coconut and pecans.

Diva Note

Nuts that are stirred into the batter will steam, not toast, so sprinkle the nuts on just before baking to bring out a toasted flavor. The choice of nut is up to you: walnuts are delicious, and peanuts, cashews, sliced almonds, and macadamia nuts are all great choices.

Blondies and Their Friends

BLONDIES ARE THE FAIR COUSIN OF THE BROWNIE, a blond bar cookie with the same texture as a brownie. Here's where your creative juices can start to flow, because you can add dried fruits, nuts, chopped chocolate, and any number of other ingredients to these blondies to stud them with your favorite flavors. Try out lots of variations on your family and see how much fun this can be! Remember to sprinkle nuts on top just before baking to get that nice toasted flavor.

MAKES TWENTY-FOUR 2-INCH SQUARES

1 cup (2 sticks) unsalted butter, softened

1½ cups firmly packed light brown sugar

1 tablespoon pure vanilla extract or vanilla bean paste (see Diva Note, page 112)

2 large eggs

1⅔ cups unbleached all-purpose flour

1 teaspoon baking soda

¼ teaspoon salt

1¼ cups chopped chocolate of your choice

½ cup chopped dried fruits of your choice

Make It Now

1. Coat the inside of a 9 x 13-inch baking dish with nonstick cooking spray.

2. In a large bowl using an electric mixer, cream together the butter, brown sugar, and vanilla at medium speed until light and fluffy. Add the eggs one at a time, beating after each addition.

3. Add the flour, baking soda, salt, chocolate, and fruit to the batter, and beat until just combined and the flour has disappeared into the batter.

4. Spread the batter in the pan in an even layer. Cover and refrigerate for up to 2 days or freeze for up to 2 months.

1½ cups chopped nuts of your choice

Bake It Later

1. Defrost the blondies in the refrigerator overnight, if necessary.

2. Preheat the oven to 325°F. Allow the blondies to come to room temperature for 30 minutes.

3. Sprinkle the nuts over the top of the blondies. Bake for 25 to 28 minutes, until a toothpick or cake tester inserted into the center comes out dry. Remove from the

oven and allow to cool completely on a wire rack before cutting into squares. Store in an airtight container at room temperature for up to 2 days or freeze for up to 6 weeks.

VARIATIONS

Try these combos in the blondies, or make up your own.

- White chocolate, dried cranberries, and pecans

- Milk chocolate, dried cherries, and pistachios

- White chocolate, dried apples, and pine nuts

- Semisweet chocolate, dried blueberries, and walnuts

- Milk chocolate, dried pineapple, and macadamia nuts or cashews

- Milk or white chocolate, flaked coconut, and macadamia nuts or pecans

Sweet 16th Brookies

SWEET 16TH IS THE BAKERY OWNED BY MY FRIENDS Ellen and Dan Einstein in Nashville, Tennessee. When I shared this recipe with them, I was delighted to see "brookies" for sale in their shop when I stopped by for coffee and a chat while I was writing this book. They are called brookies because they are a bar cookie that's part brownie. A rich chocolate chip cookie base is covered by a fudge brownie and sprinkled with pecan halves to make a scrumptious end to a casual meal, either plain or topped with a scoop of ice cream and hot fudge and/or caramel sauce. MAKES THIRTY-SIX 2-INCH SQUARES

CHOCOLATE CHIP COOKIE LAYER

1 cup (2 sticks) unsalted butter, softened

1 cup firmly packed light brown sugar

½ cup granulated sugar

2 teaspoons pure vanilla extract

2 large eggs

2½ cups unbleached all-purpose flour

One 12-ounce bag milk chocolate or semisweet chocolate chips

BROWNIE LAYER

1 cup (2 sticks) unsalted butter, softened

2 cups granulated sugar

4 large eggs

1 cup unbleached all-purpose flour

1 cup Dutch-processed cocoa powder

Make It Now

1. Line a 12 x 15-inch jellyroll pan with aluminum foil, parchment paper, or a silicone baking liner.

2. To make the chocolate chip cookie dough layer, in a large bowl, using an electric mixer, beat together the butter, brown sugar, and granulated sugar at medium speed, until light and fluffy. Blend in the vanilla and eggs until combined. Add the flour and chips and mix on low speed until blended and the flour has disappeared. Wet your hands and pat the dough in an even layer in the prepared pan, leaving about ¾ inch of space around the edge; the dough should be about ½ inch thick. Set aside.

3. To make the brownie layer, in another large bowl, using the mixer, beat together the butter and sugar at medium speed, until light and fluffy. Add the eggs and mix until thoroughly combined. Add the flour and cocoa and mix on low speed. Using an offset spatula dipped into hot water, spread the brownie batter evenly over the chocolate chip cookie dough. Cover and freeze for up to 2 months.

1 ½ cups chopped pecans

Bake It Later

1. Defrost the brookies in the refrigerator overnight.

2. Preheat the oven to 350°F. Allow the brookies to come to room temperature for 30 minutes.

3. Sprinkle the top of the brookies evenly with the chopped nuts. Bake for 25 to 35 minutes, until a toothpick or cake tester inserted into the center comes out with a few crumbs attached but is not gooey. Remove from the oven and let cool completely on a rack before cutting into squares. Store any leftovers in an airtight container at room temperature for up to 3 days, or cover and freeze for up to 6 weeks.

Diva Note
Sometimes cookie dough is sticky and hard to move around in the pan; if you have this problem, cut a large piece of plastic wrap and use it to help you push the dough down to the right thickness and to spread it out in the pan. A small dough roller (it looks like a mini rolling pin) will also help.

Maple Praline Pumpkin Cheesecake Streusel Bars

I LOVE PUMPKIN PIE, and I make lots of different variations on the theme throughout the year. I'm not sure if it's the pumpkin, or the spices, or the creamy texture, but I feel like I could eat my weight in pumpkin pies! When I wanted a dessert variation for this book, I came up with this recipe, which is not only delicious, but can be made ahead. The creamy maple-flavored pumpkin cheesecake filling sits on top of a caramel-and-pecan crust, and it is topped with a pecan and brown sugar streusel. You can serve these cold or at room temperature, but store them in the refrigerator if you have any leftovers. MAKES TWENTY-FOUR 2-INCH SQUARES

CRUST

3 cups unbleached all-purpose flour

³/₄ teaspoon baking powder

1 teaspoon salt

1 cup firmly packed light or dark brown sugar

1¹/₈ cups (2 sticks plus 2 tablespoons) cold unsalted butter, cut into small pieces

1¹/₂ cups chopped pecans

FILLING

2 cups pumpkin puree

1 cup firmly packed light or dark brown sugar

2 large eggs

Two 8-ounce packages cream cheese, softened

1 teaspoon pumpkin pie spice (see Diva Note)

2 tablespoons pure maple syrup

Make It Now

1. Preheat the oven to 350°F. Coat the inside of a 9 x 13-inch baking pan with nonstick cooking spray.

2. To make the crust, in the bowl of a food processor or electric mixer fitted with the paddle attachment, combine the flour, baking powder, salt, and brown sugar. Drop the butter pieces on the dry ingredients. Blend on low speed or pulse on and off until the mixture comes together like coarse crumbs. Stir in the pecans. Press 2¹/₂ cups of the mixture evenly into the bottom of the prepared baking pan. Set aside the remaining mixture for the topping. Bake the crust for 20 minutes, until golden brown. Allow to cool on a wire rack.

3. To make the filling, in a large bowl using an electric mixer or in a food processor, beat the pumpkin puree, brown sugar, eggs, cream cheese, pie spice, and maple syrup together until they are smooth. Pour over the cooled crust, then sprinkle with the reserved topping mixture. Cover and freeze for up to 6 weeks.

Bake It Later

1. Defrost the bars overnight in the refrigerator.

2. Preheat the oven to 350°F. Allow the bars to come to room temperature for about 30 minutes.

3. Bake the cheesecake bars for 40 to 45 minutes, until the filling is set.

4. Immediately cut into squares with a sharp knife, wiping the knife between cuts. Let the bars cool, then remove from the pan. Serve the squares warm, at room temperature, or chilled. Refrigerate any leftovers in an airtight container for up to 5 days.

Diva Note

To make your own pumpkin pie spice, mix together ½ teaspoon ground cinnamon, ⅛ teaspoon ground cloves, and ⅛ teaspoon ground nutmeg.

Apple Praline Cheesecake Bars

A CRUMB CRUST AND CRUMBLE TOPPING encases sweet Golden Delicious apples in a cheesecake-like filling for a great dessert for a casual meal. You can substitute firm ripe pears for the apples.

MAKES ABOUT THIRTY-SIX 2-INCH SQUARES

CRUST AND CRUMBLE TOPPING

2¾ cups unbleached all-purpose flour

¼ teaspoon salt

½ cup granulated sugar

½ cup firmly packed light brown sugar

½ cup (4 ounces) cream cheese, softened

½ cup (1 stick) unsalted butter, softened

1 teaspoon pumpkin pie spice (see Diva Note, page 287)

1½ cups chopped pecans

FILLING

8 ounces cream cheese, softened

1 cup granulated sugar

2 large eggs

1 tablespoon freshly squeezed lemon juice

Grated zest of 1 lemon

5 medium-size Golden Delicious apples, peeled, cored, and thinly sliced

Make It Now

1. Line a 12 x 15-inch jellyroll pan with aluminum foil, parchment paper, or a silicone baking liner.

2. To make the crust and topping, in a large bowl using an electric mixer with a paddle attachment, stir together the flour, salt, granulated sugar, and brown sugar. Cut in the cream cheese, butter, pumpkin pie spice, and pecans until crumbly. Press two-thirds of the mixture evenly into the bottom of the prepared pan. Reserve the remaining mixture for the topping.

3. To make the filling, in a large bowl using an electric mixer, beat together the cream cheese, sugar, eggs, lemon juice, and lemon zest until smooth.

4. Arrange the apples over the crust in the pan, then pour the cream cheese mixture over the apples. Sprinkle with the reserved crumble mixture. Cover and refrigerate for up to 2 days or freeze for up to 1 month.

Bake It Later

1. Defrost the bars overnight in the refrigerator, if necessary.

2. Preheat the oven to 350°F. Allow the bars to come to room temperature for 30 minutes.

3. Bake the bars for 40 to 45 minutes, until the topping is golden brown and the cream cheese mixture is set. Cut into squares immediately, but allow to cool completely before serving. Serve cool or at room temperature. **Store in an airtight container in the refrigerator for up to 3 days or freeze for up to 1 month.**

Brandied Pear Phyllo Squares

THIS STRUDEL WITH A RICH PEAR AND NUT FILLING couldn't be simpler to make. Phyllo dough becomes crackly and crunchy when brushed with butter, but sometimes the sheets can stick together or tear, and that's the beauty of this recipe—it's for all those torn sheets. Save them in a zipper-top plastic bag and freeze them until you have enough to make this dessert.

MAKES TWENTY-FOUR 2½-INCH SQUARES

½ cup granulated sugar

1 teaspoon ground cinnamon

8 ounces phyllo dough, crumbled

1 cup (2 sticks) unsalted butter, clarified (see Diva Note, page 106)

4 cups peeled, cored, and coarsely chopped firm red pears (about 6 large pears)

1 cup firmly packed light brown sugar

⅛ teaspoon ground nutmeg

2 tablespoons unbleached all-purpose flour

2 tablespoons brandy

1 cup toasted slivered almonds, chopped

Confectioners' sugar for garnish

Make It Now

1. Coat the inside of a 9 x 13-inch baking dish with nonstick cooking spray.

2. In a small bowl, combine the sugar with ½ teaspoon of the cinnamon.

3. In a large bowl, separate the phyllo if it is sticking together. Pour ½ cup of the clarified butter over the phyllo and toss to coat. Sprinkle with ¼ cup of the cinnamon sugar. Spread half of the phyllo in the prepared pan.

4. In a large mixing bowl, combine the pears, brown sugar, remaining ½ teaspoon cinnamon, nutmeg, flour, brandy, and almonds. Spread the pear mixture over the phyllo and top with the remaining phyllo. Drizzle with the remaining ½ cup clarified butter and ¼ cup cinnamon sugar. Cover and freeze for up to 1 month.

Bake It Later

1. Defrost the baking dish in the refrigerator overnight.

2. Preheat the oven to 300°F. Allow the dish to come to room temperature for 30 minutes.

3. Bake, covered, for 25 minutes. Uncover and bake for another 30 minutes, until the phyllo is golden brown and crisp. Allow to cool on a wire rack for 20 minutes.

4. Cut into squares and sift confectioners' sugar over the top to garnish. Store at room temperature for up to 1 day.

Fruit Turnovers

DESSERT DOESN'T GET MUCH EASIER THAN THIS: frozen puff pastry dough is rolled out, topped with delicious fruit fillings, then frozen till you are ready to bake. You can even bake the turnovers without defrosting them first. These will have your family watching at the oven door; the smells of the fruit and crackly puff pastry are intoxicating. Fruit choices are up to you, but these are my favorites: apples (Golden Delicious or Gala), red pears, peaches, plums, nectarines, blueberries, blackberries, or a mixture of berries. If you decide to use frozen fruit, don't defrost the fruit, but just cover it with the sugar and flavorings and freeze as directed. MAKES 12 PASTRIES

½ cup unbleached all-purpose flour, for rolling

1 sheet frozen puff pastry, defrosted

3 cups finely chopped peeled and pitted fruit of your choice

⅔ cup firmly packed light brown sugar

⅔ cup granulated sugar

2 tablespoons cornstarch

½ teaspoon ground cinnamon

Make It Now

1. Line a baking sheet with aluminum foil, parchment paper, or a silicone baking liner.

2. Sprinkle some of the flour onto a flat, clean work surface, and roll out the puff pastry into a 12-inch square, trimming the sides as necessary and discarding the excess pastry. Cut the square in half, then each half into 6 equal pieces.

3. Mound ¼ cup of the fruit in the center of each piece of pastry. In a small bowl, stir together the brown sugar, granulated sugar, cornstarch, and cinnamon. Sprinkle 1 tablespoon of the sugar mixture over the fruit. Fold the top of the pastry over the filling, like you would fold a letter (see Diva Note), and crimp around the edges with the tines of a fork or a pastry crimper. Transfer the turnover to the prepared baking sheet. Repeat with the remaining puff pastry and fruit. Cover and refrigerate for up to 1 day or freeze for up to 1 month.

1 large egg

2 tablespoons heavy cream

Bake It Later

1. Preheat the oven to 400°F. Remove the turnovers from the freezer 45 minutes before baking.

2. Beat together the egg and cream. Brush the top of the turnovers with the egg mixture and snip a few vent holes in each turnover. Bake for 15 to 20 minutes, until the pastry is golden brown and the filling is bubbling. Allow to cool on a wire rack for 10 minutes before serving. Cover and refrigerate for up to 2 days.

Diva Note

So often in my own kitchen I'm not measuring precisely how large the piece of puff pastry is, and I may not get exact squares cut from the pastry to make the traditional triangle-type turnover. I found that by forming the pastry into a simple rectangular letter-fold shape, there was actually more filling distributed throughout the turnover, instead of just a dollop in the center of a triangular-shaped pastry.

Mini Chocolate-Pecan Tarts

THESE LITTLE BITES OF CHOCOLATE PECAN PIE will be a terrific addition to your holiday baking repertoire and look gorgeous on a dessert buffet. You can choose to make these in mini-muffin tins or in individual 2- to 3-inch tart pans. Either way, they are a delicious make-ahead and bake dessert.

MAKES ABOUT 24 MINI TARTS OR TWELVE 3-INCH TARTS

CRUST

2¼ cups unbleached all-purpose flour

½ teaspoon salt

2 tablespoons light brown sugar

One 3-ounce package cream cheese, cut into small cubes

½ cup (1 stick) cold unsalted butter, cut into small cubes

FILLING

2 cups chopped pecans

1 cup chopped semisweet or bittersweet chocolate or mini chips

½ cup (1 stick) unsalted butter, softened

1 cup firmly packed brown sugar

2 large eggs

¼ cup light corn syrup

1 tablespoon bourbon (optional)

Make It Now

1. Coat the inside of mini-muffin tins or shallow tart pans with nonstick cooking spray.

2. To make the crust, combine the flour, salt, and brown sugar in the bowl of a food processor. Distribute the cream cheese and butter over the dry ingredients and pulse on and off until the ingredients begin to come together in a ball. Remove from the food processor and pinch off pieces of dough to fit into the muffin tins. If you are making tarts, push the dough evenly into the tart pans, using a piece of plastic wrap to help. (At this point, you may cover and freeze for up to 2 months.)

3. To make the filling, evenly distribute the pecans and chocolate among the pastry shells. In a large bowl using an electric mixer, beat together the butter and brown sugar at medium speed until creamy. Add the eggs, corn syrup, and bourbon, if using, stirring until blended.

4. Pour the mixture into each muffin well, filling to within ¼ inch of the top of the pan, or into each tart shell, filling halfway. Cover and freeze for up to 6 weeks.

Bake It Later

1. Defrost the tarts in the refrigerator overnight.

2. Preheat the oven to 350°F.

3. Bake the tarts in the muffin tins for 20 minutes or in tart pans for 30 minutes, until they are puffed and barely set, but not jiggly, in the center. Allow to cool completely and serve at room temperature. Cover and refrigerate for up to 3 days, or freeze for up to 2 months.

VARIATIONS

- Substitute walnuts for the pecans and pure maple syrup for the bourbon.

- Substitute macadamia nuts for the pecans and dark rum for the bourbon.

Chocolate Lava Cakes

ROY YAMAGUCHI, THE CHEF-OWNER OF ROY'S RESTAURANTS, which began in Hawaii, became famous for his molten chocolate lava cakes. They come from the kitchen with a crisp outside and a gooey, chocolaty center, and are served with unsweetened whipped cream in a pool of bittersweet chocolate sauce. The secret that I discovered about these outrageous desserts is that you can make them ahead and refrigerate or freeze them, and then just bake them when you're ready, without even defrosting them. This dessert takes about 10 minutes to put together, and then it can be refrigerated for up to 8 hours or frozen for up to 1 month. Try serving them in a pool of raspberry sauce or caramel sauce. MAKES 8 CAKES

³/₄ cup (1¹/₂ sticks) unsalted butter

¹/₂ cup confectioners' sugar

8 ounces bittersweet or semisweet chocolate, coarsely chopped

4 large eggs

1 large egg yolk

1 teaspoon pure vanilla extract

¹/₃ cup granulated sugar

2 tablespoons unbleached all-purpose flour

8 chocolate truffle candies (such as Lindt or Ghirardelli)

Make It Now

1. Using ¹/₄ cup of the butter, generously butter eight 6-ounce ramekins and dust them with the confectioners' sugar. Set aside on a baking sheet.

2. Melt the remaining ¹/₂ cup butter and the chocolate in a medium-size saucepan over low heat, stirring once or twice until smooth. Set the chocolate aside and allow to cool slightly.

3. In a large bowl using an electric mixer fitted with a whisk attachment, beat the eggs, egg yolk, vanilla, and sugar at high speed, until the volume nearly triples, the color is very light, and the mixture drops from the beaters in a thick stream (this may take 5 minutes). Whisk in the chocolate mixture, then sprinkle the flour over the mixture and fold it in until the flour is incorporated.

4. Ladle or pour the mixture into the prepared ramekins and place a truffle into the center of the batter in each ramekin. Cover and refrigerate the cakes for up to 8 hours or freeze for up to 1 month.

Unsweetened whipped cream
for serving

1. Preheat the oven to 400°F. Allow the ramekins to come to room temperature for 30 minutes.

2. Bake refrigerated cakes for 10 to 12 minutes; bake frozen cakes for 15 to 17 minutes. The cakes are done when they are puffed and appear set on the top. Run a paring knife around the inside edges of the ramekins to loosen the cakes, invert them onto individual serving plates, let cool for 1 minute, and then lift off the ramekins. Serve with a dollop of unsweetened whipped cream. Cover and refrigerate for up to 1 day, but do not freeze.

Plain Old Vanilla Cheesecake with Many Variations

THIS CHEESECAKE IS TALL, creamy, and scrumptious all by itself, but pair it with a special sauce or a topping, such as caramel-pecan sauce, raspberry puree, or fresh fruits, and it becomes a showstopper dessert. The batter also adapts well to tinkering, so you can add ingredients to it to get a totally different look and flavor. Vary the crusts and the add-ins, and you'll soon be making all kinds of exotic creations. No one has to know it all started with just one batter.

MAKES ONE 9-INCH CHEESECAKE

CRUST

1½ cups crushed graham crackers
(10 to 11 whole graham crackers)

2 tablespoons light brown sugar

6 tablespoons (¾ stick) unsalted
butter, melted

FILLING

Four 8-ounce packages cream
cheese, softened

½ cup firmly packed light
brown sugar

1 cup granulated sugar

3 large eggs

2 large egg yolks

1 tablespoon pure vanilla extract or
vanilla bean paste (see Diva Note,
page 112)

½ teaspoon salt

2 tablespoons unbleached
all-purpose flour

1 cup sour cream

¼ cup heavy cream

Make It Now

1. Line a 9-inch springform pan with aluminum foil and coat it with nonstick cooking spray.

2. To make the crust, in a mixing bowl stir together the cracker crumbs, brown sugar, and butter, until the mixture begins to come together in clumps. Press the crumbs into the bottom and about 1 inch up the sides of the pan.

3. To make the filling, in a large bowl using an electric mixer, beat together the cream cheese, brown sugar, and granulated sugar at medium speed, until fluffy. Add the eggs, one at a time, and the yolks one at a time, beating thoroughly after each addition. Stir in the vanilla, salt, flour, sour cream, and heavy cream, and blend until smooth. Pour the filling into the prepared crust. Cover and freeze for up to 6 weeks.

Bake It Later

1. Defrost the cheesecake in the refrigerator overnight.

2. Preheat the oven to 300°F. Allow the cheesecake to come to room temperature for 30 minutes.

3. Bake the cheesecake for 1 hour and 10 minutes, until it is no longer liquid in the center. Turn off the oven and allow the cheesecake to cool in the oven for 1 hour.

Cheesecakes

What's better than digging into a 3-inch-deep layer of creamy, rich cheesecake with its crunchy graham cracker or Oreo cookie crust and enjoying all the taste sensations that it brings? I'm not sure anything can top it, and the fact that you can make the cheesecake and freeze it sure is a bonus! Since cheesecakes have a basic formula, I'll start with that and then branch out. The crusts are also your choice. The standard graham cracker crust is simple, and definitely a winner, but by adding different ingredients the crusts have even more flavor and texture: try adding chopped nuts, shredded coconut, and even peanut butter, and see what happens!

To prepare a springform pan, I line the pan entirely with aluminum foil, then coat it thoroughly with nonstick cooking spray before I press in the crumbs. There are several advantages to this: one is that when the cheesecake is chilled, you can peel the aluminum foil right off the bottom; the other is that it takes away the need to cut the cheesecake directly on the springform pan and possibly damage the bottom of the pan.

Cheesecakes are best when they are served at room temperature, as that allows the flavors in the cheesecake to open up, rather than keeping them locked together in the cold.

Remove to a wire rack and let cool completely at room temperature. Store in an airtight container in the refrigerator for up to 5 days or freeze for up to 6 weeks. Serve at room temperature.

CRUST VARIATIONS

- For a chocolate crust, use 2½ cups Oreo cookie crumbs (about 24 cookies) or 2½ cups chocolate wafer cookie crumbs mixed with ½ cup sugar and ½ cup (1 stick) melted unsalted butter.

- For a peanut butter crust, increase the amount of graham cracker crumbs to 2 cups, add ¼ cup smooth peanut butter to the crumbs, and proceed as directed.

- For a coconut crust, add 1 cup shredded coconut and increase the butter to ½ cup (1 stick).

- For a nutty crust, add ½ cup finely chopped hazelnuts, pecans, walnuts, or macadamia nuts.

Cracking in the tops of cheesecakes is a common complaint from home cooks. I have had great success by baking the cheesecakes until they are no longer liquid in the center, then turning off the oven and letting them cool down in the turned-off oven. Cooling them without a dramatic change in the temperature seems to prevent the cracking that occurs when you take the cakes immediately out of the oven and leave them on the counter to cool.

FILLING VARIATIONS

Pineapple Cheesecake

Substitute dark rum for the vanilla extract. Thoroughly drain one 15.5-ounce can pineapple chunks and blot dry with paper towels. Add to the batter after you have blended in all the other ingredients. Add 1 cup shredded coconut at the same time for a piña colada cheesecake.

White Chocolate-Raspberry Cheesecake

Melt 1 cup chopped white chocolate together with 2 tablespoons unsalted butter, and allow it to cool slightly. Add the chocolate slowly to the batter after you have blended in all the other ingredients, and beat to blend. Pour the batter into the prepared pan and, using a butter knife, swirl ½ cup seedless raspberry preserves through the batter.

Chocolate Cheesecake

Melt 8 ounces bittersweet or semisweet chocolate, let cool slightly, and stir into the batter after you have blended in all the other ingredients.

Lemon Cheesecake

Substitute 2 teaspoons lemon extract for the vanilla extract, add 1 tablespoon lemon zest, and proceed as directed. This will give you a subtle lemon flavor; for added flavor, spread a thin layer of lemon curd over the cooled cheesecake.

Banana-Rum Cheesecake

Blend 4 tablespoons melted unsalted butter with ⅓ cup firmly packed brown sugar. Spread 3 sliced bananas over the bottom crust and top with the butter-sugar mixture. Substitute dark rum for the vanilla extract and add 1 teaspoon banana extract.

Praline Cheesecake

Before baking, sprinkle 1 cup pecan halves over the batter in the pan and sprinkle with ½ cup raw sugar.

Awesome Apple or Pear Pie

SERVE THIS CLASSIC WITH FRENCH VANILLA ICE CREAM or unsweetened whipped cream. Or you could lay a slice of cheddar cheese on top of each slice of pie; try sharp cheddar with apple or aged cheddar with pear. MAKES ONE 9-INCH PIE

4 large Granny Smith or your favorite tart apples, peeled, cored, and thinly sliced (5½ to 6 cups), *or* 6 to 8 red pears (still slightly firm), peeled, cored, and thinly sliced

½ cup granulated sugar

½ cup firmly packed light brown sugar

2 tablespoons cornstarch

1 teaspoon ground cinnamon

¼ teaspoon ground nutmeg

2 teaspoons freshly squeezed lemon juice

1 recipe Basic Pie Crust (page 303)

Make It Now

1. In a large bowl, combine the apples, granulated sugar, brown sugar, cornstarch, cinnamon, nutmeg, and lemon juice, stirring until the apples are thoroughly coated.

2. Sprinkle some flour onto a flat, clean work surface and roll the pie crust balls out into 11-inch circles. Coat the inside of a 9-inch pie plate with nonstick cooking spray. Transfer a dough circle to the pie plate and trim the edges. Fill the pie with the fruit filling and top with the remaining pie crust. Tuck the excess top pie crust underneath the bottom crust and flute or crimp the edges. Cover and seal airtight in aluminum foil, plastic wrap, or a 2-gallon zipper-top plastic bag, and freeze for up to 2 months.

Bake It Later

1. Preheat the oven to 425°F.

2. Cut slits in the top of the pie crust to allow steam to escape; bake for 15 minutes. Decrease the oven temperature to 375°F and bake for an additional 35 to 45 minutes, until the juices begin to bubble and the pie crust is golden brown.

3. Allow to cool on a wire rack for 25 minutes. Serve warm or at room temperature.

Diva Note

Brushing the crust with milk and then sprinkling it with sugar before cutting the slits will give you a nicely caramelized crust and an extra taste treat.

Cherry Brandy Pie

DELICIOUS AND GLORIOUSLY COLORED, cherry pies are almost as popular as apple pies, according to my friends at Marie Callender's pie shops. Frozen fruit works well here; don't defrost it, just mix it with the other ingredients, and freeze. MAKES ONE 9-INCH PIE

Two 16-ounce bags frozen pitted sweet cherries

3/4 cup sugar

1/4 cup instant tapioca

1 teaspoon brandy

1 recipe Basic Pie Crust (page 303)

Make It Now

1. In a large bowl, combine the frozen cherries with the sugar, tapioca, and brandy, tossing to coat the fruit.

2. Sprinkle some flour onto a flat, clean work surface and roll the pie crust balls out into 11-inch circles. Coat the inside of a 9-inch pie plate with nonstick cooking spray. Transfer a dough circle to the pie plate, and trim the edges. Fill the pie with the fruit filling and top with the remaining pie crust. Tuck the excess top pie crust underneath the bottom crust and flute or crimp the edges. Cover and seal airtight in aluminum foil, plastic wrap, or a 2-gallon zipper-top plastic bag, and freeze for up to 2 months.

Bake It Later

1. Preheat the oven to 425°F.

2. Cut slits in the top of the pie crust to allow steam to escape. Bake for 15 minutes. Decrease the oven temperature to 375°F and bake for an additional 35 to 45 minutes, until the juices begin to bubble and the crust is golden brown.

3. Allow to cool on a wire rack for 25 minutes. Serve warm or at room temperature.

Stone Fruit Pie

THIS GREAT FORMULA CAN BE USED WITH ANY STONE FRUITS, such as peaches, nectarines, apricots, or plums. If you have fresh fruit, drain it thoroughly before mixing with the sugar and other ingredients; if you are using frozen fruit, don't defrost it. MAKES ONE 9-INCH PIE

5 cups peeled, pitted, and thinly sliced stone fruits, *or* two 16-ounce bags frozen sliced fruit

1 cup granulated sugar

¼ cup firmly packed light brown sugar

¼ cup instant tapioca

½ teaspoon ground cinnamon

⅛ teaspoon ground nutmeg

1 teaspoon freshly squeezed lemon juice

1 recipe Basic Pie Crust (page 303)

Make It Now

1. In a large bowl, combine the fruit with the granulated sugar, brown sugar, tapioca, cinnamon, nutmeg, and lemon juice, tossing to coat the fruit.

2. Sprinkle some flour onto a flat, clean work surface and roll the pie crust balls out into 11-inch circles. Coat the inside of a 9-inch pie plate with nonstick cooking spray. Transfer a dough circle to the pie plate and trim the edges. Fill the pie with the fruit filling and top with the remaining pie crust. Tuck the excess top pie crust underneath the bottom crust and flute or crimp the edges. Cover and seal airtight in aluminum foil, plastic wrap, or a 2-gallon zipper-top plastic bag, and freeze for up to 2 months.

Bake It Later

1. Preheat the oven to 425°F.

2. Cut slits in the top of the pie crust to allow steam to escape. Bake for 15 minutes. Decrease the oven temperature to 375°F and bake for an additional 35 to 45 minutes, until the juices begin to bubble and the crust is golden brown.

3. Allow to cool on a wire rack for 25 minutes. Serve warm or at room temperature.

Berry Pie

BERRY PIES ARE AMONG MY FAVORITES; they are jewel colored, sweet, and tart, and they go so well with vanilla ice cream! This is where you can become quite creative and mix the berries, if you'd like. One of my favorite combinations is raspberries mixed with boysenberries, marionberries, or blackberries. Not only is the combination stunning to look at, but the sweet and tart notes of the filling are also a great complement to the flaky pie crust. As with the Stone Fruit Pie (page 301), if you're using frozen fruit, don't defrost it. MAKES ONE 9-INCH PIE

5 to 6 cups fresh berries, washed and picked over for stems, *or* two 16-ounce bags frozen berries

1/2 cup firmly packed light brown sugar

1/4 cup granulated sugar

1/4 cup instant tapioca

1/2 teaspoon ground nutmeg

1 teaspoon grated citrus zest (orange for raspberries, blackberries, and boysenberries; lemon for blueberries)

1 recipe Basic Pie Crust (opposite page)

Make It Now

1. In a large bowl, combine the berries with the brown sugar, granulated sugar, tapioca, nutmeg, and citrus zest, tossing to coat the fruit.

2. Sprinkle some flour onto a flat, clean work surface and roll the pie crust balls out into 11-inch circles. Coat the inside of a 9-inch pie plate with nonstick cooking spray. Transfer a dough circle to the pie plate and trim the edges. Fill the pie with the berry filling and top with the remaining pie crust. Tuck the excess top pie crust underneath the bottom crust and flute or crimp the edges. Cover and seal airtight in aluminum foil, plastic wrap, or a 2-gallon zipper-top plastic bag, and freeze for up to 2 months.

Bake It Later

1. Preheat the oven to 425°F.

2. Cut slits in the top of the pie crust to allow steam to escape. Bake for 15 minutes. Decrease the oven temperature to 375°F and bake for an additional 35 to 45 minutes, until the juices begin to bubble and the crust is golden brown.

3. Allow to cool on a wire rack for 25 minutes. Serve warm or at room temperature.

Pies and Crisps

Pies and crisps are great make-ahead desserts. The secret to freezing them is to make sure that the filling has been thickened with enough cornstarch, flour, or tapioca so that there isn't a lot of runny juice in the baking dish. Both pies and crisps can be frozen and then baked directly from the freezer, rather than waiting for them to thaw. This is a great time-saver if you have fresh fruit from your yard that you would like to make into pies, but you don't want to have to eat them all in one sitting! You can also freeze pie crusts by themselves for up to two months.

Without a bottom crust, crisps need only prepared fruit, which is topped with your choice of crumbly topping. You can certainly add flavorings to the crumble toppings, such as cinnamon, nutmeg, or your favorite flavors, but I've chosen to leave them plain so that you can customize them. Double any of the crisp recipes and bake in a 9 x 13-inch baking dish.

Basic Pie Crust

This recipe will yield two 9-inch pie crusts, enough for one double-crust or two single-crust pies. I use a food processor or electric mixer to mix my crust, but if you don't have either one, use a pastry blender to cut the shortening and butter into the dry ingredients.

> 3¼ cups unbleached all-purpose flour, plus more for rolling
> 2 teaspoons salt
> 1 cup (2 sticks) cold unsalted butter, cut into ½-inch cubes
> ½ cup cold vegetable shortening, cut into small bits
> ⅓ to ½ cup ice water (see Diva Note)

1. In a food processor or the bowl of an electric mixer, toss together the flour and salt. Distribute the butter and shortening on top of the flour and pulse or mix on low speed until the ingredients begin to resemble coarse meal.

2. Gradually mix in a few tablespoons of water, pulsing or mixing on low, until the ingredients just begin to hold together when pinched together. Form the dough into 2 equal balls, flatten each ball on a large sheet of waxed paper, parchment paper, or plastic wrap, and refrigerate for 1 hour or freeze for up to 2 months. Defrost overnight in the refrigerator before proceeding.

Diva Note

Atmospheric conditions can affect how much water you will need for a pie crust. If the air is humid, your flour may be a bit "wetter" than on a dry day. Butter differs in its water content as well. I usually have a measuring cup of ice water and begin with a few tablespoons, and add as I go to make sure that I don't add too much water and end up with a sticky dough.

Sour Cream Apple Pie

THIS CREATIVE RIFF ON TRADITIONAL APPLE PIE has a layer of apples topped by a layer of cheesecake-like filling topped by a layer of sugared pecans. It's heaven on a plate!

MAKES ONE 9-INCH PIE

½ recipe Basic Pie Crust (page 303)

APPLE FILLING

4 large Granny Smith or your favorite tart apples, peeled, cored, and thinly sliced (5½ to 6 cups)

½ cup granulated sugar

½ cup firmly packed light brown sugar

2 tablespoons cornstarch

1 teaspoon ground cinnamon

¼ teaspoon ground nutmeg

2 teaspoons freshly squeezed lemon juice

CHEESECAKE FILLING

One 8-ounce package cream cheese, softened

½ cup granulated sugar

1 large egg

½ cup sour cream

1½ cups chopped pecans

¼ cup raw sugar

Make It Now

1. Preheat the oven to 400°F.

2. Sprinkle some flour onto a flat, clean work surface and roll out the pie crust ball into an 11-inch circle. Coat the inside of a 9-inch pie plate with nonstick cooking spray. Transfer the dough circle to the pie plate and trim the edges. Butter or coat one side of a piece of aluminum foil with nonstick cooking spray and press onto the pie crust, butter side down. Pour pie weights or dry beans onto the aluminum foil and bake the pie crust for 20 minutes. Remove the pie weights, press down on any parts of the crust that may have risen, and bake for an additional 10 to 12 minutes, until light golden brown. Remove from the oven and cool on a rack.

3. Meanwhile, make the apple filling. In a large bowl, combine the apples, granulated sugar, brown sugar, cornstarch, cinnamon, nutmeg, and lemon juice, and toss until the apples are thoroughly coated.

4. To make the cheesecake filling, in a medium-size bowl, beat together the cream cheese, sugar, egg, and sour cream.

5. Pour the apple mixture into the prepared, cooled pie crust, then pour the cheese mixture over the apples. Top with the pecans and the raw sugar. Cover and seal airtight in aluminum foil, plastic wrap, or a 2-gallon zipper-top plastic bag, and freeze for up to 6 weeks.

Bake It Later

1. Preheat the oven to 400°F.

2. Bake the pie for 20 minutes. Lower the oven temperature to 350°F and bake for an additional 35 minutes, until the apples are bubbling, the topping appears set, and the pecans are golden brown. Allow to cool completely on a wire rack. Serve at room temperature or cold.

Old-Fashioned Fruit Crisp

LIKE THE PIES IN THIS CHAPTER, fruit crisps can go directly from freezer to oven. And since crisps are even easier to make than pies, they can be a real dessert lifesaver! Serve this with your favorite ice cream. MAKES ONE 9-INCH CRISP

¾ cup unbleached all-purpose flour

¾ cup firmly packed light brown sugar

¼ cup granulated sugar

½ teaspoon salt

½ cup (1 stick) cold unsalted butter, cut into ½-inch pieces

Fruit filling of your choice (pages 299 to 304)

Make It Now

1. Combine the flour, brown sugar, granulated sugar, and salt in the bowl of a food processor. Pulse on and off to blend. Distribute the butter over the dry ingredients and pulse on and off about 10 times, until the crumble topping begins to come together.

2. Pour the fruit filling into a 9-inch pie plate or 9-inch square baking dish. Sprinkle the topping over the fruit. Cover and freeze for up to 2 months.

Bake It Later

1. Preheat the oven to 350°F.

2. Bake the crisp for 45 to 55 minutes, until the fruit is bubbling and the topping is golden brown. Allow to rest for about 10 minutes, then serve warm.

Nutty Fruit Crisp

THE NUTTY, CARAMEL-FLAVORED TOPPING in this recipe goes beautifully with any of the fruit fillings in this chapter. Try pecans with the apple filling, almonds with the berry filling, and macadamias with the peach filling. MAKES ONE 9-INCH CRISP

1 cup unbleached all-purpose flour

1 cup firmly packed dark brown sugar (see Diva Note)

½ teaspoon salt

½ cup (1 stick) cold unsalted butter, cut into ½-inch cubes

⅔ cup chopped mixed nuts (such as pecans, walnuts, almonds, cashews, and macadamias)

Fruit filling of your choice (pages 299 to 304)

Make It Now

1. Combine the flour, brown sugar, and salt in the bowl of a food processor. Pulse on and off to blend. Distribute the butter over the dry ingredients and pulse on and off about 10 times, until the mixture begins to come together. Remove the crumble to a mixing bowl and stir in the nuts.

2. Pour the fruit filling into a 9-inch pie plate or 9-inch square baking dish. Sprinkle the crumble over the fruit. Cover and freeze for up to 2 months.

Bake It Later

1. Preheat the oven to 350°F.

2. Bake the crumble for 45 to 55 minutes, until the fruit is bubbling and the topping is golden brown. Allow to rest for about 10 minutes, then serve warm.

Diva Note

Using dark brown sugar in this recipe will give a caramel-like flavor to the crumble topping. If you only have light brown sugar on hand, you can certainly substitute it, but be aware that the finished crisp will have less caramel flavor.

Oatmeal Fruit Crisp

THE ADDITION OF OATS makes this a more rustic and hearty dessert. A sprinkling of cinnamon or a touch of maple extract will add a special touch. MAKES ONE 9-INCH CRISP

$^3/_4$ cup old-fashioned rolled oats (not instant)

$^2/_3$ cup unbleached all-purpose flour

$^3/_4$ cup firmly packed light brown sugar

$^1/_4$ cup granulated sugar

$^1/_2$ teaspoon salt

$^1/_2$ cup (1 stick) cold unsalted butter, cut into $^1/_2$-inch cubes

Fruit filling of your choice (pages 299 to 304)

Make It Now

1. Combine the oats, flour, brown sugar, granulated sugar, and salt in the bowl of a food processor. Pulse on and off to blend. Distribute the butter over the dry ingredients and pulse on and off about 10 times, until the mixture begins to come together.

2. Pour the fruit filling into a 9-inch pie plate or 9-inch square baking dish. Sprinkle the crumble over the fruit. Cover and freeze for up to 2 months.

Bake It Later

1. Preheat the oven to 350°F.

2. Bake the crumble for 45 to 55 minutes, until the fruit is bubbling and the topping is golden brown. Allow to rest for about 10 minutes, then serve warm.

Measurement Equivalents

Please note that all conversions are approximate.

Liquid Conversions

U.S.	Metric	U.S.	Metric
1 tsp	5 ml	1 cup	240 ml
1 tbs	15 ml	1 cup + 2 tbs	275 ml
2 tbs	30 ml	1¼ cups	300 ml
3 tbs	45 ml	1⅓ cups	325 ml
¼ cup	60 ml	1½ cups	350 ml
⅓ cup	75 ml	1⅔ cups	375 ml
⅓ cup + 1 tbs	90 ml	1¾ cups	400 ml
⅓ cup + 2 tbs	100 ml	1¾ cups + 2 tbs	450 ml
½ cup	120 ml	2 cups (1 pint)	475 ml
⅔ cup	150 ml	2½ cups	600 ml
¾ cup	180 ml	3 cups	720 ml
¾ cup + 2 tbs	200 ml	4 cups (1 quart)	945 ml
			(1,000 ml is 1 liter)

Weight Conversions

U.S. / U.K.	Metric	U.S. / U.K.	Metric
½ oz	14 g	7 oz	200 g
1 oz	28 g	8 oz	227 g
1½ oz	43 g	9 oz	255 g
2 oz	57 g	10 oz	284 g
2½ oz	71 g	11 oz	312 g
3 oz	85 g	12 oz	340 g
3½ oz	100 g	13 oz	368 g
4 oz	113 g	14 oz	400 g
5 oz	142 g	15 oz	425 g
6 oz	170 g	1 lb	454 g

Oven Temperature Conversions

°F	Gas Mark	°C
250	½	120
275	1	140
300	2	150
325	3	165
350	4	180
375	5	190
400	6	200
425	7	220
450	8	230
475	9	240
500	10	260
550	Broil	290

Index

C

Cakes
  Chocolate Lava, 294–95
  freezer shelf life, 11
  Plain Old Vanilla Cheesecake
    with Many Variations,
    296–98
Caramelized Onion and Gruyère
  Dip, 15
Caramelized Onion Mac and
  Swiss Cheese, 65
Caramelized Onions, 65
Caramelized Pears, 264
Carol's Spicy Vodka Cream Sauce,
  57
Cashews, adding to blondie
  recipe, 283
Cauliflower au Gratin, 242–43
Cheddar
  adding to appetizer recipe, 35
  adding to gratin recipe, 148
  Arroz con Pollo Casserole,
    74–75
  Baked Mushroom, and Bacon
    Puffs, 22–23
  Beef Enchiladas, 89
  Beer Dip with Smoked
    Sausage, 18
  Broccoli au Gratin, 240–41
  Cheese Enchiladas with Red
    Chile Sauce, 85
  Chicken Chili Casserole,
    166–67
  Chicken Enchiladas with Salsa
    Verde, 87–88
  Chile con Queso Dip, 16
  Chile Relleno Soufflé,
    109–10
  Chili Cheese Spuds, 249
  Chipotle Corn Casserole with
    Variations, 238–39
  Crab Melts, 36
  Eastern Ham Casserole, 106
  Jalapeño Pepper Poppers,
    33–34
  King Ranch Turkey Casserole,
    195–96
  Loaded Stuffed Spuds, 249

  Midwest Breakfast Casserole,
    105–6
  Old-Fashioned Mac and
    Cheese with Variations,
    63–65
  Queso Chile con Carne, 17
  Refried Bean Casserole, 262
  Southern Turkey Casserole,
    106
  Totally Veggie Western Casse-
    role, 106
  White, and Bacon Grits Casse-
    role, 82
Cheese. *See also* Cheddar; Cream
  cheese; Gruyère; Monterey
  Jack; Parmesan
  Artichoke, Salmon, and
    Boursin Strata, 99
  Baked Brie, 27–28
  Beef Pot Pie with
    Boursin–Mashed Potato
    Crust, 131–32
  Blue, Bacon-Wrapped Figs
    Stuffed with, 35
  Blue, Dressing, Buffalo Wing, 43
  Blue Cider Sauce, 190
  Blue Heaven Stuffed Spuds,
    249
  Cheesy Squash Casserole, 257
  Chicken, Sun-Dried Tomato,
    and Artichoke Bake, 174–75
  Creamy Boursin Baked Stuffed
    Shrimp, 233
  Eggplant Rollatini, 245–46
  Egg Stratas, 94–99
  Filet Mignon Pizzaiola, 136–37
  Garlic-Herb Mashed Potatoes,
    251
  Gorgonzola, Apple, and
    Bacon–Stuffed Chicken
    Breasts with Blue Cider
    Sauce, 189–90
  Mac and, Old-Fashioned, with
    Variations, 63–65
  Mediterranean Halibut
    with Tomatoes, Feta, and
    Mint, 204
  More Cheesy Mashed
    Potatoes, 251

  Penne, Sausage, and Meatball
    Bake, 55–56
  Pigs in a Blanket, 26
  Pizza Spuds, 249
  Potato Gratin, 252
  Roasted Tomato and Moz-
    zarella Strata, 97
  soft, crumbling, tip for, 99
  Spinach, and Bacon Pasta
    Bake, 59
  Spinach and Feta Puffs, 24–25
  Strawberry Mascarpone French
    Toast, 115
  Stuffed Leg of Lamb, 150–51
  Timpano, 68–70
  Tuscan Stuffed Chicken
    Breasts, 191–92
  Vegetarian Lasagna, 53–54
  Zucchini Pizzaiola, 258
Cheesecake
  Bars, Apple Praline, 288
  cooling, in turned-off oven,
    298
  crumb crusts for, 297
  Plain Old Vanilla, with Many
    Variations, 296–98
  preparing pan for, 297
  serving temperature, 297
  Streusel Bars, Maple Praline
    Pumpkin, 286–87
Cherry(ies)
  Brandy Pie, 300
  dried, adding to blondie
    recipe, 283
  dried, adding to cookie recipe,
    273
Chicken
  adding to appetizer recipe, 36
  All-Purpose Formula for
    Poultry Casseroles to
    Serve 6, 193
  Arroz con Pollo Casserole,
    74–75
  Artichoke, and Penne
    Alfredo, 58
  Balsamico with Roasted
    Potatoes, 179
  Barbecued, Old-Fashioned,
    Diva Style, 161